The Mystical Theology of the Eastern Church

VLADIMIR LOSSKY

ST VLADIMIR'S SEMINARY PRESS
CRESTWOOD, NEW YORK, 10707
2002

LIBRARY OF CONGRESS CATALOGING-IN-PUBLICATION DATA

Lossky, Vladimir, 1903-1958.
    The mystical theology of the Eastern Church.

    Translation of Essai sur la théologie mystique de l'Église d'Orient.
    Reprint of the ed. published by J. Clarke, London.

    Includes bibliographical references.
        1. Mysticism—Orthodox Eastern Church. I. Title.
BV5082.2.L6713   1976   230'.1'9   76-25448
ISBN 0-913836-31-1

    This book was first published in Paris, in 1944, under the title
Essai sur la Théologie Mystique de L'Église d'Orient. Translated by a
small group of members of the Fellowship of St Alban and St Sergius,
it was first published in English in 1957. This edition is published by
arrangement with the copyright holder James Clarke & Co. Ltd.,
7 All Saints' Passage, Cambridge CB2 3L3, England.

The Mystical Theology of the Eastern Church

ST VLADIMIR'S SEMINARY PRESS
575 Scarsdale Road, Crestwood, New York, 10707-1699
1-800-204-2665

First printing 1976
Reprinted 1984, 1991, 1998, 2002

ISBN 0-913836-31-1

THE MYSTICAL THEOLOGY
OF THE EASTERN CHURCH

Contents

5

CHAPTER ONE

Introduction: Theology and Mysticism in the Tradition of the Eastern Church

It is our intention, in the following essay, to study certain aspects of eastern spirituality in relation to the fundamental themes of the Orthodox dogmatic tradition. In the present work, therefore, the term 'mystical theology' denotes no more than a spirituality which expresses a doctrinal attitude.

In a certain sense all theology is mystical, inasmuch as it shows forth the divine mystery: the data of revelation. On the other hand, mysticism is frequently opposed to theology as a realm inaccessible to understanding, as an unutterable mystery, a hidden depth, to be lived rather than known; yielding itself to a specific experience which surpasses our faculties of understanding rather than to any perception of sense or of intelligence. If we adopted this latter conception unreservedly, resolutely opposing mysticism to theology, we should be led in the last resort to the thesis of Bergson who distinguishes, in his *Deux Sources*, the 'static religion' of the Churches from the 'dynamic religion' of the mystics; the former social and conservative in character, the latter personal and creative.

To what extent was Bergson justified in stating this opposition? This is a difficult question, all the more so since the two terms which Bergson opposes on the religious plane are rooted in the two poles of his philosophical vision of the universe—nature and the *élan vital*. Quite apart from this attitude of Bergson, however, one frequently hears expressed the view which would see in mysticism a realm reserved for the few, an exception to the common rule, a privilege vouchsafed to a few souls who enjoy direct experience of the truth, others, meanwhile, having to rest content with a more or less blind submission to dogmas imposed from without, as to a coercive authority. This opposition is sometimes carried to great lengths, especially if the historical reality be forced into a preconceived pattern. Thus the mystics are set up against the theologians, the contemplatives against the prelates, the saints against the Church. It will suffice to recall many a passage of Harnack, Paul Sabatier's *Life of St. Francis*, and other works, most frequently by protestant historians.

The eastern tradition has never made a sharp distinction between mysticism and theology; between personal experience of the divine mysteries and the dogma affirmed by the Church. The following words spoken a century ago by a great Orthodox theologian, the Metropolitan Philaret of Moscow, express this attitude perfectly: 'none of the mysteries of the most secret wisdom of God ought to appear alien or altogether transcendent to us, but in all humility we must apply our spirit to the contemplation of divine things'.[1] To put it in another way, we must live the dogma expressing a revealed truth, which appears to us as an unfathomable mystery, in such a fashion that instead of assimilating the mystery to our mode of understanding, we should, on the contrary, look for a profound change, an inner transformation of spirit, enabling us to experience it mystically. Far from being mutually opposed, theology and mysticism support and complete each other. One is impossible without the other. If the mystical experience is

[1] *Sermons and Addresses of the Metropolitan Philaret*, Moscow, 1844, Part II, p. 87. (In Russian.)

8

a personal working out of the content of the common faith, theology is an expression, for the profit of all, of that which can be experienced by everyone. Outside the truth kept by the whole Church personal experience would be deprived of all certainty, of all objectivity. It would be a mingling of truth and of falsehood, of reality and of illusion: 'mysticism' in the bad sense of the word. On the other hand, the teaching of the Church would have no hold on souls if it did not in some degree express an inner experience of truth, granted in different measure to each one of the faithful. There is, therefore, no Christian mysticism without theology; but, above all, there is no theology without mysticism. It is not by chance that the tradition of the Eastern Church has reserved the name of 'theologian' peculiarly for three sacred writers of whom the first is St. John, most 'mystical' of the four Evangelists; the second St. Gregory Nazianzen, writer of contemplative poetry; and the third St. Symeon, called 'the New Theologian', the singer of union with God. Mysticism is accordingly treated in the present work as the perfecting and crown of all theology: as theology *par excellence*.

Unlike gnosticism,[1] in which knowledge for its own sake constitutes the aim of the gnostic, Christian theology is always in the last resort a means: a unity of knowledge subserving an end which transcends all knowledge. This ultimate end is union with God or deification, the $\theta\acute{\epsilon}\omega\sigma\iota\varsigma$ of the Greek Fathers. Thus, we are finally led to a conclusion which may seem paradoxical enough: that Christian theory should have an eminently practical significance; and that the more mystical it is, the more directly it aspires to the supreme end of union with God. All the development of the dogmatic battles which the Church has waged down the centuries appears to us, if we regard it from the purely spiritual standpoint, as

[1] See the article by M. H.-Ch. Puech: 'Où en est le problème du gnosticisme?', *Revue de l'Université de Bruxelles*, 1934, Nos. 2 and 3.

dominated by the constant preoccupation which the Church has had to safeguard, at each moment of her history, for all Christians, the possibility of attaining to the fullness of the mystical union. So the Church struggled against the gnostics in defence of this same idea of deification as the universal end: 'God became man that men might become gods'. She affirmed, against the Arians, the dogma of the consubstantial Trinity; for it is the Word, the Logos, who opens to us the way to union with the Godhead; and if the incarnate Word has not the same substance with the Father, if he be not truly God, our deification is impossible. The Church condemned the Nestorians that she might overthrow the middle wall of partition, whereby, in the person of the Christ himself, they would have separated God from man. She rose up against the Apollinarians and Monophysites to show that, since the fullness of true human nature has been assumed by the Word, it is our whole humanity that must enter into union with God. She warred with the Monothelites because, apart from the union of the two wills, divine and human, there could be no attaining to deification—'God created man by his will alone, but He cannot save him without the co-operation of the human will.' The Church emerged triumphant from the iconoclastic controversy, affirming the possibility of the expression through a material medium of the divine realities—symbol and pledge of our sanctification. The main preoccupation, the issue at stake, in the questions which successively arise respecting the Holy Spirit, grace and the Church herself—this last the dogmatic question of our own time—is always the possibility, the manner, or the means of our union with God. All the history of Christian dogma unfolds itself about this mystical centre, guarded by different weapons against its many and diverse assailants in the course of successive ages.

The theological doctrines which have been elaborated

in the course of these struggles can be treated in the most direct relation to the vital end—that of union with God— to the attainment of which they are subservient. Thus they appear as the foundations of Christian spirituality. It is this that we shall understand in speaking of 'mystical theology'; not mysticism properly so-called, the personal experiences of different masters of the spiritual life. Such experiences, for that matter, more often than not remain inaccessible to us: even though they may find verbal expression. What, in reality, can one say of the mystical experience of St. Paul: 'I knew a man in Christ above fourteen years ago (whether in the body, I cannot tell; or whether out of the body, I cannot tell: God knoweth); such an one caught up to the third heaven. And I knew such a man (whether in the body, or out of the body, I cannot tell: God knoweth); how that he was caught up into paradise, and heard unspeakable words, which it is not lawful for a man to utter'.[1] To venture to pass any judgement upon the nature of this experience it would be necessary to understand it more fully than did St. Paul, who avows his ignorance: 'I cannot tell: God knoweth.' We deliberately leave on one side all question of mystical psychology. Nor is it theological doctrines as such that we propose to set forth in the present work, but only such elements of theology as are indispensable for the under-standing of a spirituality: the dogmas which constitute the foundation of mysticism. Here, then, is the first definition and limitation of our subject, which is the mystical theology of the Eastern Church.

The second limitation circumscribes our subject, so to say, in space. It is the Christian East, or, more precisely, the Eastern Orthodox Church, which will form the field of our studies in mystical theology. We must recognize that this limitation is somewhat artificial. In reality, since

[1] II Cor. xii, 2–4.

the cleavage between East and West only dates from the middle of the eleventh century, all that is prior to this date constitutes a common and indivisible treasure for both parts of a divided Christendom. The Orthodox Church would not be what it is if it had not had St. Cyprian, St. Augustine and St. Gregory the Great. No more could the Roman Catholic Church do without St. Athanasius, St. Basil or St. Cyril of Alexandria. Thus, when one would speak of the mystical theology of the East or of the West, one takes one's stand within one of the two traditions which remained, down to a certain moment, two local traditions within the one Church, witnessing to a single Christian truth; but which subsequently part, the one from the other, and give rise to two different dogmatic attitudes, irreconcilable on several points. Can we judge the two traditions by taking our stand on neutral ground equally foreign to the one as to the other? That would be to judge Christianity from a non-Christian standpoint: in other words, to refuse in advance to understand anything whatever about the object of study. For objectivity in no wise consists in taking one's stand outside an object but, on the contrary, in considering one's object in itself and by itself. There are fields in which what is commonly styled 'objectivity' is only indifference, and where indifference means incomprehension. In the present state of dogmatic difference between East and West it is essential, if one wishes to study the mystical theology of the Eastern Church, to choose between two possible standpoints. Either, to place oneself on western dogmatic ground and to examine the eastern tradition across that of the West—that is, by way of criticism—or else to present that tradition in the light of the dogmatic attitude of the Eastern Church. This latter course is for us the only possible one.

It will, perhaps, be objected that the dogmatic dissension between East and West only arose by chance, that it

Introduction

has not been of decisive importance, that it was rather a question of two different historical spheres which must sooner or later have separated in order that each might follow its own path; and, finally, that the dogmatic dispute was no more than a pretext for the breaking asunder once and for all of an ecclesiastical unity which had in fact long ceased to be a reality.

Such assertions, which are heard very frequently in the East as in the West, are the outcome of a purely secular mentality and of the widespread habit of treating Church history according to methods which exclude the religious nature of the Church. For the 'historian of the Church' the religious factor disappears and finds itself displaced by others; such, for instance, as the play of political or social interests, the part played by racial or cultural conditions, considered as determining factors in the life of the Church. We think ourselves shrewder, more up to date, in invoking these factors as the true guiding forces of ecclesiastical history. While recognizing their importance, a Christian historian can scarcely resign himself to regarding them otherwise than as accidental to the essential nature of the Church. He cannot cease to see in the Church an autonomous body, subject to a different law than that of the determinism of this world. If we consider the dogmatic question of the procession of the Holy Spirit, which divided East and West, we cannot treat it as a fortuitous phenomenon in the history of the Church. From the religious point of view it is the sole issue of importance in the chain of events which terminated in the separation. Conditioned, as it may well have been, by various factors, this dogmatic choice was—for the one party as for the other—a spiritual commitment, a conscious taking of sides in a matter of faith.

If we are often led to minimize the importance of the dogmatic question which determined all the subsequent development of the two traditions, this is by reason of a certain insensitivity towards dogma—which is considered as something external and abstract. It is said that it is spirituality which matters. The dogmatic difference is of no consequence. Yet spirituality and dogma, mysticism and theology, are inseparably linked in the life of the Church. As regards the Eastern Church, we have already remarked that she makes no sharp distinction between theology and mysticism, between the realm of the common faith and that of personal experience. Thus, if we would speak of mystical theology in the eastern tradition we cannot do otherwise than consider it within the dogmatic setting of the Orthodox Church.

Before coming to grips with our subject it is necessary to say a few words about the Orthodox Church, little known down to the present day in the West. Father Congar's book *Divided Christendom*, though very remarkable in many respects, remains, despite all his striving after objectivity, subject, in those pages which he devotes to the Orthodox Church, to certain preconceived notions. 'Where the West,' he says, 'on the basis at once developed and narrow of Augustinian ideology, claimed for the Church independence in life and organization, and thus laid down the lines of a very definite ecclesiology, the East settled down in practice, and to some extent in theory, to a principle of unity which was political, non-religious, and not truly universal.'[1] To Father Congar, as to the majority of Catholic and Protestant writers who have expressed themselves on this subject, Orthodoxy presents itself under the form of a federation of national churches, having as its basis a political principle—the state-church. One can venture upon such generalizations as these only by ignoring both the canonical groundwork and the history of the Eastern Church. The view which would base the unity of

---

[1] M. J. Congar, O.P., *Chrétiens désunis. Principes d'un 'oecuménisme' catholique*, Paris, 1937, p. 15. English translation by M. A. Bousfield, *Divided Christendom*, London, 1939, p. 13.

a local church on a political, racial or cultural principle is considered by the Orthodox Church as a heresy, specially known by the name of *philetism*.[1] It is the ecclesiastical territory, the area sanctified by more or less ancient Christian tradition which forms the basis of a metropolitan province, administered by an archbishop or metropolitan, with the bishops from every diocese coming together from time to time in synod. If metropolitan provinces are grouped together to form local churches under the jurisdiction of a bishop who often bears the title of patriarch, it is still the community of local tradition and of historical destiny (as well as convenience in calling together a council from many provinces), which determines the formation of these large circles of jurisdiction, the territories of which do not necessarily correspond to the political boundaries of a state.[2] The Patriarch of Constantinople enjoys a certain primacy of honour, arbitrating from time to time in disputes, but without exercising a jurisdiction over the whole body of the oecumenical Church. The local churches of the East had more or less the same attitude towards the apostolic patriarchate of Rome—first see of the Church before the separation, and symbol of her unity. Orthodoxy recognizes no visible head of the Church. The unity of the Church expresses itself through the communion of the heads of local churches among themselves, by the agreement of all the churches in regard to a local council—which thus acquires a universal import; finally, in exceptional cases, it may manifest itself

[1] Synod of Constantinople, 1872. v. Mansi, *Coll. concil.*, vol. 45, 417–546. See also the article by M. Zyzykine: 'L'Eglise orthodoxe et la nation,' *Irénikon*, 1936, pp. 265–77.

[2] Thus the Patriarchate of Moscow includes the dioceses of N. America and that of Tokyo beyond the frontiers of Russia. By contrast, the Catholicate of Georgia, though within the bounds of the U.S.S.R., does not form part of the Russian Church. The territories of the Patriarchates of Constantinople, Alexandria, Antioch and Jerusalem are politically dependent on many different powers.

through a general council.[1] The catholicity of the Church, far from being the privilege of any one see or specific centre, is realized rather in the richness and multiplicity of the local traditions which bear witness unanimously to a single Truth: to that which is preserved always, everywhere and by all. Since the Church is catholic in all her parts, each one of her members—not only the clergy but also each layman—is called to confess and to defend the truth of tradition; opposing even the bishops should they fall into heresy. A Christian who has received the gift of the Holy Spirit in the sacrament of the Holy Chrism must have a full awareness of his faith: he is always responsible for the Church. Hence the restless and sometimes agitated character of the ecclesiastical life of Byzantium, of Russia and of other countries in the Orthodox world. This, however, is the price paid for a religious vitality, an intensity of spiritual life which penetrates the whole mass of believers, united in the awareness that they form a single body with the hierarchy of the Church. From this, too, comes the unconquerable energy which enables Orthodoxy to go through all trials, all cataclysms and upheavals, adapting itself continually to the new historical reality and showing itself stronger than outward circumstances. The persecutions of the faithful in Russia, the systematic fury of which has not been able to destroy the Church, are the best witness to a power which is not of this world.

The Orthodox Church, though commonly referred to as *Eastern*, considers herself none the less the universal Church; and this is true in the sense that she is not limited by any particular type of culture, by the legacy of

[1] The name *Oecumenical Council* given in the East to the first seven general synods corresponds to a reality of a purely historical character. These are the councils of the 'oecumenical' territories, that is to say of the Byzantine Empire which extended (theoretically, at least) throughout the Christian world. In later epochs the Orthodox Church has known general councils which, without bearing the title of 'oecumenical' were neither smaller nor less important.

any one civilization (Hellenistic or otherwise), or by strictly eastern cultural forms. Moreover, *eastern* can mean so many things: from the cultural point of view the East is less homogeneous than the West. What have Hellenism and Russian culture in common, notwithstanding the Byzantine origins of Christianity in Russia? Orthodoxy has been the leaven in too many different cultures to be itself considered a cultural form of eastern Christianity. The forms are different: the faith is one. The Orthodox Church has never confronted national cultures with another which could be regarded as specifically Orthodox. It is for this reason that her missionary work has been able to expand so prodigiously: witness the conversion of Russia to Christianity during the tenth and eleventh centuries, and, at a later date, the preaching of the Gospel across the whole of Asia. Towards the end of the eighteenth century Orthodox missions reached the Aleutian Islands and Alaska, passed thence to North America, creating new dioceses of the Russian Church beyond the confines of Russia, spreading to China and Japan.[1] The anthropological and cultural variations which one encounters from Greece to the remotest parts of Asia, and from Egypt to the Arctic, do not destroy the homogeneous character of this kinship of spirituality, very different from that of the Christian West.

There is a great richness of forms of the spiritual life to be found within the bounds of Orthodoxy, but monasticism remains the most classical of all. Unlike western monasticism, however, that of the East does not include a multiplicity of different orders. This fact is explained by the conception of the monastic life, the aim of which can only be union with God in a complete renunciation of the life of this present world. If the secular clergy (married priests and deacons), or confraternities of laymen may

[1] See S. Bolshakoff, *The Foreign Missions of the Russian Orthodox Church*, London, 1943.

occupy themselves with social work, or devote themselves to other outward activities, it is otherwise with the monks. The latter take the habit above all in order to apply themselves to prayer, to the interior life, in cloister or hermitage. Between a monastery of the common life and the solitude of an anchorite who carries on the traditions of the Desert Fathers there are many intermediate types of monastic institution. One could say broadly that eastern monasticism was exclusively contemplative, if the distinction between the two ways, active and contemplative, had in the East the same meaning as in the West. In fact, for an eastern monk the two ways are inseparable. The one cannot be exercised without the other, for the ascetic rule and the school of interior prayer receive the name of spiritual *activity*. If the monks occupy themselves from time to time with physical labours, it is above all with an ascetic end in view: the sooner to overcome their rebel nature, as well as to avoid idleness, enemy of the spiritual life. To attain to union with God, in the measure in which it is realizable here on earth, requires continual effort, or, more precisely, an unceasing vigil that the integrity of the inward man, 'the union of heart and spirit' (to use an expression of Orthodox asceticism), withstand all the assaults of the enemy: every irrational movement of our fallen nature. Human nature must undergo a change; it must be more and more transfigured by grace in the way of sanctification, which has a range which is not only spiritual but also bodily—and hence cosmic. The spiritual work of a monk living in community or a hermit withdrawn from the world retains all its worth for the entire universe even though it remain hidden from the sight of all. This is why monastic institutions have always enjoyed great veneration in every country of the Orthodox world.

The part played by the great centres of spirituality was very considerable not only in ecclesiastical life but also in the realm of culture and politics. The monasteries of

Introduction

Mount Sinai and of Studion, near Constantinople, the monastic republic of Mount Athos, bringing together religious of all nations (there were Latin monks there prior to the schism), other great centres beyond the bounds of the Empire such as the monastery of Tirnovo, in Bulgaria, and the great *lavras* of Russia—Petcheri at Kiev and the Holy Trinity near Moscow—have all been strongholds of Orthodoxy, schools of the spiritual life, whose religious and moral influence was of the first importance in the moulding of peoples newly converted to Christianity.[1] But if the monastic ideal had so great an influence upon souls, it was, nevertheless, not the only type of the spiritual life which the Church offered to the faithful. The way of union with God may be pursued outside the cloister, amid all the circumstances of human life. The outward forms may change, the monasteries may disappear, as in our own day they disappeared for a time in Russia, but the spiritual life goes on with the same intensity, finding new modes of expression.

Eastern hagiography, which is extremely rich, shows beside the holy monks many examples of spiritual perfection acquired by simple laymen and married people living in the world. It knows also strange and unwonted paths to sanctification: that, for instance, of the 'fools in Christ', committing extravagant acts that their spiritual gifts might remain hidden from the eyes of those about them under the hideous aspect of madness; or, rather, that they

---

[1] There is some useful information about eastern monasticism in the little book by Fr. N. F. Robinson, S.S.J.E., entitled *Monasticism in the Orthodox Churches* (London, 1916). For Mount Athos, see Hasluck: *Athos and its Monasteries* (London, 1924) and F. Spunda, *Der heilige Berg Athos* (Leipzig, 1928). For the monastic life in Russia, see the following studies of Igor Smolitsch, 'Studien zum Klosterwesen Russlands', in *Kyrios*, No. 2 (1937), pp. 95–112, and No. 1 (1939), pp. 29–38, and, above all, the same author's 'Das altrussische Mönchtum' (XI-XVI Jhr.), Würzburg, 1940, in *Das östliche Christentum*, XI, and *Russischer Mönchtum*, Würzburg, 1953.

might be freed from the ties of this world in their most intimate and most spiritually troublesome expression, that of our social 'ego'.[1] Union with God sometimes manifests itself through charismatic gifts as, for example, in that of spiritual direction exercised by the *starets* or elder. These latter are most frequently monks who, having passed many years of their life in prayer and secluded from all contact with the world, towards the end of their life throw open to all comers the door of their cell. They possess the gift of being able to penetrate to the unfathomable depths of the human conscience, of revealing sins and inner difficulties which normally remain unknown to us, of raising up overburdened souls, and of directing men not only in their spiritual course but also in all the vicissitudes of their life in the world.[2]

The individual experiences of the greatest mystics of the Orthodox Church more often than not remain unknown to us. Apart from a few rare exceptions the spiritual literature of the Christian East possesses scarcely any autobiographical account dealing with the interior life, such as those of Angela of Foligno and Henry Suso, or the *Histoire d'une âme* of St. Teresa of Lisieux. The way of mystical union is nearly always a secret between God and the soul concerned, which is never confided to others unless, it may be, to a confessor or to a few disciples. What is published abroad is the fruit of this union: wisdom, understanding of the divine mysteries, expressing itself in theological or moral teaching or in advice for the edification of one's brethren. As to the inward and personal aspect of the mystical experience, it remains hidden from

[1] See on this subject E. Benz, 'Heilige Narrheit', in *Kyrios*, 1938, Nos. 1 and 2, pp. 1–55; Mme Behr-Sigel, 'Les Fous pour le Christ et la sainteté laïque dans l'ancienne Russie', in *Irénikon*, Vol. XV (1939), pp. 554–65; Gamayoun, 'Etudes sur la spiritualité populaire russe: les fous pour le Christ', in *Russie et Chrétienté*, 1938–9, I, pp. 57–77.

[2] Smolitsch, *Leben und Lehre der Starzen*, Vienna, 1936.

the eyes of all. It must be recognized that it was only at a
comparatively late period, towards the thirteenth century
in fact, that mystical individualism made its appearance
in western literature. St. Bernard speaks directly of his
personal experience only very seldom—on but a single
occasion in the Sermons on the Song of Songs—and then
with a sort of reluctance, after the example of St. Paul.
It was necessary that a certain cleavage should occur
between personal experience and the common faith, between the life of the individual and the life of the Church,
that spirituality and dogma, mysticism and theology,
could become two distinct spheres; and that souls unable
to find adequate nourishment in the theological *summae*
should turn to search greedily in the accounts of individual
mystical experience in order to reinvigorate themselves in
an atmosphere of spirituality. Mystical individualism has
remained alien to the spirituality of the Eastern Church.

Father Congar is right when he says: 'We have become
different men. We have the same God but before him we are
different men, unable to agree as to the nature of our
relationship with him.'[1] But in order to estimate accurately this spiritual divergency it would be necessary to
examine it in its most perfect manifestations: in the different types of sanctity in East and West since the schism.
We should then be able to give an account of the close
link which always exists between the dogma which the
Church confesses and the spiritual fruit which it bears.
For the inner experience of the Christian develops within
the circle delineated by the teaching of the Church: within the dogmatic framework which moulds his person. If
even now a political doctrine professed by the members of
a party can so fashion their mentality as to produce a type
of man distinguishable from other men by certain moral
or psychical marks, *a fortiori* religious dogma succeeds in
transforming the very souls of those who confess it. They

[1] Congar, op. cit., p. 47.

are men different from other men, from those who have been formed by another dogmatic conception. It is never possible to understand a spirituality if one does not take into account the dogma in which it is rooted. We must accept facts as they are, and not seek to explain the difference between eastern and western spirituality on racial or cultural grounds when a greater issue, a dogmatic issue, is at stake. Neither may we say that the questions of the procession of the Holy Spirit or of the nature of grace have no great importance in the scheme of Christian doctrine, which remains more or less identical among Roman Catholics and among Orthodox. In dogmas so fundamental as these it is this 'more or less' which is important, for it imparts a different emphasis to all doctrine, presents it in another light; in other words, gives place to another spirituality.

We do not wish to embark on a 'comparative theology'; still less to renew confessional disputes. We confine ourselves here to stating the fact of a dogmatic dissimilarity between the Christian East and the Christian West, before examining certain of the elements of the theology which forms the foundation of eastern spirituality. It will be for the reader to judge in what measure these theological aspects of Orthodox mysticism can be of use for the comprehension of a spirituality which is alien to western Christianity. If while remaining loyal to our respective dogmatic standpoints we could succeed in getting to know each other, above all in those points in which we differ, this would undoubtedly be a surer way towards unity than that which would leave differences on one side. For, in the words of Karl Barth, 'the union of the Churches is not made, but we discover it'.[1]

[1] 'The Church and the churches', *Oecumenica*, III, No. 2, July, 1936.

CHAPTER TWO

The Divine Darkness

T he problem of the knowledge of God has been stated in its fundamentals in a short treatise whose very title—Περὶ μυστικῆς θεολογίας, *Concerning Mystical Theology*—is significant. This remarkable book, the importance of which for the whole history of Christian thought cannot be exaggerated, is the work of the unknown author of the so-called *Areopagitic* writings: a person whom widespread opinion over a very long period of time has sought to identify with a disciple of St. Paul—Dionysius the Areopagite. The defenders of this attribution, however, have had to take into account a disturbing fact: complete silence reigns for nearly five centuries in regard to these *Areopagitic* works. They were neither quoted nor referred to by any ecclesiastical writer before the beginning of the sixth century, and it was the heterodox monophysites who, in seeking to lean upon their authority, first made them known. St. Maximus the Confessor wrested this weapon from the hands of the heretics during the course of the following century by demonstrating in his commentaries (or *scholia*) the orthodox meaning of the Dionysian writings.[1] From that time onwards these works

[1] The *Scholia* or commentaries on the *Corpus Dionysiacum* which pass under the name of St. Maximus are in great part the work of John of Scythopolis (fl. 530–40) whose notes have been confused with those of Maximus by Byzantine copyists. The text of the *Scholia* presents a fabric in which it is practically impossible to unravel the part which

have enjoyed an undisputed authority in the theological tradition of the East, as well as in that of the West.

Modern critics, so far from agreeing as to the identity of the 'Pseudo Dionysius' and as to the date of the composition of his works, wander amidst the most diverse hypotheses.[1] The way in which the critical researches waver between dates as far apart as the third and sixth centuries shows how small a measure of agreement has as yet been reached in regard to the origins of this mysterious

belongs to St. Maximus himself. See on this subject the researches of S. Epiphanovitch, *Materials for the study of the life and works of St. Maximus the Confessor*, Kiev, 1917 (in Russian); and an article by Fr. von Balthasar entitled 'Das Scholienwerk des Johannes von Scythopolis', in *Scholastik*, XV (1940), pp. 16–38.

[1] Thus, for H. Koch, the Areopagitic writings were the work of a forger of the end of the fifth century, 'Pseudo-Dionysius Areopagita in seinen Beziehungen zum Neoplatonismus und Mysterienwesen' (*Forsch. zu christl. Litter. und Dogmengeschichte* 86, I, 1 and 2, Mainz, 1900). The same date is accepted by Bardenhewer (*Les Pères de l'Eglise*; Paris, 1905). Fr. Stiglmayr would identify the Pseudo-Dionysius with Severus of Antioch, a monophysite of the sixth century, 'Der sogennante Dionysius Areopagita und Severus von Antiochen' (*Scholastik III*, 1928). In criticising this thesis M. Robert Devreesse carries the date of composition of the Dionysian writings back to a period before the year 440, 'Denys l'Aréopagite et Sévère d'Antioche' (*Archives d'histoire doctrinale et littéraire du moyen age*, IV, 1930). M. H.-Ch. Puech revindicated the attribution of the writings to a date at the close of the fifth century, 'Liberatus de Carthage et la date de l'apparition des écrits dionysiens' (*Annuaire de l'Ecole des Hautes Etudes*, 1930–31). For Mgr Athenagoras, Dionysius was a disciple of Clement of Alexandria. He identifies him with Dionysius the Great, Bishop of Alexandria (middle of the third century), 'Ο γνήσιος συγγραφεὺς τῶν εἰς Διονύσιον τὸν 'Αρεοπαγίτην ἀποδιδομένων συγγραμμάτων (Athens, 1932), and 'Διονύσιος ὁ Μέγας, ἐπίσκοπος 'Αλεξανδρείας, ὁ συγγραφεὺς τῶν ἀρεοπαγιτικῶν συγγραμμάτων' (Alexandria, 1934). Finally, Fr. Ceslas Pera, in his article 'Denys le Mystique et la θεομαχία' (*Revue des sciences philosophiques et théologiques*, XXV, 1936) detects the influence of Cappadocian thought in the Dionysian writings, and seeks to attribute them to an unknown disciple of St. Basil.

work. But whatever the results of all this research may be, they can in no way diminish the theological value of the *Areopagitica*. From this point of view it matters little who their author was. What is important is the Church's judgement on the contents of the work and the use which she has made of it. Does not the author of the Epistle to the Hebrews say in quoting a psalm of David: 'But one in a certain place testified . . .'[1]? thus showing to what extent the question of authorship is of secondary importance in the case of a text inspired by the Holy Spirit. What is true of Holy Scripture is also true of the theological tradition of the Church.

Dionysius distinguishes two possible theological ways. One—that of cataphatic or positive theology—proceeds by affirmations; the other—apophatic or negative theology— by negations. The first leads us to some knowledge of God, but is an imperfect way. The perfect way, the only way which is fitting in regard to God, who is of His very nature unknowable, is the second—which leads us finally to total ignorance. All knowledge has as its object that which is. Now God is beyond all that exists. In order to approach Him it is necessary to deny all that is inferior to Him, that is to say, all that which is. If in seeing God one can know what one sees, then one has not seen God in Himself but something intelligible, something which is inferior to Him. It is by *unknowing* (ἀγνωσία) that one may know Him who is above every possible object of knowledge. Proceeding by negations one ascends from the inferior degrees of being to the highest, by progressively setting aside all that can be known, in order to draw near to the Unknown in the darkness of absolute ignorance. For even as light, and especially abundance of light, renders darkness invisible; even so the knowledge of created things, and especially excess of knowledge, destroys the ignorance which is the only way by which one can attain to God in Himself.[2]

[1] Heb. ii, 6.   [2] Ep. I., *Migne P.G.*, III, 1065.

Mystical Theology of the Eastern Church

If we transfer Dionysius' distinction between negative and affirmative theology to the plane of dialectic, we are faced with an antinomy, which we then seek to resolve; in the attempt to make a synthesis of the two opposed ways we bring them together as a single method of knowing God. It is thus that St. Thomas Aquinas reduces the two ways of Dionysius to one, making negative theology a corrective to affirmative theology. In attributing to God the perfections which we find in created beings, we must (according to St. Thomas) deny the mode according to which we understand these finite perfections, but we may affirm them in relation to God *modo sublimiori*. Thus, negations correspond to the *modus significandi*, to the always inaccurate means of expression; affirmations to the *res significata*, to the perfection which we wish to express, which is in God after another fashion than it is in creatures.[1] We may indeed ask how far this very ingenious philosophical invention corresponds to the thought of Dionysius. If, for the author of the *Areopagitica*, there is an antinomy between the two 'theologies' which he distinguishes, does he admit this synthesis of the two ways? Is it possible, moreover, speaking in general terms, to oppose the two ways by dealing with them on the same level, by putting them on the same plane? Does not Dionysius say time and time again that apophatic theology surpasses cataphatic? An analysis of the treatise on mystical theology, which is devoted to the negative way, will show what this method means to Dionysius. It will at the same time enable us to judge of the true nature of that apophaticism which constitutes the fundamental characteristic of the whole theological tradition of the Eastern Church.[2]

[1] *Quaestiones disputatae*, VII, 5.

[2] The 'Mystical Theology' is printed in *Migne P.G.*, III, 997–1048. There is an English translation by C. E. Rolt (S.P.C.K. translations of Christian Literature, London, 1920), and a more recent French version by M. de Gandillac, *Oeuvres complètes du pseudo-Denys l'Aréopagite*, Aubier, 1943.

The Divine Darkness

Dionysius begins his treatise with an invocation of the Holy Trinity, whom he prays to guide him 'to the supreme height of mystical writings, which is beyond what is known, where the mysteries of theology, simple, unconditional, invariable, are laid bare in a darkness of silence beyond the light'. He invites Timothy, to whom the treatise is dedicated, to 'mystical comtemplation' (μυστικὰ θεάματα). It is necessary to renounce both sense and all the workings of reason, everything which may be known by the senses or the understanding, both that which is and all that is not, in order to be able to attain in perfect ignorance to union with Him who transcends all being and all knowledge. It is already evident that this is not simply a question of a process of dialectic but of something else: a purification, a κάθαρσις, is necessary. One must abandon all that is impure and even all that is pure. One must then scale the most sublime heights of sanctity leaving behind one all the divine luminaries, all the heavenly sounds and words. It is only thus that one may penetrate to the darkness wherein He who is beyond all created things makes his dwelling.[1]

This way of ascent, in the course of which we are gradually delivered from the hold of all that can be known, is compared by Dionysius to Moses' ascent of Mount Sinai to meet with God. Moses begins by purifying himself. Then he separates himself from all that is unclean. It is then that he hears 'the many notes of the trumpets, he sees the many lights which flash forth many pure rays; then he is separated from the many, and with the chosen priests he raches the height of the divine ascents. Even here he does not associate with God, he does not contemplate God (for He is unseen), but the place where He is. I think this means that the highest and most divine of the things which are seen and understood are a kind of hypothetical account of what is subject to Him who is over all.

[1] 'Mystical Theology', I, 3, P.G., III, 1000.

Through them is revealed the presence of Him who is above all thought, a presence which occupies the intelligible heights of His holy places. It is then that Moses is freed from the things that see and are seen (τῶν ὁρωμένων καὶ τῶν ὁρώντων): he passes into the truly mystical darkness of ignorance, where he shuts his eyes to all scientific apprehensions, and reaches what is entirely untouched and unseen, belonging not to himself and not to another, but wholly to Him who is above all. He is united to the best of his powers with the unknowing quiescence of all knowledge, and by that very unknowing he knows what surpasses understanding (καὶ τῷ μηδὲν γινώσκειν, ὑπὲρ νοῦν γινώσκων).'[1]

It is now clear that the apophatic way, or mystical theology—for such is the title of the treatise devoted to the way of negations—has for its object God, in so far as He is absolutely incomprehensible. It would even be inaccurate to say that it has God for its object. The latter part of the passage which we have just quoted shows that once arrived at the extreme height of the knowable one must be freed from that which perceives as much as from that which can be perceived: that is to say, from the subject as well as from the object of perception. God no longer presents Himself as object, for it is no more a question of knowledge but of union. Negative theology is thus a way towards mystical union with God, whose nature remains incomprehensible to us.

The second chapter of the *Mystical Theology* opposes the affirmative way, that of 'positions' (θέσεις), to the negative way, that of successive 'abstractions' or 'detachments' (ἀφαιρέσεις). The former is a descent from the superior degrees of being to the inferior; the latter an ascent towards the divine incomprehensibility. In chapter three Dionysius enumerates his theological works, arranging them in order of 'prolixity', which increases as one

[1] Ibid. 1000–1001.

descends from the higher theophanies to the lower. The treatise *Concerning Mystical Theology* is the briefest of all, for it deals with the negative way which leads towards the silence of the divine union. In the fourth and fifth chapters Dionysius considers a whole series of attributes borrowed from the world of sense and of intelligence and refuses to relate them to the divine nature. He concludes his treatise by recognizing that the universal Cause eludes all affirmation as well as all negation. 'When we make affirmations and negations about the things which are inferior to it, we affirm and deny nothing about the Cause itself, which, being wholly apart from all things, is above all affirmation, as the supremacy of Him who, being in His simplicity freed from all things and beyond everything, is above all denial.'[1]

There have been many attempts to make a neoplatonist of Dionysius. Indeed, if we compare the Dionysian ecstasy with that which we find described at the close of the Sixth Ennead of Plotinus we are bound to record some striking resemblances. To approach the One (ἕν) it is necessary, according to Plotinus, 'to reach out towards what is first, to detach oneself from sensible objects, which are the last things, and to be freed from all evil because one is eager for the good; to go back to the beginning within oneself, and to become one instead of many in contemplation of the beginning and of the One'.[2] It is the first step in the ascent, where we find ourselves freed from things of sense and recollected in the intelligence. But it is necessary to go beyond the intelligence since the attainment of an object which is superior thereto is in question. 'It is not something, but before everything; neither is it being, for that which is being has the form of its being; but this is formless, lacking even intelligible form. For since the nature of the One procreates all things, it does not itself form part of them.'[3] To this nature are applied negative

---

[1] Ibid., 1048 B.   [2] *Enn.*, VI, ix, 3.   [3] Ibid.

definitions which recall those of the *Mystical Theology* of Dionysius: 'it is not something, neither is it of any kind or degree; it is not mind, it is not soul; it is not moved, nor again does it remain still; it is neither in space nor in time; it is in itself, of one kind, or, rather, without kind, being before all kind, before movement, before stillness, *for all these things concern being, and make it many.*'[1]

Here there appears an idea which one never finds in Dionysius, and which draws a line of demarcation between Christian mysticism and the mystical philosophy of the neo-platonists. If Plotinus rejects the attributes proper to being in seeking to attain to God, it is not, as with Dionysius, on account of the absolute unknowability of God: an unknowability obscured by all which can be known in creatures. It is because the realm of being, even at its highest levels, is necessary multiple: it has not the absolute simplicity of the One. The God of Plotinus is not incomprehensible by nature. If we can neither comprehend the One by discursive reason nor by intellectual intuition, it is because the soul, when it grasps an object by reason, falls away from unity and is not absolutely one.[2] It is therefore necessary to have recourse to the way of ecstasy, to the union in which we are wholly at one with our subject, in which all multiplicity disappears and the distinction between subject and object no longer exists. 'When they come together they are one: it is only when separated that they are two. . . . How can anyone state that, it is other, when he does not see it as such, but in contemplating it, as one with himself?'[3] What is discarded in the negative way of Plotinus is multiplicity, and we arrive at the perfect unity which is beyond being—since being is linked with multiplicity and is subsequent to the One.

The ecstasy of Dionysius is a going forth from being as such. That of Plotinus is rather a reduction of being to absolute simplicity. This is why Plotinus describes his

[1] Ibid. The italics are ours.   [2] *Enn.*, VI, ix, 4.   [3] *Enn.*, VI, ix, 10.

ecstasy by a name which is very characteristic: that of 'simplification' (ἅπλωσις). It is a reintegration in the simplicity of the object of contemplation which can be positively defined as the One (ἕν) and which, in this capacity, is not distinguished from the subject contemplating. Despite all the outward resemblances (due primarily to a common vocabulary), we are far removed from the negative theology of the *Areopagitica*. The God of Dionysius, incomprehensible by nature, the God of the Psalms: 'who made darkness his secret place', is not the primordial God-Unity of the neo-platonists. If He is incomprehensible it is not because of a simplicity which cannot come to terms with the multiplicity with which all knowledge relating to creatures is tainted. It is, so to say, an incomprehensibility which is more radical, more absolute. Indeed, God would no longer be incomprehensible by nature if this incomprehensibility were, as in Plotinus, rooted in the simplicity of the One. Now it is precisely the quality of incomprehensibility which, in Dionysius, is the one definition proper to God—if we may speak here of proper definitions. In his refusal to attribute to God the properties which make up the matter of affirmative theology, Dionysius is aiming expressly at the neo-platonist definitions: 'He is neither One, nor Unity' (οὐδὲ ἕν, οὐδὲ ἑνότης).[1] In his treatise *Of the Divine Names*, in examining the name of the One, which can be applied to God, he shows its insufficiency and compares with it another and 'most sublime' name—that of the Trinity, which teaches us that God is neither one nor many but that He transcends this antinomy, being unknowable in what He is.[2]

If the God of revelation is not the God of the philosophers, it is this recognition of His fundamental unknowability which marks the boundary between the two con-

---

[1] *P.G.*, III, 1048 A.
[2] *Of the Divine Names*, XIII, 3; *P.G.*, III, 981 A.

ceptions. All that can be said in regard to the platonism of the Fathers, and especially in regard to the dependence of the author of the *Areopagitica* on the neo-platonist philosophers, is limited to outward resemblances which do not go to the root of their teaching, and relate only to a vocabulary which was common to the age. To a philosopher of the platonist tradition, even though he speak of the ecstatic union as the only way by which to attain to God, the divine nature is nevertheless an object, something which may be explicitly defined—the ἕν —a nature whose unknowability lies above all in the fact of the weakness of our understanding, inseparable as it is from multiplicity. As we have just said, this ecstatic union will be a reduction to simplicity rather than a going forth from the realm of created beings, as in Dionysius. For outside revelation nothing is known of the difference between the created and the uncreated, of creation *ex nihilo*, of the abyss which has to be crossed between the creature and the Creator. The heterodox doctrines with which Origen was charged had their root in a certain insensitivity towards the unknowability of God on the part of this great Christian thinker. An attitude which was not fundamentally apophatic made the Alexandrine teacher a religious philosopher rather than a mystical theologian, in the sense proper to the eastern tradition. For Origen, in fact, God is 'a simple, intellectual nature admitting of no complexity whatever in itself. . . . He is Monad (μονὰς) and Unity (ἑνάς) and Spirit; the source and origin of all intellectual and spiritual nature.'[1] It is interesting to note that Origen was equally insensitive towards creation *ex nihilo*: a God who is not the *Deus absconditus* of the Scripture does not easily lend himself to the truths of revelation. With Origen, Hellenism attempts to creep into the Church. This conception coming from outside has its origin in human nature, in modes of thought proper to

[1] 'Περὶ ἀρχῶν', *P.G.* XI, 125 A.

men—'to the Greeks and to the Jews'. This is not the tradition in which God reveals Himself and speaks to the Church. It is for this reason that the Church has had to fight against 'Origenism' as she has always fought against doctrines which, in striking at the divine incomprehensibility, replaced the experience of the unfathomable depths of God by philosophical concepts.

It is the apophatic basis of all true theology which the great Cappadocians were defending in their controversy with Eunomius. The latter maintained the possibility of expressing the divine essence in those innate concepts by which it reveals itself to the reason. For St. Basil, not the divine essence alone but also created essences could not be expressed in concepts. In contemplating any object we analyse its properties: it is this which enables us to form concepts. But this analysis can in no case exhaust the content of the object of perception. There will always remain an 'irrational residue' which escapes analysis and which cannot be expressed in concepts; it is the unknowable depth of things, that which constitutes their true, indefinable essence. In regard to the names which we apply to God, these reveal his energies which descend towards us yet do not draw us closer to his essence, which is inaccessible.[1] For St. Gregory of Nyssa every concept relative to God is a simulacrum, a false likeness, an idol. The concepts which we form in accordance with the understanding and the judgement which are natural to us, basing ourselves on an intelligible representation, create idols of God instead of revealing to us God Himself.[2] There is only one name by which the divine nature can

[1] 'Adversus Eunomium', I, i, c. 6, *P.G.*, XXIX, 521–4; I. ii. c. 4. 570–80; I. ii. c., 648 'Ad Amphilochium, Epist. 234', *P.G.*, XXXII, 869 A C. Cf. Gregory of Nyssa, 'Con. Eunom', X, *P.G.*, XLV, 828.

[2] 'De Vita Moysis', *P.G.*, XLIV, 377 B., new edition by J. Daniélou, S.J., Series *Sources chrétiennes* (Paris, 1955), p. 82. 'Con. Eunom.', III, *P.G.*, XLV, 604 B-D; XII, ibid., 944 C.

be expressed: the wonder which seizes the soul when it thinks of God.[1] St. Gregory Nazianzen, in quoting Plato without naming him ('one of the Greek divines'), corrects a passage from the *Timaeus* on the difficulty of knowing God and the impossibility of expressing His nature, in the following way: 'It is difficult to conceive God, but to define Him in words is impossible.'[2] This rearrangement of a sentence of Plato by a Christian author who is often regarded as a platonizer, itself demonstrates how far is the thought of the Fathers from that of the philosophers.

Apophaticism, as a religious attitude towards the incomprehensibility of God, does not belong exclusively to the *Areopagitica*, but is found in most of the Fathers. Clement of Alexandria, for example, says in the *Stromata* that we can attain to God not in that which He is, but in that which He is not.[3] The very awareness of the inaccessibility of 'the unknown God' cannot, according to him, be acquired except by grace: 'by this God-given wisdom which is the power of the Father'.[4] This awareness of the incomprehensibility of the divine nature thus corresponds to an experience: to a meeting with the personal God of revelation. In the power of this grace Moses and St. Paul experienced the impossibility of knowing God: the former, when he penetrated to the darkness of inaccessibility: the latter, when he heard the words conveying the divine ineffability.[5] The theme of Moses drawing near to God in the darkness of Sinai—a theme which we have already come across in Dionysius and which was adopted in the first instance by Philo of Alexandria as an image of ecstasy, is the favourite symbol of the Fathers for convey-

[1] 'In Cantica Canticorum. Homil.', XII, *P.G.*, XLIV, 1028 D.
[2] Oratio XXVIII (theol. II) 4, *P.G.*, XXXVI, 29–32. Ed. A. J. Mason (*The Five Theological Orations of Gregory of Nazianzus*), Cambridge, 1899, p. 26.
[3] 'Stromata', V, 2; *P.G.*, IX, 109 A.
[4] Ibid., V, 13, 124 B–125 A.
[5] Ibid., V, 12, 116–124.

ing the experience of the incomprehensibility of the divine nature. St. Gregory of Nyssa devotes a special treatise to the *Life of Moses*,[1] in which the assent of Mount Sinai towards the darkness of incomprehensibility represents the way of contemplation, superior to Moses' first meeting with God when He appeared to him in the burning bush. Then Moses saw God in light; now he enters the darkness, leaving behind him all that can be seen or known; there remains to him only the invisible and unknowable, but in this darkness is God.[2] For God makes His dwelling there where our understanding and our concepts can gain no admittance. Our spiritual ascent does but reveal to us, ever more and more clearly, the absolute incomprehensibility of the divine nature. Filled with an ever-increasing desire the soul grows without ceasing, goes forth from itself, reaches out beyond itself, and, in so doing, is filled with yet greater longing. Thus the ascent becomes infinite, the desire insatiable. This is the love of the bride in the Song of Songs: she stretches out her hands towards the lock, she seeks Him who cannot be grasped, she calls Him to whom she cannot attain . . . she attains to Him in the perception that the union is endless, the ascent without limit.[3]

St. Gregory Nazianzen takes up the same images, especially that of Moses. 'I was running,' he says, 'to lay hold on God, and thus I went up into the mount, and drew aside the curtain of the cloud, and entered away from matter and from material things, and as far as I could I withdrew within myself. And then when I looked up, I scarce saw the back parts of God; although I was sheltered by the Rock, the Word that was made flesh for

---

[1] *P.G.*, XLIV, 297–430. Ed. J. Daniélou, *Sources Chrétiennes*, 1bis.

[2] See the article by M. Henri-Charles Puech, 'La ténèbre mystique chez le pseudo-Denys l'Aréopagite et dans la tradition patristique,' in *Etudes Carmélitaines*, Oct. 1938, pp. 33–53.

[3] 'In Cant. Canticorum', *P.G.*, XLIV, 755–1120.

us. And when I looked a little closer, I saw, not the first and unmingled nature, known to itself—to the Trinity, I mean; not that which abideth within the first veil, and is hidden by the Cherubim; but only that nature, which at last even reaches to us. And that, so far as I can learn, is the majesty, or as holy David calls it, the glory, which is manifested amongst creatures.'[1] As to the divine essence in itself, it is 'the Holy of Holies which remains hid even from the Seraphim'.[2] The divine nature is like a sea of essence, indeterminate and without bounds, which spreads far and wide beyond all notion of time or of nature. If the mind tries to form a faint image of God, considering Him not in Himself but in that which compasses Him, this image eludes it even before it can attempt to seize it, illuminating the superior faculties as a flash of lightning which dazzles the eyes.[3] St. John Damascene expresses himself in the same manner: 'God, then, is infinite and incomprehensible, and all that is comprehensible about Him is His infinity and incomprehensibility. All that we can say cataphatically concerning God does not show forth His nature but the things that relate to His nature ($\tau\grave{\alpha}$ $\pi\epsilon\rho\grave{\iota}$ $\tau\grave{\eta}\nu$ $\phi\acute{\upsilon}\sigma\iota\nu$). . . . God does not belong to the class of existing things: not that He has no existence, but that He is above all existing things, nay even above existence itself. For if all forms of knowledge have to do with what exists, assuredly that which is above knowledge must certainly be also above essence ($\acute{\upsilon}\pi\grave{\epsilon}\rho$ $o\dot{\upsilon}\sigma\acute{\iota}\alpha\nu$); and, conversely, that which is above essence will also be above knowledge.'[4]

It would be possible to go on indefinitely finding ex-

---

[1] 'Oratio XXVIII (theologica II)', 3, *P.G.*, XXXVI, 29 AB.
[2] 'Oratio XXXVII, In Theophaniam', 8, ibid., 320 BC. Cf. 'Or. XLV, In sanct. Pascha', 4, ibid., 628D–629 A.
[3] 'Oratio XXXVIII', 7, ibid., 317 BC; 'Oratio XLV', 3, 625–628 A.
[4] 'De fide orthodoxa', I, 4, *P.G.*, XCIV, 800 BA.

amples of apophaticism in the theology of the eastern tradition. We will confine ourselves to quoting a passage from a great Byzantine theologian of the fourteenth century, St. Gregory Palamas: 'The super-essential nature of God is not a subject for speech or thought or even contemplation, for it is far removed from all that exists and more than unknowable, being founded upon the uncircumscribed might of the celestial spirits—incomprehensible and ineffable to all for ever. There is no name whereby it can be named, neither in this age nor in the age to come, nor word found in the soul and uttered by the tongue, nor contact whether sensible or intellectual, nor yet any image which may afford any knowledge of its subject, if this be not that perfect incomprehensibility which one acknowledges in denying all that can be named. None can properly name its essence or nature if he be truly seeking the truth that is above all truth.'[1] 'For if God be nature, then all else is not nature. If that which is not God be nature, God is not nature, and likewise He is not being if that which is not God is being.'[2]

Face to face with this radical apophaticism, characteristic of the theological tradition of the East, we may ask whether or not it corresponds to an ecstatic approach: whether there is a quest of ecstasy whenever the knowledge of God is sought by the way of negations. Is this negative theology necessarily a theology of ecstasy, or is it susceptible of a more general interpretation? We have seen, in examining the *Mystical Theology* of Dionysius, that the apophatic way is not merely an intellectual quest, that it is something more than a spinning of abstractions. As in the ecstatic platonists, as also in Plotinus, it is a question of a κάθαρσις: of an inward purification. There is, however, this difference: the Platonic purification was

---

[1] 'Theophanes', *P.G.*, CL, 937 A.

[2] 'Capita 150 physica, theologica, moralia et practica, cap. 78', *P.G.*, CL, 1176 B.

above all of an intellectual nature, intended to free the understanding from the multiplicity which is inseparable from being. For Dionysius, on the other hand, it is a refusal to accept being as such, in so far as it conceals the divine non-being: it is a renunciation of the realm of created things in order to gain access to that of the un-created; a more existential liberation involving the whole being of him who would know God. In both cases it is a question of union. But union with the ἕν of Plotinus can in fact mean a perception of the primordial and onto-logical union of man with God: in Dionysius the mystical union is a new condition which implies a progress, a series of changes, a transition from the created to the un-created, the acquiring of something which man did not hitherto possess by nature. Indeed, not only does he go forth from his own self (for this happens also in Plotinus), but he belongs wholly to the Unknowable, being deified in this union with the uncreated. Here union means deification. At the same time, while intimately united with God he knows Him only as Unknowable, in other words as infinitely set apart by His nature, remaining even in union, inaccesible in that which He is in His essential being. Though Dionysius speaks of ecstasy and of union, though his negative theology, far from being a purely intellectual exercise involves a mystical experience, an ascent towards God; he makes it none the less clear that even though we attain to the highest peaks accessible to created beings, the only rational notion which we can have of God will still be that of His incomprehensibility. Consequently, theology must be not so much a quest of positive notions about the divine being as an experience which surpasses all understanding. 'It is a great thing to speak of God, but still better to purify oneself for God,' says St. Gregory Nazianzen.[1] Apophaticism is not neces-sarily a theology of ecstasy. It is, above all, an attitude of

[1] 'Oratio XXXII, 12, *P.G.*, XXXVI, 188 C.

The Divine Darkness

mind which refuses to form concepts about God. Such an
attitude utterly excludes all abstract and purely intellectual theology which would adapt the mysteries of the
wisdom of God to human ways of thoughts. It is an
existential attitude which involves the whole man: there
is no theology apart from experience; it is necessary to
change, to become a new man. To know God one must
draw near to Him. No one who does not follow the path
of union with God can be a theologian. The way of the
knowledge of God is necessarily the way of deification.
He who, in following this path, imagines at a given
moment that he has known what God is has a depraved
spirit, according to St. Gregory Nazianzen.[1] Apophaticism
is, therefore, a criterion: the sure sign of an attitude of
mind conformed to truth. In this sense all true theology is
fundamentally apophatic.

It will naturally be asked what is the function of
'cataphatic' or affirmative theology, the theology of the
'divine names' which we find made manifest in the order
of creation? Unlike the negative way, which is an ascent
towards union, this is a way which comes down towards
us: a ladder of 'theophanies' or manifestations of God in
creation. It may even be said to be one and the same way
which can be followed in two different directions: God
condescends towards us in the 'energies' in which He is
manifested; we mount towards Him in the 'unions' in
which He remains incomprehensible by nature. The
'supreme theophany', the perfect manifestation of God in
the world by the incarnation of the Word, retains for us
its apophatic character. 'In the humanity of Christ,' says
Dionysius, 'the Super-essential was manifested in human
substance without ceasing to be hidden after this manifestation, or, to express myself after a more heavenly
fashion, in this manifestation itself.'[2] 'The affirmations of

[1] 'Carmina moralia. X: Περὶ ἀρετῆς', P.G., XXXVII, 748.
[2] 'Epist. III', P.G., III, 1069 B.

which the sacred humanity of Jesus Christ are the object
have all the force of the most pre-eminent negations.'[1] So
much the more the partial theophanies of inferior degree
conceal God in that which He is, whilst manifesting Him
in that which He is not by nature. The ladder of cataphatic theology which discloses the divine names drawn,
above all, from Holy Scripture, is a series of steps up
which the soul can mount to contemplation. These are
not the rational notions which we formulate, the concepts with which our intellect constructs a positive science
of the divine nature; they are rather images or ideas
intended to guide us and to fit our faculties for the contemplation of that which transcends all understanding.[2]
On the lower steps, especially, these images are fashioned
from the material objects least calculated to lead spirits
inexperienced in contemplation into error. It is, indeed,
more difficult to identify God with stone or with fire than
with intelligence, unity, being or goodness.[3] What
seemed evident at the beginning of the ascent—'God is not
stone, He is not fire'—is less and less so as we attain to the
heights of contemplation, impelled by that same apophatic
spirit which now causes us to say: 'God is not being, He is
not the good.' At each step of this ascent as one comes
upon loftier images or ideas, it is necessary to guard
against making of them a concept, 'an idol of God'.
Then one can contemplate the divine beauty itself: God,
in so far as He manifests Himself in creation. Speculation
gradually gives place to contemplation, knowledge to
experience; for, in casting off the concepts which shackle
the spirit, the apophatic disposition reveals boundless
horizons of contemplation at each step of positive theology.
Thus, there are different levels in theology, each appropriate to the differing capacities of the human under-

[1] 'Epist. IV', ibid., 1072 B.
[2] Gregory of Nyssa, 'Con. Eunom.', *P.G.*, XLV, 939–41.
[3] 'De Coel. hier., II, 3–5', ibid., 140–5.

standings which reach up to the mysteries of God. In this connection St. Gregory Nazianzen takes up again the image of Moses on Mount Sinai: 'God commands me to enter within the cloud and hold converse with Him; if any be an Aaron, let him go up with me, and let him stand near, being ready, if it must be so, to remain outside the cloud. But if any be a Nadad or an Abihu, or of the order of the elders, let him go up indeed, but let him stand afar off. . . . But if any be of the multitude, who are unworthy of this height of contemplation, if he be altogether impure let him not approach at all, for it would be dangerous to him; but if he be at least temporarily purified, let him remain below and listen to the voice alone, and the trumpet, the bare words of piety, and let him see the mount smoking and lightening. . . . But if any be an evil and savage beast, and altogether incapable of taking in the matter of contemplation and theology, let him not hurtfully and malignantly lurk in his den amongst the woods, to catch hold of some dogma or saying by a sudden spring . . . but let him stand yet afar off and withdraw from the mount, or he shall be stoned.'[1] This is not a more perfect or esoteric teaching hidden from the profane; nor is it a gnostic separation between those who are spiritual, psychic or carnal, but a school of contemplation wherein each receives his share in the experience of the Christian mystery lived by the Church. This contemplation of the hidden treasures of the divine Wisdom can be practised in varying degrees, with greater or lesser intensity: whether it be a lifting up of the spirit towards God and away from creatures, which allows His splendour to become visible; whether it be a meditation on the Holy Scriptures in which God hides Himself, as it were behind a screen, beneath the words which express the revelation (so Gregory of Nyssa); whether it be through the dogmas of the Church or through her liturgical life; whether, finally,

[1] 'Oratio XXVIII (theologica II), 2'; *P.G.*, XXXVI, 28 AC.

it be through ecstasy that we penetrate to the divine mystery, this experience of God will always be the fruit of that apophatic attitude which Dionysius commends to us in his *Mystical Theology*.

All that we have said about apophaticism may be summed up in a few words. Negative theology is not merely a theory of ecstasy. It is an expression of that fundamental attitude which transforms the whole of theology into a contemplation of the mysteries of revelation. It is not a branch of theology, a chapter, or an inevitable introduction on the incomprehensibility of God from which one passes unruffled to a doctrinal exposition in the usual terminology of human reason and philosophy in general. Apophaticism teaches us to see above all a negative meaning in the dogmas of the Church: it forbids us to follow natural ways of thought and to form concepts which would usurp the place of spiritual realities. For Christianity is not a philosophical school for speculating about abstract concepts, but is essentially a communion with the living God. That is why, despite all their philosophical learning and natural bent towards speculation, the Fathers of the eastern tradition in remaining faithful to the apophatic principle of theology, never allowed their thought to cross the threshold of the mystery, or to substitute idols of God for God Himself. That is also why there is no philosophy *more* or *less* Christian. Plato is not more Christian than Aristotle. The question of the relations between theology and philosophy has never arisen in the East. The apophatic attitude gave to the Fathers of the Church that freedom and liberality with which they employed philosophical terms without running the risk of being misunderstood or of falling into a 'theology of concepts'. Whenever theology is transformed into a religious philosophy (as in the case of Origen) it is always the result of forsaking the apophaticism which is truly characteristic of the whole tradition of the Eastern Church.

The Divine Darkness

Unknowability does not mean agnosticism or refusal to know God. Nevertheless, this knowledge will only be attained in the way which leads not to knowledge but to union—to deification. Thus theology will never be abstract, working through concepts, but contemplative: raising the mind to those realities which pass all understanding. This is why the dogmas of the Church often present themselves to the human reason as antinomies, the more difficult to resolve the more sublime the mystery which they express. It is not a question of suppressing the antinomy by adapting dogma to our understanding, but of a change of heart and mind enabling us to attain to the contemplation of the reality which reveals itself to us as it raises us to God, and unites us, according to our several capacities, to Him.

The highest point of revelation, the dogma of the Holy Trinity, is pre-eminently an antinomy. To attain to the contemplation of this primordial reality in all its fullness, it is necessary to reach the goal which it set before us, to attain to the state of deification; for, in the words of St. Gregory Nazianzen, 'they will be welcomed by the ineffable light, and the vision of the holy and sovereign Trinity . . . uniting themselves wholly to the whole Spirit; wherein alone and beyond all else I take it that the Kingdom of Heaven consists.'[1] The apophatic way does not lead to an absence, to an utter emptiness; for the unknowable God of the Christian is not the impersonal God of the philosophers. It is to the Holy Trinity, 'superessential, more than divine and more than good' ($T\rho\iota\grave{a}s \ \acute{v}\pi\epsilon\rho o\acute{v}\sigma\iota\epsilon,$ $\kappa a\grave{\iota} \ \acute{v}\pi\acute{\epsilon}\rho\theta\epsilon\epsilon, \ \kappa a\grave{\iota} \ \acute{v}\pi\epsilon\rho\acute{a}\gamma a\theta\epsilon$)[2] that the author of the *Mystical Theology* commends himself in entering upon the way which is to bring him to a presence and a fullness which are without measure.

[1] 'Oratio XVI', *P.G.*, XXXV, 945 C.
[2] 'Myst. Theology, I, 1', *P.G.*, III, 997.

CHAPTER THREE

God in Trinity

The apophaticism characteristic of the theological thought of the Eastern Church is not an impersonal mysticism, an experience of the absolute, divine nothingness in which both the human person and God as person are swallowed up.

The goal to which apophatic theology leads—if, indeed, we may speak of goal or ending when, as here, it is a question of an ascent towards the infinite; this infinite goal is not a nature or an essence, nor is it a person; it is something which transcends all notion both of nature and of person: it is the Trinity.

St. Gregory Nazianzen, who is sometimes called the minstrel of the Holy Trinity, tells us in one of his theological poems: 'From the day whereon I renounced the things of the world to consecrate my soul to luminous and heavenly contemplation, when the supreme intelligence carried me hence to set me down far from all that pertains to the flesh, to hide me in the secret places of the heavenly tabernacle; from that day my eyes have been blinded by the light of the Trinity, whose brightness surpasses all that the mind can conceive; for from a throne high exalted the Trinity pours upon all, the ineffable radiance common to the Three. This is the source of all that is here below, separated by time from the things on high. . . . From that day forth I was dead to the world and the world was dead to me.'[1] At the close of his life he longs to be 'there where

---

[1] 'Poemata de seipso I', *P.G.*, XXXVII, 984-5.

my Trinity is, and the gathered brightness of Its splendour. . . . Trinity, whose dim shadows exalt me'.[1]

If the very foundation of created being is change, the transition from non-being to being, if the creature is contingent by nature, the Trinity is an absolute stability. One would say, an absolute necessity of perfect being: and yet the idea of necessity is not proper to the Trinity, for It transcends the antinomy of what is necessary, and the contingent; entirely personal and entirely nature; liberty and necessity are one, or, rather, can have no place in God. There is no dependence in relation to created being on the part of the Trinity; no determination of what is called 'the eternal procession of the divine persons' by the act of the creation of the world. Even though the created order did not exist, God would still be Trinity—Father, Son and Holy Ghost—for creation is an act of will: the procession of the persons is an act 'according tona ture' (κατὰ φύσιν).[2] There is no interior process in the Godhead; no 'dialectic' of the three persons; no becoming; no 'tragedy in the Absolute', which might necessitate the trinitarian development of the divine being in order that it be surmounted or resolved. These conceptions, proper to the romantic tradition of nineteenth-century German philosophy, are wholly foreign to the dogma of the Trinity. If we speak of processions, of acts, or of inner determinations, these expressions—involving, as they do, the ideas of time, becoming and intention—only show to what extent our language, indeed our thought, is poor and deficient before the primordial mystery of revelation. Again we are forced to appeal to apophatic theology in order to rid ourselves of concepts proper to human thought, transforming them into steps

[1] Ibid., XI; *P.G.*, XXXVII, 1165–6.
[2] St. Athanasius of Alexandria, 'Contra Arianos', I, 18, *P.G.*, XXVI, 49. St. John Damascene, 'De fide orthodoxa', I, 8, *P.G.*, XCIV, 812–13.

by which we may ascend to the contemplation of a reality which the created intelligence cannot contain.

It is in such a spirit as this that St. Gregory Nazianzen speaks in his oration on baptism: 'No sooner do I conceive of the One than I am illumined by the splendour of the Three; no sooner do I distinguish them than I am carried back to the One. When I think of any One of the Three, I think of Him as the whole, and my eyes are filled, and the greater part of what I am thinking of escapes me. I cannot grasp the greatness of that One so as to attribute a greater greatness to the rest. When I contemplate the Three together, I see but one torch, and cannot divide or measure out the undivided light.'[1] Our thought must be in continuous motion, pursuing now the one, now the three, and returning again to the unity; it must swing ceaselessly between the two poles of the antinomy, in order to attain to the contemplation of the sovereign repose of this threefold monad. How can the antinomy of unity and trinity be contained in an image? How can this mystery be grasped save by the aid of an idea—be it that of movement or of development—which is inadmissible? Nazianzen's conscious adoption of the language of Plotinus can delude only those unimaginative and pedestrian souls who are incapable of rising above rational concepts: those who ransack the thought of the Fathers for traces of 'Platonism' or 'Aristotelianism'. St. Gregory speaks to the philosophers as a philosopher, that he may win the philosopher to the contemplation of the Trinity. 'The monad is set in motion in virtue of its richness; the dyad is surpassed (for the deity is above matter and form); the triad contains itself in perfection, for it is the first which surpasses the composition of the dyad. Thus, the Godhead does not dwell within bounds, nor does it spread itself indefinitely. The one would be without honour, the other would be contrary to order. The

[1] 'Oratio XL, 41', *P.G.*, XXXVI, 417 BC.

one would be wholly Judaic, the other Hellenistic and polytheistic.'[1] One gains a glimpse of the mystery of the number, three; the deity is neither one nor many; its perfection goes beyond the multiplicity of which duality is the root (we recall the interminable dyads of the gnostics, and the dualism of the Platonists), and expresses itself in the Trinity. The term 'expresses itself' is improper, for the divinity has no need to manifest its perfection, either to itself or to others. It *is* the Trinity, and this fact can be deduced from no principle nor explained by any sufficient reason, for there are neither principles nor causes anterior to the Trinity.

Τριάς : 'name which unites things united by nature, and never allows those which are inseparable to be scattered by a number which separates,' says St. Gregory Nazianzen.[2] Two is the number which separates, three the number which transcends all separation: the one and the many find themselves gathered and circumscribed in the Trinity. 'When I say *God*, I mean Father, Son and Holy Ghost; for Godhead is neither diffused beyond these, so as to introduce a multitude of gods, nor yet bounded by a smaller compass than these, so as to condemn us for a poverty-stricken conception of deity, either Judaizing to save the monarchy, or falling into Hellenism by the multitude of our gods.'[3] St. Gregory Nazianzen is not seeking to vindicate the trinity of persons before the human reason: he simply shows the insufficiency of any number other than three. But we may ask whether the idea of number can be applied to God; whether we do not thus submit the divinity to an exterior determination, to a form proper to our understanding—that of the number, three. To this objection St. Basil replies as follows: 'we do not count by addition, passing from the one to the many by increase;

---

[1] 'Oratio XXII, 8', *P.G.*, XXXV, 1160 CD.
[2] 'Oratio XXIII, 10', *P.G.*, XXXV, 1161 C.
[3] 'Oratio XLV, 4', *P.G.*, XXXVI, 628 C.

we do not say: one, two, three, or first, second and third. '*For I am God, the first, and I am the last.*[1] Now we have never, even to the present time, heard of a second God; but adoring God of God, confessing the individuality of the hypostases, we dwell in the monarchy without dividing the theology into fragments.'[2] In other words, there is no question here of a material number which serves for calculation and is in no wise applicable in the spiritual sphere, where there is no quantitative increase. The threefold number is not, as we commonly understand it, a quantity; when it relates to the indivisibly united divine hypostases, the 'sum' of which is always the unity, $3 = 1$, it expresses the ineffable order within the Godhead.

The contemplation of this absolute perfection, of this divine plenitude which is the Trinity—God who is personal and who is not a person confined in his own self—the very thought, the mere 'pale shade of the Trinity', lifts the human soul beyond the world of being, changing and confused, in bestowing upon it this stability in the midst of passions; this serenity, or ἀπάθεια which is the beginning of deification. For the creature, subject to change by nature, can by grace attain to the state of eternal stability; can partake of infinite life in the light of the Trinity. This is why the Church has defended so vehemently the mystery of the Holy Trinity against the natural tendencies of the human mind, which strive to suppress it by reducing the Trinity to unity, in making it an essence of the philosophers with three modes of manifestation (the modalism of Sabellius), or even by dividing it into three distinct beings, as did Arius.

The Church has expressed by the ὁμοούσιος the

---

[1] Is. xliv, 6: 'Ἐγὼ [γὰρ] θεὸς πρῶτος, καὶ ἐγὼ μετα ταῦτα' in the lxx. 'I am the first and I am the last', in A.V.

[2] 'De Spiritu Sancto', cap. 45, *P.G.*, XXXII, 149 B. Edited with French translation by Benoit Pruche, O.P., Paris, 1947 (*Sources chrétiennes*), pp. 192–3.

consubstantiality of the Three, the mysterious identity of the monad and of the triad; identity of the one nature and distinction of the three hypostases. It is interesting to note that the expression τό ὁμοούσιον εἶναι is found in Plotinus.[1] The trinity of Plotinus comprises three consubstantial hypostases: the One, the Intelligence, and the Soul of the world. Their consubstantiality does not rise to the trinitarian antinomy of Christian dogma: it appears as a descending hierarchy and realizes itself through the ceaseless flow of the hypostases which pass the one into the other, reciprocally reflecting each other. This demonstrates once again the unsoundness of the method of those historians who would express the thought of the Fathers of the Church by explaining the terms they use in the light of Hellenistic philosophy. Revelation sets an abyss between the truth which it declares and the truths which can be discovered by philosophical speculation. If human thought guided by the instinct for truth—which is faith, though confused and uncertain—could, apart from Christianity, grope its way towards certain notions which approximated to the Trinity, the mystery of God-in-Trinity remained inscrutable to it. A 'change of spirit' was needed—a μετάνοια, which also means 'penitence', like the penitence of Job when he found himself face to face with God: 'I have heard of thee by the hearing of the ear: but now mine eye seeth thee. Wherefore I abhor myself, and repent in dust and ashes.'[2] The mystery of the Trinity only becomes accessible to that ignorance which rises above all that can be contained within the concepts of the philosophers. Yet this *ignorantia*, not only *docta* but charitable also, redescends again upon these concepts that it may mould them; that it may transform the expressions

---

[1] *Ennead*, IV, 4, 28. It is a question of the passions of the soul having the same nature.

[2] Job xlii, 5–6.

of human wisdom into the instruments of that Wisdom of God which is to the Greeks foolishness.

It required the superhuman efforts of an Athanasius of Alexandria, of a Basil, of a Gregory Nazianzen and of many others, to purify the concepts of Hellenistic thought, to break down the watertight bulkheads by the introduction of a Christian apophaticism which transformed rational speculation into a contemplation of the mystery of the Trinity. It was a question of finding a distinction of terms which should express the unity of, and the differentiation within, the Godhead, without giving the pre-eminence either to the one or to the other; that thought might not fall into the error of a Sabellian unitarianism or a pagan tritheism. The Fathers of the fourth century—trinitarian century *par excellence*—availed themselves by preference of the terms οὐσία and ὑπόστασις to lead the intellect towards the mystery of the Trinity. The term οὐσία is frequently employed by Aristotle, who defines it as follows: 'That is principally, primarily and properly called οὐσία which is stated of no subject and which is in no subject—for example, this man, or this horse. We call "second ousias" (δεύτεραι οὐσίαι) those species wherein the "first ousias" exist with their corresponding description: thus, "this man" is specifically man and generically animal. Man and animal, then, are called "second ousias".'[1] In other words, 'first ousias' are individual subsistences, the individual subsisting; 'second ousias'—essences, in the realistic sense of the word. Ὑπόστασις, without having the value of a philosophical term, signifies in current terminology that which really subsists, subsistence (from the verb ὑφίσταμαι, to subsist). St. John Damascene gives the following definition of the conceptual value of the two terms in his Dialectic: 'οὐσία is a thing that exists by itself, and which has need of nothing else for its consistency. Again, *ousia* is all that *subsists* by

[1] *Categories*, V.

itself and which has not its being in another. It is thus that which is not for another, that which does not have its existence in another, that which has no need of another for its consistency, but is in itself and in which the accident has its existence. . . . The term *hypostasis* has two meanings. Sometimes it means simply existence. From this definition it follows that *ousia* and *hypostasis* are the same thing. Hence certain of the holy fathers have said: natures, or hypostases. Sometimes it denotes that which exists by itself and in its own consistency; from which meaning it comes that it denotes the individual, differing numerically from every other—Peter, Paul, this particular horse.'[1] The two terms would thus appear to be more or less synonymous; *ousia* meaning an individual substance, while being capable at the same time of denoting the essence common to many individuals; *hypostasis*, on the other hand, meaning existence in general, but capable also of application to individual substances. According to the testimony of Theodoret of Cyrus: 'for profane wisdom there is no difference between ousia and hypostasis. For ousia means that which is, and hypostasis that which subsists. But according to the teaching of the fathers, there is between ousia and hypostasis the same difference as between common and particular.'[2] The genius of the Fathers made use of the two synonyms to distinguish in God that which is common—ousia, substance or essence—from that which is particular—ὑπόστασις or person.

This latter expression, *persona*, πρόσωπον, which was widely adopted especially in the West, at first occasioned lively disputes in Eastern Christendom. In reality, this word far from having its modern sense of *person* (human personality, for example), denoted rather the outward aspect of the individual—the appearance, visage, mask; or the character assumed by an actor. St. Basil saw in this

[1] 'Πηγὴ γνώσεως', 39 and 42', *P.G.*, XCIV, 605 and 612.
[2] *P.G.*, LXXXIII, 33 AB.

term, as applied to trinitarian doctrine, a tendency peculiar to western thought: a tendency which had already shown itself in Sabellianism in making of the Father, the Son and the Holy Ghost no more than three modalities of a unique substance. In the West, on the other hand, the term hypostasis (which was translated by *substantia*), was regarded as an expression of tritheism and even of Arianism. These misunderstandings were nevertheless dispelled. The term hypostasis, as expressing the notion of person in the concrete sense, passed to the West. The term *persona*, or προσώπον, was received and suitably interpreted in the East. Thus, in the freeing of men's minds from natural limitations due to differences of mentality and culture, the catholicity of the Church was made manifest. Though the Latins might express the mystery of the Trinity by starting from one essence in order to arrive at the three persons; though the Greeks might prefer the concrete as their starting point (that is to say, the three hypostases), seeing in them the one nature; it was always the same dogma of the Trinity that was confessed by the whole of Christendom before the separation. St. Gregory Nazianzen thus brings together the two methods of approach: 'When I speak of God you must be illumined at once by one flash of light and by three. Three in Properties, or Hypostases, or Persons, if any prefer so to call them, for we will not quarrel about names so long as the syllables amount to the same meaning; but One in respect of the οὐσία— that is, the Godhead. For they are divided indivisibly, if I may so say; and they are conjoined dividedly. For the Godhead is one in three, and the three are one, in whom the Godhead is, or, to speak more accurately, Who are the Godhead.'[1] And in another oration he thus sums up the distinction between the hypostatic characteristics: 'The very fact of being unbegotten, or begotten, or proceeding, has given the name of Father to the First, of the Son to

[1] 'In sancta lumina, Oratio XXXIX, xi', *P.G.*, XXXVI, 345 CD

the Second, and to the Third, Him of whom we are speaking, of the Holy Ghost, that the distinction of the Three Hypostases may be preserved in the one nature and dignity of the Godhead. For neither is the Son Father, for the Father is One, but He is what the Father is; nor is the Spirit Son because He is of God, for the Only-begotten is One, but He is what the Son is. The Three are One in Godhead, and the One Three in properties; so that neither is the Unity a Sabellian one, nor does the Trinity countenance the present evil division.' (i.e. Arianism).[1]

Purged of its Aristotelian content, the theological notion of hypostasis in the thought of the eastern Fathers means not so much *individual* as *person*, in the modern sense of this word. Indeed, our ideas of human personality, of that *personal* quality which makes every human being unique, to be expressed only in terms of itself: this idea of *person* comes to us from Christian theology. The philosophy of antiquity knew only human individuals. The human person cannot be expressed in concepts. It eludes all rational definitions, indeed all description, for all the properties whereby it could be characterized can be met with in other individuals. Personality can only be grasped in this life by a direct intuition; it can only be expressed in a work of art. When we say 'this is by Mozart', or 'this is by Rembrandt', we are in both cases dealing with a personal world which has no equivalent anywhere. And yet human persons, or hypostases, are isolated and, in the words of St. John Damascene, 'do not exist the one within the other'; while, 'in the Holy Trinity it is quite the reverse . . . the hypostases dwell in one another.'[2] The works of human persons are distinct. Not so those of the divine Persons; for the Three, having but one nature, have but a single will, a single power, a single operation. To quote St. John Damascene again: 'The persons are

[1] 'Oratio XXXI (Theologica V), ix' *P.G.*, XXXVI, 144 A.
[2] 'De Fide Orthodoxa, I, 8', *P.G.*, XCIV, 828–9.

made one not so as to commingle, but so as to cleave to each other, and they have their being in each other (τὴν ἐν ἀλλήλαις περιχώρησιν ἔχουσι) without any coalescence or commingling. Nor do the Son and Spirit stand apart, nor are they sundered in essence as in the heresy of Arius. For, to put it concisely, the Godhead is undivided; and it is just like three suns cleaving to each other without separation, and giving out light mingled and conjoined into one.'[1] 'Each one of the persons contains the unity by this relation to the others no less than by this relation to Himself.'[2]

Indeed, each of the three hypostastes contains the unity, the one nature, after the manner proper to it, and which, in distinguishing it from the other two persons, recalls at the same time the indissoluble bond uniting the Three. 'For in their hypostatic or personal properties alone', says Damascene—'the properties of being unbegotten, of filiation and of procession—do the three divine hypostases differ from each other, being indivisibly divided, not by essence but by the distinguishing mark of their proper and peculiar hypostasis.'[3] 'The Father, the Son, and the Holy Ghost are one in all respects save those of being unbegotten, of filiation and of procession.'[4]

The only characteristic of the hypostases which we can state to be exclusively proper to each, and which is never found in the others, by reason of their consubstantiality, is thus the relation of origin. Nevertheless, this relation must be understood in an apophatic sense. It is above all a negation, showing us that the Father is neither the Son nor the Holy Spirit; that the Son is neither the Father nor the Spirit; that the Holy Spirit is neither the Father nor the Son. Otherwise to regard it would be to submit the Trinity to a category of Aristotelian logic, that of relation. Understood apophatically, the relation of origin describes

[1] Ibid., 829.　　[2] Ibid., 828 C.
[3] Ibid., 821–4.　　[4] Ibid., 828 D.

54

the difference but nevertheless does not indicate the manner of the divine processions. 'The mode of generation and the mode of procession are incomprehensible,' says St. John Damascene. 'We have learned that there is a difference between generation and procession, but the nature of the difference we in no wise understand.'[1] St. Gregory Nazianzen had already been forced to reject the attempts made to define the mode of the divine procession. 'You ask,' he says, 'what is the procession of the Holy Spirit? Do you tell me first what is the unbegottenness of the Father, and I will then explain to you the physiology of the generation of the Son, and the procession of the Spirit, and we shall both of us be stricken with madness for prying into the mystery of God.'[2] 'You hear that there is generation? Do not waste your time in seeking after the *how*. You hear that the Spirit proceeds from the Father? Do not busy yourself about the *how*.'[3] Indeed, if the relations of origin—to be unbegotten, begotten and proceeding—which cause us to distinguish the three hypostases, lead our thought to the sole source of the Son and of the Holy Spirit, to the πηγαία θεότης, to the Father, Source of Divinity,[4] they do not establish a separate relation between the Son and the Holy Spirit. These two persons are distinguished by the different mode of their origin: the Son is begotten, the Holy Spirit *proceeds* from the Father. This is sufficient to distinguish them.

The reaction of St. Gregory Nazianzen shows that trinitarian speculation, not content with the formula of the procession of the Holy Spirit διὰ υἱοῦ, 'through the Son', or 'in connexion with the Son' (an expression which is found in the Fathers and which usually refers to the mission of the Holy Spirit in the world through the

---

[1] Ibid., 820 A, 824 A.

[2] 'Oratio XXXI (Theologica V), 8', *P.G.*, XXXVI, 141 B.

[3] 'Oratio XX, ii', *P.G.*, XXXV, 1077 C.

[4] The expression is that of Dionysius, D.N., II, 7, *P.G.*, III, 645 B.

mediation of the Son), was seeking to establish a relationship between the Son and the Holy Spirit as to their
hypostatic origins. This relationship between the two
persons who take their origin from the Father was established by the western doctrine of the procession of the
Holy Spirit *ab utroque*, that is to say from the two persons
at once; from the Father and from the Son. The *filioque*
was the primordial cause, the only dogmatic cause, of the
breach between East and West. The other doctrinal disputes were but its consequences. In order to understand
what the East desired to safeguard in protesting against
the western formula it will suffice to compare the two
trinitarian conceptions which confronted each other about
the middle of the ninth century.

As we have already observed, in expounding the dogma
of the Trinity, western thought most frequently took as its
starting point the one nature, and thence passed to the
consideration of the three persons, while the Greeks followed the opposite course—from the three persons to the
one nature. St. Basil preferred this latter way, which in
conformity to Holy Scripture and to the baptismal formula which names the Father, the Son and the Holy
Ghost, starts from the concrete. Human thought does not
run the risk of going astray if it passes from the consideration of the three persons to that of the common nature.
Nevertheless, the two ways were both equally legitimate
so long as the first did not attribute to the essence a
supremacy over the three persons, nor the second to the
three persons a supremacy over the common nature. In
fact, as we have seen, the Fathers made use of two
synonyms (οὐσία and ὑπόστασις) to establish the distinction between the nature and the persons, without putting the emphasis upon either. Where one spoke of the
persons (or person) one spoke at the same time of the
nature, and vice versa. The nature is inconceivable apart
from the persons or as anterior to the three persons, even

in the logical order. If the balance of this antinomy between nature and persons, absolutely different and absolutely identical at the same time, is upset, there will be in the one case a tendency towards a Sabellian unitarianism (the God-essence of the philosophers), or else towards tritheism. The Greeks saw in the formula of the procession of the Holy Spirit from the Father and the Son a tendency to stress the unity of nature at the expense of the real distinction between the persons. The relationships of origin which do not bring the Son and the Spirit back directly to the unique source, to the Father—the one as begotten, the other as proceeding—become a system of relationships within the one essence: something logically posterior to the essence. Indeed, according to the western conception the Father and the Son cause the Holy Spirit to proceed, inasmuch as they represent the one nature; while the Holy Spirit, who, for western theologians, becomes 'the bond between the Father and the Son', stands for a natural unity between the first two persons. The hypostatic characteristics (paternity, generation, procession), find themselves more or less swallowed up in the nature or essence which, differentiated by relationships—to the Son as Father, to the Holy Spirit as Father and Son—becomes the principle of unity within the Trinity. The relationships, instead of being characteristics of the hypostases, are identified with them. As St. Thomas was later to write: 'Persona est relatio',[1] inner relationship of the essence which it diversifies. It can scarcely be denied that there is a difference between this trinitarian conception and that of Gregory Nazianzen with his 'Thrice-repeated Holy, meeting in one ascription of the title Lord and God.'[2] As Father de Régnon very justly observes: 'Latin

---

[1] *Summa theologica*, Ia, q. 29, a. 4.
[2] 'In Theophaniam, Oratio XXXVIII, 8', *P.G.*, XXXVI, 320 BC. The reference is, of course, to the Triumphal Hymn: 'Holy, holy, holy, Lord God of hosts. . . .'

philosophy first considers the nature in itself and proceeds
to the agent; Greek philosophy first considers the agent
and afterwards passes through it to find the nature. The
Latins think of personality as a mode of nature; the
Greeks think of nature as the content of the person.'[1]

The Greek Fathers always maintained that the principle of unity in the Trinity is the person of the Father. As
Principle of the other two persons, the Father is at the
same time the Source of the relations whence the hypostases receive their distinctive characteristics. In causing
the persons to proceed, he lays down their relations of
origin—generation and procession—in regard to the
unique principle of Godhead. This is why the East has
always opposed the formula of *filioque* which seems to im-
pair the monarchy of the Father: either one is forced to
destroy the unity by acknowledging two principles of Godhead, or one must ground the unity primarily on the
common nature, which thus overshadows the persons and
transforms them into relations within the unity of the
essence. For the West, the relations diversified the primordial unity. For the East, they signified at one and the
same time the diversity and the unity, because they had
reference to the Father who is principle, as well as
recapitulation (συγκεφαλαίωσις), of the Trinity. It is in
this sense that St. Athanasius understands the saying of
St. Dionysius of Alexandria: 'We extend the monad indivisibly into the triad, and conversely we *recapitulate* the
triad without diminution into the monad.'[2] Elsewhere he
declares: 'There is a single principle of the Godhead,
whence there is strictly a monarchy.'[3] 'A single God
because a single Father', according to the saying of the
Greek Fathers. The persons and the nature are, so to say,
given at the same time, without the one being logically

[1] *Etudes de théologie positive sur la St. Trinité*, I, 433.
[2] 'De sententiae Dionysii, 17', *P.G.*, XXV, 505 A.
[3] 'Contra Arianos, Oratio IV, 1', *P.G.*, XXVI, 468 B.

prior to the other. The Father—πηγαία θεότης, source of all divinity within the Trinity—brings forth the Son and the Holy Spirit in conferring upon them His nature, which remains one and indivisible, identical in itself in the Three. For the Greek Fathers, to confess the unity of the nature is to recognize the Father as unique Source of the persons who receive from Him this same nature. 'In my opinion,' says St. Gregory Nazianzen, 'one safeguards one only God in referring the Son and the Spirit to a single Principle, neither compounding nor confounding them; and in affirming the identity of substance and what I will call the unique and like motion and will of the Godhead.'[1] 'To us there is one God, for the Godhead is One, and all that proceedeth from Him is referred to One, though we believe in Three Persons. . . . When, then, we look at the Godhead, or the First Cause, or the Monarchy, that which we conceive is One; but when we look at the Persons in whom the Godhead dwells, and at those who timelessly and with equal glory have their being from the First Cause—there are Three whom we worship.'[2] St. Gregory Nazianzen here brings the Godhead and the Person of the Father so closely together that he might be thought to confound them. He clarifies his thought in another passage: 'The Three have one Nature—God. And the union (ἕνωσις) is the Father, from whom and to whom the order of Persons runs its course, not so as to be confounded, but so as to be possessed, without distinction of time, of will, or of power.'[3] St. John Damascene expresses the same thought with that doctrinal precision which is peculiar to him. 'The Father derives from Himself His being, nor does He derive a single quality from another. Rather He is Himself the beginning and cause of the existence of all things both as

[1] 'Oratio XX, 7', *P.G.*, XXXV, 1073.
[2] 'Oratio XXXI (Theologica V), 14', *P.G.*, XXXVI, 148D–149A.
[3] 'Oratio XLII', *P.G.*, XXXVI, 476 B.

to their nature and mode of being. All then that the Son
and the Spirit have is from the Father, even their very
being: and unless the Father is, neither the Son nor the
Spirit is. And unless the Father possesses a certain attribute, neither the Son nor the Spirit possesses it: and
through the Father, that is, because of the Father's existence, the Son and the Spirit exist. . . . When, then, we
turn our eyes to the Godhead, and the first cause, and the
sovereignty . . . what is seen by us is unity. But when we
look to those things in which the Godhead is, or, to put it
more accurately, which are the Godhead, and those
things which are in it through the first cause . . . that is
to say, the hypostases of the Son and the Spirit, it seems
to us a Trinity that we adore.'[1] It is the Father who
distinguishes the hypostases 'in an eternal movement of
love' (ἀχρόνως καί ἀγαπητικῶς), according to an expression of St. Maximus.[2] He confers His one nature
upon the Son and upon the Holy Spirit alike, in whom it
remains one and undivided, not distributed, while being
differently conferred; for the procession of the Holy Spirit
from the Father is not identical with the generation of the
Son by the same Father. Manifested by the Son and with
the Son, the Holy Spirit has His being as divine person in
proceeding from the Father, as is plainly stated by St.
Basil: ' For of the Father is the Son, by Whom are all
things and with whom the Holy Spirit is always thought
of together inseparably. For it is impossible to obtain any
comprehension of the Son without first being enlightened
by the Spirit. Since, then, the Holy Spirit, from whom
springs the whole abundance of good things distributed
to the creation, is linked on to the Son, and with Him
is apprehended without any discontinuity, He has His
being attached to the Father, from whom He proceeds.

---

[1] 'De fide orth., I, 8', *P.G.*, XCIV, 821 C, 824 B, 829 B.
[2] 'Scholia in lib. de Divin. nomin., II, 3. ἐνώσεις τε καί διακρίσεις', *P.G.*, IV, 221 A.

This is the distinguishing note characteristic of His hypostasis—that He is made known after the Son and together with Him, and that He takes His subsistence from the Father. As for the Son, who through Himself and with Himself makes known the Spirit who proceeds from the Father, and who shines forth alone only-begottenly from the unbegotten light, He has nothing in common with the Father or the Holy Spirit as to the marks whereby He is distinguished, but alone is distinguished by the notes just mentioned. But God who is above all, alone has one exceptional mark of His hypostasis—that He is Father, and has His subsistence from no cause; and by this note again He is Himself peculiarly recognized.'[1]

St. John Damascene expresses himself with no less precision in distinguishing the persons of the Holy Trinity without submitting them to the category of relation: 'It should be understood', he says, 'that we do not speak of the Father as derived from anyone, but we speak of Him as the Father of the Son. We speak of the Son neither as Cause (αἴτιον) nor Father, but we speak of Him, both as from the Father and as the Son of the Father. And we speak likewise of the Holy Spirit as from the Father, and call Him the Spirit of the Father. We do not speak of the Spirit as from the Son, but yet we call Him the Spirit of the Son. (ἐκ τοῦ υἱοῦ δὲ τὸ πνεῦμα οὐ λέγομεν, πνεῦμα δὲ υἱοῦ ὀνομάζομεν).'[2]

The Word and the Spirit, two rays of the same sun, or rather 'two new suns',[3] are inseparable in their showing forth of the Father and are yet ineffably distinct, as two persons proceeding from the same Father. If, in conformity to the Latin formula, we introduce here a new relation of origin, making the Holy Spirit to proceed from the

---

[1] 'Epist. XXXVIII, 4', *P.G.*, XXXII, 329 C–332 A.
[2] 'De fide orth., I, 8', *P.G.*, XCIV, 832 AB.
[3] St. Gregory Nazianzen, 'Oratio XXXI, 32', *P.G.*, XXXVI, 169 B.

Father and from the Son; the monarchy of the Father, this personal relation creating the unity at the same time as the trinity, gives place to another conception—that of the one substance in which the relations intervene to establish the distinction of persons, and in which the hypostasis of the Holy Spirit is no more than a reciprocal bond between the Father and the Son. Once the different emphasis of the two trinitarian doctrines has been perceived, it will be understood why the East has always defended the ineffable, apophatic character of the procession of the Holy Spirit from the Father, unique source of the persons, against a more rational doctrine which, in making of the Father and the Son a common principle of the Holy Spirit, places the common nature above the persons; a doctrine which tends to weaken the hypostases by confounding the persons of Father and Son in the natural act of spiration, and in making of the Holy Spirit a connection between the two.

In insisting upon the monarchy of the Father—— unique source of Godhead and principle of the unity of the three—the eastern theologians were defending a conception of the Trinity which they considered to be more concrete, more personal, than that against which they contended. Nevertheless, we may ask, does not this triadology fall into the opposite excess: does it not place the persons before the nature? Such would be the case, for example, if the nature were given the character of a common revelation of the persons (as in the sophiology of Father Bulgakov, a modern Russian theologian whose teaching, like that of Origen, reveals the dangers of the eastern approach, or, rather, the snares into which the Russian thinker is prone to stumble).[1] But the Orthodox

---

[1] Father Bulgakov regarded God as a 'person in three hypostases', who reveals himself in the οὐσία —Wisdom. See his *Agnus Dei* (in Russian), Ch. I. (French translation, *Du Verbe incarné*, Aubier, 1943, pp. 13–20.)

tradition is as far from this eastern exaggeration as from its western antithesis. In fact, as we have seen, if the persons exist it is precisely because they have the one nature; their very procession consists in receiving their common nature from the Father. A further objection may seem to rest on surer ground: does not this monarchy of the Father savour of subordination? Does not this conception confer upon the Father, the one unique source, a certain pre-eminence as *the* divine person?

St. Gregory Nazianzen foresaw this difficulty: 'I should like', he says, 'to call the Father the greater, because from Him flow both the equality and the being of the equals . . . but I am afraid to use the word Origin, lest I should make Him the Origin of inferiors, and thus insult Him by precedencies of honour. For the lowering of those who are from Him is no glory to the Source.'[1]

'Godhead . . . neither increased nor diminished by superiorities or inferiorities; in every respect equal, in every respect the same; just as the beauty and the greatness of the heavens is one; the infinite connaturality of Three Infinite Ones, each God when considered in Himself; as the Father so the Son, as the Son so the Holy Ghost; the Three, one God when contemplated together; each God because consubstantial; the Three, one God because of the monarchy.'[2]

Thus, in formulating the dogma of the Trinity, the apophatic character of patristic thought was able while distinguishing between nature and hypostases to preserve their mysterious equivalence. In the words of St. Maximus, 'God is identically Monad and Triad'.[3] This is the end of the endless way: the limit of the limitless ascent; the

---

[1] 'In sanct. bapt. Oratio XL, 43', *P.G.*, XXXVI, 419 B.

[2] Ibid., 41, 417 B.

[3] 'Capita theologica et oeconomica 200, Cent. II, I', *P.G.*, XC, 1125 A.

Incomprehensibility reveals Himself in the very fact of His being incomprehensible, for his incomprehensibility is rooted in the fact that God is not only Nature but also Three Persons; the incomprehensible Nature is incomprehensible inasmuch as it is the Nature of the Father, of the Son and of the Holy Ghost; God, incomprehensible because Trinity yet manifesting Himself as Trinity. Here apophaticism finds its fulfilment in the revelation of the Holy Trinity as primordial fact, ultimate reality, first datum which cannot be deduced, explained or discovered by way of any other truth; for there is nothing which is prior to it. Apophatic thought, renouncing every support, finds its support in God, whose incomprehensibility appears as Trinity. Here thought gains a stability which cannot be shaken; theology finds its foundation; ignorance passes into knowledge.

If one speaks of God it is always, for the Eastern Church, in the concrete: 'The God of Abraham, of Isaac and of Jacob; the God of Jesus Christ.' It is always the Trinity: Father, Son and Holy Ghost. When, on the contrary, the common nature assumes the first place in our conception of trinitarian dogma the religious reality of God in Trinity is inevitably obscured in some measure and gives place to a certain philosophy of essence.[1] Likewise, the idea of beatitude has acquired in the West a slightly intellectual emphasis, presenting itself in the guise of a vision of the essence of God. The personal relationship of man to the living God is no longer a relationship to the Trinity, but rather has as its object the person of Christ, who reveals to us the divine nature. Christian life and thought become christocentric, relying primarily upon the humanity of the incarnate Word; one might almost say that it is

---

[1] 'It would seem that in our time the dogma of the divine Unity had, as it were, absorbed the dogma of the Trinity of which one only speaks as a memory.' (Th. de Régnon, *Etudes de theol. pos. sur la Sainte Trinité*, I, 365.)

this which becomes their anchor of salvation.[1] Indeed, in the doctrinal conditions peculiar to the West all properly theocentric speculation runs the risk of considering the nature before the persons and becoming a mysticism of 'the divine abyss', as in the *Gottheit* of Meister Eckhart; of becoming an impersonal apophaticism of the divine-nothingness prior to the Trinity. Thus by a paradoxical circuit we return through Christianity to the mysticism of the neo-platonists.

In the tradition of the Eastern Church there is no place for a theology, and even less for a mysticism, of the divine essence. The goal of Orthodox spirituality, the blessedness of the Kingdom of Heaven, is not the vision of the essence, but, above all, a participation in the divine life of the Holy Trinity; the deified state of the co-heirs of the divine nature, gods created after the uncreated God, possessing by grace all that the Holy Trinity possesses by nature.

The Trinity is, for the Orthodox Church, the unshakeable foundation of all religious thought, of all piety, of all spiritual life, of all experience. It is the Trinity that we seek in seeking after God, when we search for the fullness of being, for the end and meaning of existence. Primordial revelation, itself the source of all revelation as of all being, the Holy Trinity presents itself to our religious consciousness as a fact the evidence for which can be grounded only upon itself. According to a modern Russian theologian, Father Florensky,[2] there is no other way in which human

---

[1] To avoid excessive generalization it must be pointed out that Cistercian mysticism, for example, remains trinitarian in its inspiration. This is above all true of Guilliame de St. Thierry whose teaching is greatly influenced by that of the Greek Fathers. Following the line of eastern theology he tends to moderate the prevailing 'filioquism'. See J.-M. Déchanet, O.S.B., 'Guillaume de Saint-Thierry, l'homme et son oeuvre' (*Bibliothèque Mediévale, Spirituels préscolastiques, I*), Bruges, 1942, pp. 103–10.

[2] See the chapter devoted to the Trinity on *Pillar and Ground of the Truth*, Moscow, 1911 (in Russian).

thought may find perfect stability save that of accepting the trinitarian antinomy. If we reject the Trinity as the sole ground of all reality and of all thought, we are committed to a road that leads nowhere; we end in an aporia, in folly, in the disintegration of our being, in spiritual death. Between the Trinity and hell there lies no other choice. This question is, indeed, crucial—in the literal sense of that word. The dogma of the Trinity is a cross for human ways of thought. The apophatic ascent is a mounting of calvary. This is the reason why no philosophical speculation has ever succeeded in rising to the mystery of the Holy Trinity. This is the reason why the human spirit was able to receive the full revelation of the Godhead only after Christ on the cross had triumphed over death and over the abyss of hell. This, finally, is the reason why the revelation of the Trinity shines out in the Church as a purely religious gift, as the catholic truth above all other.

CHAPTER FOUR

Uncreated Energies

The revelation of God the Holy Trinity—Father, Son and Holy Spirit is the basis of all Christian theology; it is, indeed, theology itself, in the sense in which that word was understood by the Greek Fathers, for whom *theology* most commonly stood for the mystery of the Trinity revealed to the Church. Moreover, it is not only the foundation, but also the supreme object of theology; for, according to the teaching of Evagrius Ponticus (developed by St. Maximus), to know the mystery of the Trinity in its fullness is to enter into perfect union with God and to attain to the deification of the human creature: in other words, to enter into the divine life, the very life of the Holy Trinity, and to become, in St. Peter's words, 'partakers of the divine nature'—θείας κοινωνοὶ φύσεως. Trinitarian theology is thus a theology of union, a mystical theology which appeals to experience, and which presupposes a continuous and progressive series of changes in created nature, a more and more intimate communion of the human person with the Holy Trinity.

The words of St. Peter are explicit: *partakers of the divine nature.* They leave us in no doubt as to the reality of the union with God which is promised us, and set before us as our final end, the blessedness of the age to come. It would be childish, not to say impious, to see in these words only a rhetorical expression or metaphor. It would be altogether too facile to try to dispose of difficulties in this way, by emptying of their meaning whatsoever words of revelation do not readily correspond with our own modes of thought, which do not square with the idea of God which we have fashioned for ourselves. It is, on the other hand, entirely legitimate for us to attempt to define the meaning of an expression which appears to be in conflict with so many other passages of Holy Scripture, and with the tradition of the Church, about the absolute incommunicability of the divine being. It would be possible to draw up two sets of texts taken from the Bible and the Fathers, contradictory to one another; the first to show the inaccessible character of the divine nature, the second asserting that God does communicate Himself, can be known experimentally, and can really be attained to in union. St. Macarius of Egypt (or the pseudo-Macarius if it be preferred: it makes no difference to the great value of the mystical writings known by this name), speaking of the soul which is entering upon union with God, insists upon the absolute difference between the two natures involved in the very union itself: 'The one is God, the other is not God; the one is Lord, the other is servant; the one is Creator, the other is creature . . . and their natures have nothing in common.'[1] On the other hand, the same writer speaks of the 'changing of the soul into the divine nature'.[2] God is thus at the same time totally inaccessible and really communicable to created beings; neither of the terms of this antinomy excluded or minimized in any way. And if it is true that Christian mysticism cannot accommodate itself to a transcendant God, still less is it able to envisage a God immanent and accessible to creatures. Etienne Gilson expresses this fundamental principle of spiritual life very well: 'Lower,' he says, 'even if only for an instant and at a single point, the barrier between God and man which is created by the contingency

[1] 'Hom. 49', *P.G.*, XXXIV, 816 B.
[2] 'Hom. 44, 8', ibid., 784 C.

of being, and you have deprived the Christian mystic of his God, and thus of his mysticism itself; any God who is not inaccessible he can dispense with; it is the God who is by His nature inaccessible whom he cannot do without.'[1]

The question of the possibility of any real union with God, and, indeed, of mystical experience in general, thus poses for Christian theology the antinomy of the accessibility of the inaccessible nature. How is it possible that the Holy Trinity should be the object of union and of mystical experience in general? Vigorous theological debates were provoked by this question in the East towards the middle of the fourteenth century, and these resulted in the conciliar decisions which clearly formulated the tradition of the Eastern Orthodox Church on the subject. St. Gregory Palamas, Archbishop of Thessalonica, and the spokesman of the councils of this great period of Byzantine theology, devoted a dialogue entitled *Theophanes* to the question of the incommunicable and yet communicable deity. When he is considering the meaning of St. Peter's words, 'partakers of the divine nature', St. Gregory of Thessalonica affirms that this statement has an antinomic character analogous to the dogma of the Trinity. Just as God is at the same time both one and three, 'the divine nature must be said to be at the same time both exclusive of, and, in some sense, open to participation. We attain to participation in the divine nature, and yet at the same time it remains totally inaccessible. We need to affirm both at the same time and to preserve the antinomy as a criterion of right devotion.'[2]

What is the nature of the relationship by which we are able to enter into union with the Holy Trinity? If we were able at a given moment to be united to the very essence of God and to participate in it even in the very least degree, we should not at the moment be what we are, we should

---

[1] *La théologie mystique de saint Bernard*, pp. 143–44.
[2] *P.G.*, CL, 932 D.

be God by nature. God would then no longer be Trinity, but '*μυριυπόστατος*', 'of myriads of hypostases'; for He would have as many hypostases as there would be persons participating in His essence. God, therefore, is and remains inaccessible to us in His essence. But can we then say that it is with one of the three divine *Persons* that we enter into union? This would be the hypostatic union proper to the Son alone, in whom God becomes man without ceasing to be the second Person of the Trinity. Even though we share the same human nature as Christ and receive in Him the name of sons of God, we do not ourselves become the divine hypostasis of the Son by the fact of the Incarnation. We are unable, therefore, to participate in either the essence or the hypostases of the Holy Trinity. Nevertheless the divine promise cannot be an illusion: we *are* called to participate in the divine nature. We are therefore compelled to recognize in God an ineffable distinction, other than that between His essence and His persons, according to which He is, under different aspects, both totally inaccessible and at the same time accessible. This distinction is that between the essence of God, or His nature, properly co-called, which is inaccessible, unknowable and incommunicable; and the energies or divine operations, forces proper to and inseparable from God's essence, in which He goes forth from Himself, manifests, communicates, and gives Himself. 'The divine and deifying illumination and grace is not the essence but the energy of God',[1] a 'divine power and energy common to the nature in three'.[2] Thus, according to St. Gregory Palamas, 'to say that the divine nature is communicable not in itself but through its energy, is to remain within the bounds of right devotion'.[3] (*εὐσέβεια.*)

[1] St. Gregory Palamas, 'Capita physica, theologica, moralia et practica', 69, *P.G.*, CL, 1169 C.
[2] 'Theophanes', ibid., 941 C.   [3] Ibid., 937 D.

Uncreated Energies

As we have already seen, it was the need to establish a dogmatic basis for union with God which impelled the Eastern Church to formulate her teaching on the distinction between God's essence and His energies. St. Gregory Palamas was not, however, the originator of this doctrine; the same distinction is found, though with less doctrinal precision, in most of the Greek Fathers—even amongst those of the first centuries of the Church. It is in fact an integral part of the tradition of the Eastern Church, and is closely bound up with the dogma of the Trinity.

In the thought of the Fathers, theology proper is always the teaching about the divine being itself—the Holy Trinity; whereas the exterior manifestations of God—the Trinity known in its relation to created being—belonged to the realm of *economy*.[1] The ecclesiastical writers of the first centuries, prior to the council of Nicaea, often mixed these two planes when they spoke of the person of the Word as the λόγος προφορικός, manifesting the divinity of the Father. It is in this order of ideas, that is to say in the order of the divine economy, that they sometimes call the Logos the force or power (δύναμις) of the Father, or his operation (ἐνέργειά). Athenagoras called Him the divine 'idea and energy' manifesting itself in creation.[2] St. Paul's saying about the invisible things of God, His eternal power and His divinity (ἥ τε ἀΐδιος αὐτοῦ δύναμις καὶ θειότης) made visible since the creation of the world, is sometimes interpreted as meaning the Logos, 'Power and Wisdom', who manifests the Father; sometimes in the more precise meaning of the 'energies'—the common operations of the Holy Trinity, showing forth in creatures, 'those things that can be known of God' (τό γνωστὸν τοῦ θεοῦ), according to the same passage of St. Paul (Rom. i, 19). In the same way, St. Basil talks of the role of the energies

---

[1] Οἰκονομία, means, literally, the construction or administration of a house, a regimen, a dispensation.

[2] 'Πρεσβεία περὶ χριστιανῶν', 10, *P.G.*, VI, 908 B.

in *manifesting*, opposing them to the unknowable essence: 'It is by His energies'—he says—'that we say we know our God; we do not assert that we can come near to the essence itself, for His energies descend to us, but His essence remains unapproachable.'[1] In creation the consubstantial Trinity makes itself known in the energies proper to its nature.

The author of the *Areopagitica* contrasts the 'unions' (ἐνώσεις) with the 'distinctions' (διακρίσεις) in God. The 'unions' are 'the secret mansions which are but seldom thrown open', the superessential nature of God where He remains as if in absolute repose, without manifesting Himself in any way. The 'distinctions', on the other hand, are the processions (πρόοδοι) beyond Himself, His manifestations (ἐκφανσεῖς), which Dionysius also calls virtues or forces (δυνάμεις), in which everything that exists partakes, thus making God known in His creatures.[2] The contrast between the two ways in the knowledge of God, between negative and positive theology, is for Dionysius founded upon this ineffable but real distinction between the unknowable essence and the self-revealing energies of the Divinity, between the 'unions' and the 'distinctions'. Holy Scripture reveals God to us by formulating the divine names according to the energies in which God communicates Himself, while remaining inaccessible in His essence, distinguishes Himself while remaining simple, and becomes manifold without leaving His unity; for in Him 'the unions prevail over the distinctions'.[3] In other words, the distinctions are not divisions or separations within the divine being. The δυνάμεις, or energies, in which God proceeds forth, are God Himself; but not according to His substance. St. Maximus the Confessor expresses the same idea when he

---

[1] 'Epistle 234 (ad Amphilochium)', *P.G.*, XXXII, 869 AB. Cf. 'Adversus Eunomium, II, 32', *P.G.*, XXIX, 648.
[2] 'De divin. nomin., II, 4', *P.G.*, III.   [3] Ibid., 649–52.

says: 'God is communicable in what He imparts to us; but He is not communicable in the incommunicability of his essence'.[1] And St. John Damascene takes up and renders more precise the thought of St. Gregory Nazianzen: 'all that we say positively (κατάφατικῶς) of God manifests not His nature but the things about His nature'.[2] The same writer uses expressive images of 'movement' (κίνησις) or of the 'rush (ἔξαλμα) of God' in describing the divine energies.[3] Like Dionysius, the Fathers apply to the energies the name of 'rays of divinity', penetrating the created universe. St. Gregory Palamas calls them quite simply 'divinities', or 'uncreated light', or 'grace'.

God's presence in His energies must be understood in a realistic sense. It is not the presence of a cause operative in its effects: for the energies are not effects of the divine cause, as creatures are; they are not created, formed *ex nihilo*, but flow eternally from the one essence of the Trinity. They are the outpourings of the divine nature which cannot set bounds to itself, for God is more than essence. The energies might be described as that mode of existence of the Trinity which is outside of its inaccessible essence. God thus exists both in His essence and outside of His essence. Palamas says, referring back to St. Cyril of Alexandria, that 'Creation is the task of energy; it is for nature to beget'.[4] If we deny the real distinction between essence and energy, we cannot fix any very clear borderline between the procession of the divine persons and the creation of the world; both the one and the other will be

---

[1] ' Μεδεκτὸς μὲν ὁ θεὸς κατὰ τὰς μεταδόσεις αὐτοῦ, ἀμέδεκτος δὲ κατά τό μηδὲν μετέχον αὐτῆς τῆς οὐσίας αὐτοῦ Quoted from Maximus in the 'Panoplia dogmatics' of Euthymius Zigabenus, III, *P.G.*, CXXX, 132 A.

[2] Gregory Nazianzen, 'In Theophaniam, Oratio XXXVIII, 7', *P.G.*, XXXVI, 317 B; John Damascene, 'De fide orth., I, 4', *P.G.*, XCIV, 800 BC.

[3] 'De fide orth., I, 14', *P.G.*, XCIV, 860 B.

[4] 'Capita physica, etc. (143)', *P.G.*, CL, 1220 D.

equally acts of the divine nature.[1] The being and the action of God would then appear to be identical and as having the same character of necessity, as is observed by St. Mark of Ephesus (fifteenth century).[2] We must thus distinguish in God His nature, which is one; and three hypostases; and the uncreated energy which proceeds from and manifests forth the nature from which it is inseparable. If we participate in God in His energies, according to the measure of our capacity, this does not mean that in His procession *ad extra* God does not manifest Himself fully. God is in no way diminished in His energies; He is wholly present in each ray of His divinity. There are in fact two main errors into which it is possible to fall in regard to the divine energies:

First, the energy is not a divine function which exists *on account* of creatures, despite the fact that it is through His energies, which penetrate everything that exists, that God creates and operates. Even if creatures did not exist, God would none the less manifest Himself beyond His essence; just as the rays of the sun would shine out from the solar disk whether or not there were any beings capable of receiving their light. Indeed, expressions, such as 'manifest Himself' and 'beyond' are really inappropriate, for the 'beyond' in question only begins to exist with the creation, and 'manifestation' is only conceivable when there is some realm foreign to Him who is manifested. In using such defective expressions, such inadequate images, we acknowledge the absolute, non-relative character of the natural and eternal expansive energy, proper to God.

But, secondly, the created world does not become infinite and coeternal with God because the natural processions, or divine energies, are so. The existence of the energies implies no necessity in the act of creation, which

[1] Ibid., 96, 1189 B.
[2] 'S. Marci Eugenici Ephes. Capita syllogistica', in W. Gass, *Die Mystik des N. Cabasilas*, Greiswald, 1849, append. II, p. 217.

is freely effected by the divine energy but determined by a decision of the common will of the three Persons. Creation is an act of the will of God which makes a new subject outside the divine being, *ex nihilo*; to the sphere of God's manifestation comes into being. As for the manifestation itself, it is eternal, for it is the glory of God.

Philaret of Moscow expresses this doctrine of the Eastern Church in a Christmas sermon, in which he speaks of the angels' hymn 'Glory to God in the highest': 'God', he says, 'has from all eternity enjoyed the sublimity of His glory . . . His glory is the revelation, the manifestation, the reflection, the garment of His inner perfection. God reveals Himself to Himself from all eternity by the eternal generation of His consubstantial Son, and by the eternal procession of His consubstantial Spirit; and thus the unity, within the Holy Trinity shines forth imperishable and unchangeable in its essential glory. God the Father is *the Father of glory* (Eph. i, 17); the Son is *the brightness of His glory* (Heb. i, 3) and He Himself has that glory which He had with the Father before the world was (John xvii, 5); likewise, the Holy Spirit of God is *the Spirit of glory* (I Pet. iv, 14). In this glory, uniquely proper to Himself, God dwells in perfect felicity above all glory, without having need of any witness, without admitting of any division. But as in His mercy and His infinite love He desires to communicate His blessedness, to create for Himself beings capable of sharing in the joyfulness of His glory, He calls forth His infinite perfections and they disclose themselves in His creatures; His glory is manifested in the celestial powers, is reflected in man, and puts on the splendour of the visible world; He bestows it, and those who become partakers thereof receive it, it returns to Him, and in this perpetual circumvolution, so to say, of the divine glory, the blessed life, the felicity of the creature consists.'[1]

---

[1] *Choix de sermons et discours de son Eminence Mgr Philarete*, French translation by A. Serpinet, Paris, 1866, I, pp. 3–4.

reatures—beings created from nothing by the
limited and subject to change—that the infinite
l energies abide, making the greatness of God
to shine forth in all things, and appearing beyond all
things as the divine light which the created world cannot
contain. This is the inaccessible light in which, as St. Paul
says, God makes His dwelling: 'dwelling in light unapproachable, whom no man hath seen nor can see'
(I Tim. vi, 16). This is the glory in which God appeared
to the righteous in the Old Testament; the eternal light
which shone through the humanity of Christ and manifested His divinity to the apostles at the Transfiguration.
This is the uncreated and deifying grace, the portion of
the saints of the Church in their life of union with God;
this is the Kingdom of God where the righteous will shine
forth as the sun (Matt. xiii, 43). The Bible abounds in texts
which, according to the tradition of the Eastern Church,
refer to the divine energies, as, for example, this passage
from the prophet Habakkuk: 'God came from Teman, and
the Holy One from Mount Paran. His glory covered the
heavens, and the earth was full of His praise. And His
brightness was as the light; He had rays coming forth from
His hand: and there was the hiding of His power.'[1]

It is clear that the doctrine concerning the energies is
not a mere abstract conception, a purely intellectual distinction. We are dealing with a strictly concrete reality of
the religious order, though it is one that is not easily
grasped. Hence the formulation of the doctrine as an
antinomy: the energies express by their procession an ineffable distinction—they are not God in His essence—
and yet, at the same time, being inseparable from His
essence, they bear witness to the unity and the simplicity
of the being of God. The opponents of St. Gregory Palamas—eastern theologians who had been strongly influenced by Aristotelianism (in particular the Calabrian

[1] Hab. iii, 3–4.

monk Barlaam who had received his theological training in Italy, and Akindynus, who quotes the Greek translation of the *Summa theologica*)—saw in the real distinction between the essence and the energies a derogation of the simplicity of God, and accused Palamas of ditheism and polytheism. Having become alienated from the apophatic and antinomical spirit of eastern theology, they set up against it a conception of God which saw Him, primarily at any rate, as a simple essence, in which even the hypostases assumed the character of relations within the essence. The philosophy of God as pure act cannot admit anything to be God that is not the very essence of God. From this point of view God is, as it were, limited by His essence; that which is not essence does not belong to the divine being, is not God. Thus, according to Barlaam and Akindynus, the energies are either the essence itself, understood as pure act, or are produced by the outward acts of the essence, that is to say, the created effects which have the essence for their cause—creatures, in other words. The adversaries of St. Gregory Palamas recognized the divine essence, they recognized also its created effects; but they did not recognize the divine operations or energies. In his reply to their strictures, the Archbishop of Thessalonica confronted his opponents with the following dilemma: either they must admit the distinction between the essence and the operations, in which case they must needs, in obedience to their philosophical conception of essence, relegate the glory of God, the light of the Transfiguration, and grace, to the status of creatures; or, on the other hand, they must deny this distinction, in which case they would be forced to identify the unknowable and the knowable, the incommunicable and the communicable, essence and grace.[1] In either case real deification would be impossible. So this defence of the divine simplicity, starting from a philosophical concept of essence, leads finally to conclu-

[1] 'Theophanes', *P.G.*, CL, 929 BC.

sions which are inadmissible for practical piety and contrary to the tradition of the Eastern Church.

For St. Gregory Palamas—as for all eastern theology, which is fundamentally apophatic—it was impossible to base the divine simplicity upon the concept of simple essence. The pre-eminent simplicity of the Trinity is the basis of his theological thought: a simplicity unimpaired by the distinction between the nature and the persons on the one hand, and that between the persons themselves on the other. Like every doctrinal statement about God, this simplicity can only be expressed in terms of an antinomy: it does not exclude distinction, but can admit neither separation nor division on the divine being. In the same way St. Gregory of Nyssa could affirm that the human intelligence remains simple, despite the diversity of its faculties; it becomes diversified in the process of going out towards the objects that it knows, while remaining undivided, without in its essence passing into other substances. But the human intelligence is not 'above all names', as are the Three Persons who possess in their common energies everything that can be attributed to the nature of God.[1] Simplicity does not mean uniformity or absence of distinction—otherwise Christianity would not be the religion of the Holy Trinity. Speaking generally, we must remark that it is too often forgotten that the idea of the divine simplicity—at least in the way in which it is presented in the manuals of theology—originates in human philosophy rather than in the divine revelation.[2] St. Mark

[1] Ibid., 949 AC. The passage of Gregory of Nyssa referred to by Palamas is undoubtedly that of the. 'De hominis opificio', ch. XI, *P.G.*, XLIV, 153–6.

[2] There is nothing more exasperating than a *simpliste* notion of the divine simplicity. Fr. Sébastien Guichardan's book, *Le problème de la simplicité divine en Orient et en Occident au XIVe et XVe siècles: Grégoire Palamas, Duns Scot, Georges Scholarios*, Lyon, 1933, is a striking example of this theological insensibility before the fundamental mysteries of faith.

of Ephesus, recognizing how difficult it is for philosophical thought to admit a mode of existence in God other than that of essence, and to reconcile His distinctions with His simplicity, draws a picture for us in which he shows the wise economy of the Church adjusting herself at different times to human capacity for receiving the truth. 'We must not be surprised', he says, 'if we do not find among the ancients any clear and defined distinction between the essence of God and His operation. If, in our time, after the solemn confirmation of the truth and the universal recognition of the divine monarchy, the partisans of profane wisdom have created so much confusion in the Church over this question, and have even accused her of polytheism, what would not have been done in earlier times by those who, puffed up with their vain learning, were seeking only an opportunity to confound our teachers? This is why the theologians have insisted more on the simplicity of God than on the distinction which exists within Him. It would have been inopportune to impose the distinction in the operations upon those who had difficulty in admitting even the distinction in the hypostases. Thus by a wise discretion the divine teachings have become clarified in due course of time, the divine wisdom making use for this purpose of the insensate attacks of heresy.'[1]

While distinguishing in God the three hypostases, the one nature and the natural energies, Orthodox theology does not admit any kind of 'composition' in Him. The energies, like the persons, are not elements of the divine being which can be conceived of apart, in separation from the Trinity of which they are the common manifestation, the eternal splendour. They are not accidents ($\sigma\upsilon\mu\beta\epsilon\beta\eta\kappa o\acute{\iota}$) of the nature in their quality as pure energies, and they

---

[1] This passage is not in W. Gass, op. cit.: it is to be found in *Canon Oxoniensis*, 49. It is quoted by M. Jugie in the article 'Palamas', *Dict. de theol. cathol.*, XI, 1759s.

imply no passivity in God.[1] Neither are they hypostatic beings, comparable to the three Persons.[2] It is not even possible to attribute any particular energy to any one of the divine hypostases exclusively, although one talks about 'the Wisdom or the Power of the Father' in speaking of the Son. One may say, to use a common expression, that the energies are attributes of God; provided, that is, that one remembers that these dynamic and concrete attributes have nothing in common with the concept-attributes with which God is credited in the abstract and sterile theology of the manuals. The energies manifest the innumerable names of God, according to the teaching of the Areopagite: Wisdom, Life, Power, Justice, Love, Being, God—and an infinity of other names which are unknown to us, for the world can no more contain the fullness of the divine manifestation which is revealed in the energies, than, as St. John says, it can contain the books which would be needed to describe all Jesus did. Like the energies, the divine names are innumerable, so likewise the nature which they reveal remains nameless and unknowable--darkness hidden by the abundance of light.

For Orthodox thought, the energies signify an exterior manifestation of the Trinity which cannot be interiorized, introduced, as it were, within the divine being, as its natural determination. This was the basis of the theological development of Fr. Bulgakov, and also his fundamental error; for he sought to see in the energy of Wisdom (*Sophia*), which he identified with the essence, the very principle of the Godhead. In fact, God is not determined by any of His attributes; all determinations are inferior to Him, logically posterior to His being in itself, in its essence. When we say that God is Wisdom, Life, Truth,

---

[1] St. Gregory Palamas, 'Capita physica, etc. (127 and 128)', *P.G.*, CL, 1209 C– 1212 A.

[2] 'Theophanes', ibid., 929 A.

Love—we understand the energies, which are subsequent to the essence and are its natural manifestations, but are external to the very being of the Trinity. That is why, in contrast to western theology, the tradition of the Eastern Church never designates the relationship between the Persons of the Trinity by the name of attributes. We never say, for example, that the Son proceeds by the mode of the intelligence and the Holy Spirit by the mode of the will. The Spirit can never be assimilated to the mutual love of the Father and the Son. The 'trinitarian psychologism' of St. Augustine is viewed rather as an analogical image than as a positive theology expressing the relationship between the Persons. St. Maximus refused to admit in the Trinity qualifications of a psychological order in connection with the notion of the will; he saw in such qualifications that which is posterior to the nature of God, in other words, His exterior determinations, His manifestations.[1] To say: 'God is love', 'the divine Persons are united by mutual love', is to think of a common manifestation, the 'love-energy' possessed by the three hypostases, for the union of the Three is higher even than love. A work hitherto attributed to St. Gregory Palamas sometimes applies to the energies—real attributes of God, inasmuch as they are posterior to the Trinity—the name of 'lesser divinity' (ὑφειμένη θεότης) in contradistinction to the essence, the 'greater divinity' (ὑπερειμένη), an expression which would have caused great scandal to St. Gregory's adversaries. Even had St. Gregory used this expression, it would in the context of his thought have referred simply to the manifestation, logically posterior to Him who manifests Himself, 'for God signifies He who acts; divinity (understood as energy) signifies His operation'.[2]

As we have already said, the Holy Trinity may be con-

---

[1] 'De ambiguis', *P.G.*, XCI, 1261–1264.

[2] Council of 1341, Synopsis Nili, MANSI, *Coll. Concil.*, XXV, 1149.

sidered either in itself—theology, properly so-called, according to patristic terminology; or it may be considered in its relation to the created order—that is to say, in the domain of 'economy', the divine activity, or dispensation. The object of theology, taken in this limited sense, is the eternal procession of the Persons; while their manifestation in the work of creation or of providence, the temporal mission of the Son and of the Holy Spirit, pertains to the sphere of 'economy'. This is what several modern theologians have somewhat inexactly called the 'economic Trinity'. According to this division of the substance of Christian doctrine, the energies hold a middle place: on the one hand they belong to theology, as eternal and inseparable forces of the Trinity existing independently of the creative act; on the other, they also belong to the domain of 'economy', for it is in His energies that God manifests Himself to His creatures: as St. Basil says, 'they descend even to ourselves.'

In the order of the economic manifestation of the Trinity in the world, all energy originates in the Father, being communicated by the Son in the Holy Spirit— ἐκ πατρὸς, διὰ υἱοῦ, ἐν ἁγίῳ πνεύματι. Thus it is said that the Father creates all things by the Son in the Holy Spirit. This is expressed very clearly by St. Cyril of Alexandria: 'The operation of the uncreated substance', he says, 'is a kind of common property, while it is the proper possession of each Person, in such a way that it is thanks to the three hypostases that the operation belongs to each as a property of a perfect person. Thus, it is the Father who acts, but by the Son in the Spirit; the Son acts also, but as the power of the Father, inasmuch as He is from Him and in Him according to His own hypostasis. The Spirit also acts, for He is the all-powerful Spirit of the Father and of the Son.'[1] In this dispensation, in which the Godhead is manifested in the energies, the Father appears

[1] 'De Sancta Trinitate, dial. VI', *P.G.*, LXXV, 1056 A.

as the possessor of the attribute which is manifested, the Son as the manifestation of the Father, the Holy Spirit as He who manifests. Thus for St. Gregory Nazianzen, the Father is He who is True, the Son is Truth, and the Holy Spirit the Spirit of Truth: Ἀληθινὸς, καὶ Ἀλήθεια, καὶ πνεῦμα τῆς Ἀληθείας.[1] According to St. Gregory of Nyssa, 'the source of Power is the Father; the Power of the Father is the Son, the Spirit of Power is the Holy Spirit.'[2] This is why the attribute of Wisdom, common to the Trinity, designates the Son in the order of the divine economy; thus: 'the Son is the hypostatic Wisdom of the Father'. The very name of the Word—λόγος—attributed to the Son is itself primarily a designation of the 'economic' order, proper to the second hypostasis as manifesting the nature of the Father. This is what St. Gregory Nazianzen means when he says: 'It seems to me that the Son is called Logos not only because He is begotten without passion, but also because He remains one with the Father whom He reveals; or, as one might also say, because He is, in relation to the Father as the definition is to the subject defined. For *logos* is another way of saying definition, and *he that hath known the Son knoweth the Father also* (John xiv, 7). The Son is thus a precise and clear declaration of the nature of the Father; for every being which is begotten is a silent definition of its begetter. And lastly, if by the word *logos* one understands the essential reason of every particular object, there will be no error in attributing this name to the Son. For there is nothing that can exist which is not dependent upon the Logos.'[3] It is not possible to express the 'economic' character of the name Logos more clearly than this—it is the exterior manifestation of the nature of the Father by the Son. St. Irenaeus expresses a

---

[1] 'Oratio XXIII (De Pace III), II', *P.G.*, XXXV, 1164 A.

[2] 'De spiritu Sancto, adversus Macedonianos, 13', *P.G.*, XLV, 1317 A.

[3] 'Oratio XXX (Theologica IV), 20', *P.G.*, XXXVI, 129 A.

similar idea, in a way which is characteristic of the Christian thought of the early centuries: 'for that which is invisible of the Son is the Father, and that which is visible of the Father is the Son.'[1] The Son who renders visible the hidden nature of the Father is here almost identified with the manifesting energies. In the same way St. Basil, when he says that 'The Son shows forth in Himself the Father in His fullness, shining forth in all His glory and splendour',[2] emphasizes the 'energetic' character of the manifestation of the Father by the Son by the use of words such as 'glory' and 'splendour'.

It is only in this sense, that is to say in the light of the 'exterior' aspect of the Trinity as manifested in the world by the energies, that the teaching of the Fathers about the persons of the Word and of the Spirit can be explained. St. John Damascene, in working out the idea contained in Heb. i, 3 (*the brightness of his glory and the express image of his substance*), says that 'The Son is the image of the Father, and the Spirit the image of the Son'.[3] Here, the image (εἰκών) is for Damascene a manifestation and a declaration of that which remains hidden.[4] And he goes on to clarify his thought in regard to the manifesting function of the two Persons who proceed from the Father: 'The Son is the image of the Father, natural, complete, and in all things like unto Him save in unbegottenness and in paternity. For the Father is the unbegotten begetter, while the Son is begotten and is in no wise Father' . . . 'The Holy Spirit is the image of the Son; for *no man can say that Jesus is the Lord, but by the Holy Ghost*. Thus it is by the Holy Spirit that we know Christ, who is both Son of God and God, and it is in the Son that we see the Father.'[5]

---

[1]. 'Contra Haereses, IV, vi, 6', *P.G.*, VII, 989 C.
[2] 'Adversus Eunomium, II, 17', *P.G.*, XXXIX, 605 B.
[3] 'De fide orth., I, 13', *P.G.*, XCIV, 856 B.
[4] 'De imaginibus, III, 17', *P.G.*, XCIV, 1337 B.
[5] Ibid., III, 18, 1340 AB.

Thus, in their operation in the world, the consubstantial Persons of the Son and of the Spirit do not manifest themselves—for they do not act in virtue of some will of their own—but the Son makes known the Father, and the Holy Spirit bears witness to the Son. It is important to note that the Person of the Holy Spirit remains unmanifested— having no image in another Person. We shall have occasion to return to this subject, in dealing with the question of the Holy Spirit and of grace; for the moment we shall say only this: the Eastern Church has criticized western theology for confounding the exterior aspect of God's manifesting activity in the world (an activity in which the Holy Spirit, as a consubstantial Person sent by the Father and the Son, reveals the Son), and the interior aspect of the Trinity, in which the Person of the Holy Spirit proceeds from the Father alone, without having any relation of origin with the Son. It is the will—which, for the eastern tradition, never intervenes in the interior relationships of the Trinity, but determines the exterior activities of the divine Persons in relation to the created order— which constitutes the difference between the two aspects. This will is common to the three Persons; that is why, in the mission of the Son and of the Holy Spirit, each of the three Persons acts in concourse with the two others: the Son becomes incarnate, but He is sent by the Father and takes flesh by the Holy Spirit; the Holy Spirit descends— sent from the Father by the Son. It is in this context of the divine economy—the love of the Holy Trinity made manifest in the mystery of the cross—that Philaret of Moscow speaks of: 'The love of the Father crucifying, the love of the Son crucified, and love of the Holy Spirit triumphant in the invincible power of the cross.'[1]

Thus the theology of the Eastern Church distinguishess in God the three hypostases, the nature or essence, and

[1] Mgr Philaret, *Oraisons funèbres, homélies et discours.* French translation by A. de Stourdza, Paris, 1849, p. 154.

the energies. The Son and the Holy Spirit are, so to say, personal processions, the energies natural processions. The energies are inseparable from the nature, and the nature is inseparable from the three Persons. These distinctions are of great importance for the Eastern Church's conception of mystical life:

1. The doctrine of the energies, ineffably distinct from the essence, is the dogmatic basis of the real character of all mystical experience. God, who is inaccessible in His essence, is present in His energies 'as in a mirror', remaining invisible in that which He is; 'in the same way we are able to see our faces, themselves invisible to us in a glass', according to a saying of St. Gregory Palamas.[1] Wholly unknowable in His essence, God wholly reveals Himself in His energies, which yet in no way divide His nature into two parts—knowable and unknowable—but signify two different modes of the divine existence, in the essence and outside of the essence.

2. This doctrine makes it possible to understand how the Trinity can remain incommunicable in essence and at the same time come and dwell within us, according to the promise of Christ (John xiv, 23). The presence is not a causal one, such as the divine omnipresence in creation; no more is it a presence according to the very essence— which is by definition incommunicable; it is a mode according to which the Trinity dwells in us by means of that in itself which is communicable—that is to say, by the energies which are common to the three hypostases, or, in other words, by grace—for it is by this name that we know the deifying energies which the Holy Spirit communicates to us. He who has the Spirit, who confers the gift, has at the same time the Son, through whom every gift is transmitted to us; he also has the Father, from whom comes every perfect gift. In receiving the gift—the

[1] *Sermon on the Presentation of the Holy Virgin in the Temple*, edited by Sophocles, Athens, 1861, pp. 176-7.

deifying energies—one receives at the same time the indwelling of the Holy Trinity—inseparable from its natural energies and present in them in a different manner but none the less truly from that in which it is present in its nature.

3. The distinction between the essence and the energies, which is fundamental for the Orthodox doctrine of grace, makes it possible to preserve the real meaning of St. Peter's words 'partakers of the divine nature'. The union to which we are called is neither hypostatic—as in the case of the human nature of Christ—nor substantial, as in that of the three divine Persons: it is union with God in His energies, or union by grace making us participate in the divine nature, without our essence becoming thereby the essence of God. In deification we are by grace (that is to say, in the divine energies), all that God is by nature, save only identity of nature (χωρὶς τῆς κατ' οὐσίαν ταυτότητα), according to the teaching of St. Maximus.[1] We remain creatures while becoming God by grace, as Christ remained God in becoming man by the Incarnation.

These distinctions in God which are made by the theology of the Eastern Church do not in any way contradict its apophatic attitude in regard to revealed truth. On the contrary, these antinomical distinctions are dictated by a concern for safeguarding the mystery, while yet expressing the data of revelation in dogma. Thus, as we have seen in the doctrine of the Trinity, the distinction between the persons and the nature revealed a tendency to represent God as a 'monad and triad in one', with the consequence that the domination of the unity of nature over the trinity of the hypostases was avoided, as was the elimination or minimizing of the primordial mystery of the identity-diversity. In the same way, the distinction between the essence and the energies is due to the antinomy

---

[1] 'De ambiguis', *P.G.*, XCI, 1308 B.

between the unknowable and the knowable, the incommunicable and the communicable, with which both religious thought and the experience of divine things are ultimately faced. These real distinctions introduce no 'composition' into the divine being; they signify the mystery of God, who is absolutely one according to His nature, absolutely three according to His persons, sovereign and inaccessible Trinity, dwelling in the profusion of glory which is His uncreated light, His eternal Kingdom which all must enter who inherit the deified state of the age to come.

Western theology which, even in the doctrine of the Trinity, puts the emphasis upon the one essence, is even less prepared to admit any distinction between the essence and the energies. On the other hand, it establishes other distinctions foreign to eastern theology: such as that between the light of glory and the light of grace—both created; and between other elements of the 'supernatural order' such as the gifts of the Holy Spirit, the infused virtues, and habitual and actual grace. Eastern tradition knows no such supernatural order between God and the created world, adding, as it were, to the latter a new creation. It recognizes no distinction, or rather division, save that between the created and the uncreated. For eastern tradition the created supernatural has no existence. That which western theology calls by the name of the *supernatural* signifies for the East the *uncreated*—the divine energies ineffably distinct from the essence of God. The difference consists in the fact that the western conception of grace implies the idea of causality, grace being represented as an effect of the divine Cause, exactly as in the act of creation; while for eastern theology there is a natural procession, the energies, shining forth eternally from the divine essence. It is in creation alone that God acts as cause, in producing a new subject called to participate in the divine fullness; preserving it, saving it, *granting* grace to it, and guiding it towards its final goal. In the energies *He is*, He exists, He eternally manifests Himself. Here we are faced with a mode of divine being to which we accede in receiving grace; which, moreover, in the created and perishable world, is the presence of the uncreated and eternal light, the real omnipresence of God in all things, which is something more than His causal presence—'the light shineth in darkness, and the darkness comprehended it not' (John i, 5).

The divine energies are within everything and outside everything. One must be raised above created being, and abandon all contact with creatures in order to attain to union with 'the rays of the Godhead', says Dionysius the Areopagite. Despite this, these divine rays penetrate the whole created universe, and are the cause of its existence. The light 'was in the world and the world was made by Him and the world knew Him not' (John 1, 10). God has created all things by His energies. The act of creation established a relationship between the divine energies and that which is not God, and constituted a limitation, a determination (προορισμός) of the infinite and eternal effulgence of God, who thereby became the cause of finite and contingent being. For the energies do not produce the created world by the mere fact of their existence, that they are the natural processions of the essence of God; if they did, either the world would be as infinite and eternal as God Himself, or the energies would be only His limited and temporal manifestation. Thus the divine energies in themselves are not the relationship of God to created being, but they do enter into relationship with that which is not God, and draw the world into existence by the will of God. For, according to St. Maximus, the will is always an active relationship towards another, towards something external to the subject which acts. This will has created all things *by* the energies in order that created being may accede freely to union with

God *in* the same energies. 'God', says St. Maximus, 'has created us in order that we may become partakers of the divine nature, in order that we may enter into eternity, and that we may appear like unto Him, being deified by that grace out of which all things that exist have come, and which brings into existence everything that before had no existence.'[1]

[1] 'Epist. 43, Ad Joannem cubicularium', *P.G.*, XCI, 640 BC.

CHAPTER FIVE

Created Being

We must now turn from the fullness of the divine Being to ourselves, and to the created universe, in itself implenitude and indeed non-being, but called to acquire that fullness. And we have at once to admit that difficult as it was to raise ourselves to the consideration of God and necessary as it proved to follow out the apophatic way in order to apprehend as far as we might the revelation of the Trinity, it is not less difficult to pass from the notion of divine Being to that of created being. A leap of faith is necessary in the second case as in the first in order to recognize outside of and alongside of God, something other than Him, a totally new subject. And we shall need a sort of apophaticism in reverse in order to arrive at the revealed truth of creation *ex nihilo*, out of nothing.

It is often forgotten that the creation of the world is not a truth of a philosophical order, but rather an article of faith. Ancient philosophy knows nothing of creation in the absolute sense of the word; the demiurge of Plato is not a creator-God, but rather an ordainer of the universe, a craftsman, a fashioner of the κόσμος, a word itself implying order and comeliness. 'Being' in hellenistic thought signifies existence in some ordered manner, the possession of an essence. The demiurge creates substances giving form to amorphous matter which exists eternally and in-

91

Creator
maker

dependently of himself as a chaotic and unqualifiable mass, capable of receiving every possible form and quality. In itself, matter is thus non-being, a pure potentiality of being, of becoming something; it is the μη ὄν, but it is not the οὐκ ὄν, which is absolute nothingness. The idea of creation *ex nihilo* is first found in the Bible (II Macc. vii, 28) where a mother, urging her son to have courage to undergo martyrdom for the faith, says: 'I beseech thee, my son, look upon the heaven and the earth, and all that is therein, and consider that God made them of things that were not; and so was mankind made likewise.' (ὅτι ἐκ οὐκ ὄντων ἐποίησεν αὐτά ὁ θεός, according to the Septuagint translation.)

'All creatures are balanced upon the creative word of God, as if upon a bridge of diamond; above them is the abyss of the divine infinitude, below them that of their own nothingness,' says Philaret of Moscow.[1] The nothingness of creatures is as mysterious and unimaginable as the divine Nothingness of apophatic theology. The very idea of absolute nothingness is contradictory and absurd: to say that nothingness exists is a contradiction in terms; to say that it does not exist is to state a pleonasm, at least unless we are trying awkwardly to express, in this way, the idea that nothing exists outside God; that, indeed, there is no such thing as 'outside God'. Yet creation *ex nihilo* does mean just such an act producing something which is 'outside of God'—the production of an entirely new subject, with no origin of any kind either in the divine nature or in any matter or potentially of being external to God. We might say that by creation *ex nihilo* God 'makes room' for something which is wholly outside of Himself; that, indeed, He sets up the 'outside' or nothingness alongside of His plenitude. The result is a subject which is entirely 'other', infinitely removed from Him,

---

[1] Quoted by Fr. Florovsky in *The Ways of Russian Theology*, Paris, 1937, p. 180 (in Russian).

'not by place but by nature' (οὐ τόπῳ, αλλὰ φύσει), as it is expressed by St. John Damascene.[1]

The creation is not a kind of spreading out or infinite diffusion of the Godhead, a spontaneous communication of the energies producing beings in virtue of some necessity of the divine nature—'the Good diffusing itself by itself' of neo-platonism is not the God of St. Paul who 'calleth those things which be not as though they were' (Rom. iv, 17). The creation is a work of will and not of nature; and it is in this sense that St. John Damascene opposes the creation of the world to the generation of the Word: 'Since,' he says, 'the generation is a work of nature and proceeds from the very substance of God, it must necessarily be that it is eternal and without beginning, otherwise the begetter would undergo a change, and there would be prior God and posterior God: God would develop. With creation, on the other hand, it is a work of the will, and is thus not coeternal with God. For it is not possible that which is brought from not-being into being should be coeternal with that which exists always and without origin.'[2] We are, therefore, dealing with a work which has had a beginning; and a beginning presupposes a change, the passage from not-being into being. The creature is thus, by virtue of its very origin, something which changes, is liable to pass from one state into another. It has no ontological foundation either in itself (for it is created from nothing), nor in the divine essence, for in the act of creation God was under no necessity of any kind whatever. There is, in fact, nothing in the divine nature which could be the necessary cause of the production of creatures: creation might just as well not exist. God could equally well not have created; creation is a free act of His will, and this free act is the sole foundation of the existence of all beings. The very intention of the

---

[1] 'De fide orthodoxa, I, 13', *P.G.*, XCIV, 853 C.

[2] Ibid., I, 8, 813 A.

divine will, in the act of God's willing it, becomes a fact, and is realized in the immediate existence of a being by the power of the Almighty, who, when in His Wisdom and creative power He desires something, does not leave His will unrealized. And created being, according to St. Gregory of Nyssa, *is* this realization of His will.[1] But though creation is contingent in its origin and began to exist, it will never cease to be; death and destruction will not involve a return to non-being, for 'the word of the Lord endureth for ever' (I Pet. i, 25), and the divine will is unchangeable.

Creation, which is thus a free act of the will, and not (like the shining forth of the divine energies) a natural out-pouring, is an act proper to a God who is personal, to the Trinity whose common will belongs to the divine nature and operates according to the determination of thought. St. John Damascene calls this 'the eternal and unchanging Counsel of God'.[2] In the book of Genesis God is repre-sented to us as saying: 'Let us make man in our image, after our likeness' (i, 26), as if the Trinity consulted within Itself before creating. 'Counsel' signifies a free and con-sidered act: 'God creates by His thought which immedi-ately becomes a work', according to the same St. John Damascene.[3] 'God,' he says, 'contemplated all things before their existence, formulating them in His mind; and each being received its existence at a particular moment, according to His eternal thought and will (κατὰ τὴν θελητικὴν αὐτοῦ ἄχρονον ἔννοιαν), which is a pre-destination (προορισμός), an image (ἐικών) and a model (πάράδειγμα).'[4] The term θελητικὴ ἔννοια ('thought-will', or, more accurately, 'volitional thought') is very important. It is a perfect expression of the Eastern doctrine of the divine ideas, of the place which the

aemeron', *P.G.*, XLIV, 69 A.
inibus, I, 20', *P.G.*, XCIV, 1240–1241.
rth., II, 2', *P.G.*, XCIV, 865 A.   [4] Ibid., 837 A.

theology of the Eastern Church gives to the ideas of created things in God. The ideas are not, according to this conception, the eternal reasons of creatures contained within the very being of God, determinations of the essence to which created things refer as to their exemplary cause, as in the thought of St. Augustine which later became the common teaching of the whole Western tradition and was more precisely formulated by St. Thomas Aquinas. In the thought of the Greek Fathers the divine ideas are more dynamic, intentional in character. Their place is not in the essence, but in 'that which is after the essence', the divine energies: for the ideas are to be identified with the will or wills ($\theta\epsilon\lambda\acute{\eta}\mu\grave{a}\tau a$) which determine the different modes according to which created beings participate in the creative energies. It is thus that Dionysius characterizes the 'ideas or models' which are 'the reasons of things which give them substance', . . . 'for it is by them that all things have been determined and are created by the supersubstantial God'.[1] And if the divine ideas are not the essence of God itself, if they are thus as it were separated from the essence by the will, then it follows that not only the act of creation but also the very thoughts of God Himself can no longer be considered as a necessary determination of His nature and part of the intelligible content of the divine Being. The created universe is thus not seen, as in platonic or platonizing thought, under the pale and attenuated aspect of a poor replica of the Godhead; rather it appears as an entirely new being, as creation fresh from the hands of the God of Genesis 'who saw that it was good', a created universe willed by God and the joy of His Wisdom, 'a harmonious ordinance', 'a marvellously composed hymn to the power of the Almighty', as St. Gregory of Nyssa says.[2]

[1] 'De divin. nomin., V, 8', *P.G.*, III, 824 C.
[2] 'In Psalmorum inscriptiones', *P.G.*, XLIV, 441 B. Cf. 'Oratio catechetica magna, c. 6', *P.G.*, XLV, 25 C.

The attempt to bring the ideas into the inner being of God necessarily gives an ideal content to the divine essence and places the platonic κόσμος νοητός in it; the consequence of this is to face us with the following alternative, which will be decided according to the view one holds of this ideal world in God: either the created world will be disparaged, and deprived of its original character as the unconditioned work of the creative Wisdom, or else creation will be introduced into the inner life of the Godhead with its ontological roots established within the Trinity itself, as in the so-called sophiological doctrines. In the first case (that of St. Augustine), the divine ideas remain static—unmoving perfections of God; in the second (that of Eastern sophiology) the essence (οὐσία) of God itself becomes dynamic. It is interesting to note that John Scotus Eriugena (whose theological system is a curious amalgam of Eastern and Western elements, a transposition of the doctrines of the Greek fathers upon a basis of Augustinian thought),[1] represents the divine ideas as creatures, the first created principles by means of which God creates the universe (*natura creata creans*). Together with the Easterns, he puts the ideas outside the divine essence, but at the same time he wants to maintain with St. Augustine their substantial character; and so they become the first created essences. Eriugena did not grasp the distinction between the essence and the energies; on this point he remained faithful to Augustinianism, and was therefore unable to identify the ideas with God's creative acts of will.

The ideas or acts of will, which Dionysius calls 'models' (πάραδείγματα), 'predestinations' (προορισμοί) or 'provi-

[1] A. Brilliantov expounds the thought of Scotus Eriugena in this sense in his fundamental work, *The influence of Eastern theology upon Western thought in the works of John Scotus Eriugena*, St. Petersburg, 1898 (in Russian).

dences' (προνοίαι),[1] are not identical with created things. While they are the foundation of everything which is established by the divine will in the simple outpourings or energies, relationships between God and the beings which He creates, the ideas remain nevertheless separate from creatures, as the will of the craftsman remains separate from the work in which it is manifested. The ideas foreordain the different modes of participation in the energies, the unequal statures of the various categories of beings, which are moved by the divine love and respond to it each according to the proportion of its nature. The creation then appears as a hierarchy of real analogies in which, as Dionysuis says, 'each order of the hierarchical disposition achieves co-operation with God according to its proper analogy, accomplishing by the grace and power which is given by God that which God possesses by nature and without measure'.[2] Thus all creatures are called to perfect union with God which is accomplished in the 'synergy', the co-operation of the created wills with the idea-willings of God. The notion of creation in Dionysuis is so close to that of deification that it is hard to distinguish between the first state of creatures and their final end, union with God. In fact, because this union, according to Dionysuis, presupposes 'co-operation', the agreement of wills and therefore liberty, it is possible to see in the initial state of the created cosmos an unstable perfection in which the fullness of union is not yet achieved and in which created beings have still to grow in love in order to accomplish fully the thought-will of God.

This consideration is developed by St. Maximus, for whom creatures are defined in the first place as beings who are limited, which is as much as to say (according to

---

[1] 'De divin. nomin., V, 2, 8', *P.G.*, III, 817 and 824.
[2] 'De coel. Hier., III, 3', *P.G.*, III, 168.

St. Maximus) that their end is outside of themselves, that
there is something towards which they tend, that they are
in a perpetual state of becoming. Wherever there is
diversity and multiplicity there is becoming; everything
in the created world is in a state of becoming, the intelligible as well as the sensible, and this limitation and this
movement of becoming are the domain of the forms of
space and time. God alone remains in absolute repose;
and His perfect unmovability places him outside space
and time. If one attributes movement to Him in His relationship to created being, it is meant that He produces in
creatures the love which makes them tend towards Himself, that He draws them to Him, 'desiring to be desired
and loving to be loved'.[1] His will for us is a mystery, for
the will is a relationship with another, and there is
nothing which is 'other' to God: creation *ex nihilo* is incomprehensible to us. We only know the will of God in
so far as it is His relationship to the world which is already
created; it is the point of contact between the infinite and
the finite, and in this sense the divine 'willings' are the
creative ideas of things, the *logoi*, the 'words'. In spite of the
terminological identity, these 'words' have little in common with the λόγοι σπερματικοί or 'seminal reasons' of the
stoics. Rather they are the 'words' of creation and of
providence which are found in Genesis and the Psalms
(Ps. cxlvii). Every created thing has its point of contact
with the Godhead; and this point of contact is its idea,
reason or *logos* which is at the same time the end towards
which it tends. The ideas of individual things are contained within the higher and more general ideas, as are
the species within a genus. The whole is contained in the
Logos, the second person of the Trinity who is the first
principle and the last end of all created things. Here the
Logos, God the Word, has the 'economical' emphasis
proper to antenicene theology: He is the manifestation of

[1] 'De ambiguis', *P.G.*, XCI, 1260 C.

the divine will, for it is by Him that the Father has created all things in the Holy Spirit. When we are examining the nature of created things, seeking to penetrate into the reason of their being, we are led finally to the knowledge of the Word, causal principle and at the same time end of all beings. All things were created by the Logos who is as it were a divine nexus, the threshold from which flow the creative outpourings, the particular *logoi* of creatures, and the centre towards which in their turn all created beings tend, as to their final end. For creatures, from the moment of their first condition, are separate from God; and their end and final fulfilment lies in union with Him or deification. Thus the primitive beatitude was not a state of deification, but a condition of order, a perfection of the creature which was ordained and tending towards its end.[1]

Revealing himself through His creative 'thought-wills', God can be known in creatures and by means of creatures, but He can also be known immediately in mystical contemplation, in His uncreated energies which are the splendour of His face. It is thus, in His Godhead, that Christ appeared to the apostles on Mount Tabor, and it is thus that He makes Himself known to the saints who detach themselves from all created things, renouncing all finite knowledge in order to attain to union with God. And we see here why, when they have abandoned all, the saints receive in the end perfect knowledge of the created world, for in being lifted up to the contemplation of God, they possess in the same instant the knowledge of the whole world of being in its first reasons which are the 'thought-wills' of God, contained in His simple energies. We are reminded here of the ecstasy of St. Benedict of

[1] See the principal texts of St. Maximus on the ontology of created being in Hans Urs von Balthasar, *Kosmische Liturgie* Breisgau, 1941; especially in the chapter, 'Die Kosm thesen', pp. 108–60.

Nursia, who saw the whole universe as if it had been gathered together into a beam of the divine light.[1]

All things were created by the Logos. St. John tells us this—*all things were made by Him* (i, 3)—and we repeat it in the creed: *by whom all things were made*. But the same symbol of Nicaea teaches us that it is the Father who created the heavens and the earth and all things visible and invisible; and, later on, the Holy Spirit is called 'life-giving', ζωοποιόν. 'The Father created all things by the Son in the Holy Spirit—says St. Athanasius—for where the Word is, there also is the Spirit, and whatever is created by the Father receives its existence by the Word in the Holy Spirit; as the Psalm (xxxii) says: *By the word of the Lord were the heavens made; and all the host of them by the breath of his mouth*.'[2] Here we have the 'economical' manifestation of the Trinity: the Father operating by the Son in the Holy Spirit. This is why St. Irenaeus calls the Son and the Spirit 'the two hands of God'.[3] The work of creation is common to the whole Trinity, but each of the three persons is the cause of created being in a way which is different though in each case united to the others. St. Basil, when he is speaking of the creation of the angels, traces the manifestation of the three persons in the work of creation in the following way: 'In the creation, he says, consider first the primordial cause (τὴν προκαταρτικὴν αἰτίαν) of all that has been made—this is the Father; then the operating cause (τὴν δεμιουργικήν)—which is the Son; and the perfecting cause (τὴν τελειωτικήν)—the Holy Spirit: so that it is by the will of the Father that the heavenly spirits are, by the operation of the Son that they come into existence, and by the presence of the Spirit

[1] St. Gregory the Great, 'Dialogorum liber II, cap. 35', *P.G.*, LXVI, 198–200.
[2] 'Epistola III ad Serapionem, 5', *P.G.*, XXVI, 632 BC.
[3] 'Contra Haereses, IV, praefatio', *P.G.*, VII, 975 B.

that they are made perfect.'[1] It is this common action of the Trinity, manifested thus in the double economy of the effecting Word and of the perfecting Spirit, that confers upon all creatures not simply being, but also 'good being' —τὸ εὖ εἶναι—the faculty of being according to the good, to perfection.

The Eastern tradition knows nothing of 'pure nature' to which grace is added as a supernatural gift. For it, there is no natural or 'normal' state, since grace is implied in the act of creation itself. The eternal determinations of the 'divine Counsel', the divine ideas cannot really be made to correspond with the 'essences' of things which are postulated in the so-called natural philosophy of Aristotle and of every other philosopher whose experience reaches only to nature in its fallen state. 'Pure nature', for Eastern theology, would thus be a philosophical fiction corresponding neither to the original state of creation, nor to its present condition which is 'against nature', nor to the state of deification which belongs to the age to come. The world, created in order that it might be deified, is dynamic, tending always towards its final end, predestined in the 'thought-wills'. These latter have their centre in the Word, the hypostatic Wisdom of the Father who gives expression to Himself in all things and who brings all things, in the Holy Spirit, towards union with God. For there is no 'natural beatitude' for the creation, which can have no other end than deification. All the distinctions which we may try to make between the state which was proper to the first creatures according to their nature and that which was conferred upon them by their ever-increasing participation in the divine energies can never be more than fictions; fictions, moreover, which tend to separate into distinct moments an indivisible reality whose appearance is simultaneous: created

---

[1] 'Liber de Spiritu Sancto, XVI, 38', *P.G.*, XXXII, 136 AB.

beings have the faculty of being assimilated to God because such was the very object of their creation.

In Genesis we read that the heavens and the earth, the universe in its entirety in fact, was created 'in the beginning'. St. Basil saw this as the beginning of time; but 'as the beginning of a road is not yet the road, and the beginning of a house is not yet a house, so the beginning of time is not yet time, not even the smallest part of it.'[1] If the divine will created 'in the beginning', it means that 'its action was instantaneous and outside of time'; but with the universe time also begins. According to St. Maximus it is motion, the change which is proper to created things whose very origin was in change, which is also the origin of time, the form of sensible being (τὰ αἰσθητά). It is time whose nature is to begin, to endure, and to have an end; however, there is also another form of created existence outside of time, and which is proper to intelligible being (τὰ νοητὰ): the aeon—αἰῶνι. 'The aeon —says St. Maximus—is motionless time, while time is the aeon measured according to motion.'[2] The intelligible is not eternal: it has its beginning 'in the age' —ἐν αἰῶνι, in passing from not-being to being, but it remains none the less without any change, being part of a non-temporal mode of existence. The aeon is outside of time, but having, like time, a beginning, it is commensurable to it. The divine eternity alone is incommensurable: in relation both to time and to the aeon.

It is in this extra-temporal condition that God created the angelic world, according to St. Basil.[3] This is why the angels are no longer capable of falling into sin: their un-

---

[1] 'In Hexaemeron, homilia I, 6', *P.G.*, XXIX, 16 C.

[2] 'De ambiguis', *P.G.*, XCI, 1164 BC.

[3] 'In Hexaemeron, homil. I, 5', *P.G.*, XXIX, 13; 'Adversus Eunomium, IV, 2', ibid., 680 B.

wavering attachment to God or their eternal enmity against Him having been realized instantaneously and for all the ages at the moment of their creation. For St. Gregory of Nyssa, as for St. Maximus, however, the angelic nature is none the less able to grow without ceasing in the acquisition of eternal good things in an unending development such as is proper to everything which is created, but excluding all temporal succession.

The nature of matter in the teaching of St. Gregory of Nyssa, later adopted by St. Maximus, is the result of the uniting of simple qualities, which are intelligible in themselves but of which the sum, the joining together or concretion produces the substratum or corporeity of sensible things. 'No one thing in the body—neither its shape nor its size nor its bulk nor its weight nor its colour, nor any of its other qualities taken in themselves *are* the body: they are in themselves simply intelligible. Their concourse (συνδρομή), nevertheless, does make the body.'[1] This dynamic theory of matter makes it possible to conceive of different degrees of materiality, bodies which are material to a greater or lesser extent; it also makes it easier to comprehend the change which took place in the original nature after the coming of sin, as also the resurrection of the body. The material elements pass from one body to another, so that the universe is in fact but a single body. All things exist in each other—says St. Gregory of Nyssa— and all things mutually support each other, for there is a kind of transmuting power which, by a movement of rotation causes the terrestrial elements to pass from one to the other and gathers them in again to the point from which they started. 'And thus in this process nothing becomes greater or less, but everything remains within its primordial limits.'[2] Moreover, each element of the body is

[1] 'De anima et resurrectione', *P.G.*, XLVI, 124 C.
[2] 'In Hexaemeron', *P.G.*, XLIV, 104 BC; 'De anima et resurrectione', *P.G.*, XLVI, 28 A.

'as if guarded by a sentinel'[1] by the intellectual faculty of the soul whose character it is imprinted, for the soul knows its own body even when its elements are dispersed throughout the world. Thus in the condition of mortality which is the consequence of the coming of sin, the spiritual nature of the soul maintains a certain link with the dis-united elements of the body, a link which it will find again at the moment of the resurrection in order that the parts may be transformed into a 'spiritual body', which is in-deed our true body, different from the grossness of those we now have, the 'garments of skin' which God made for Adam and Eve after their sin.

The cosmology of the Greek Fathers is necessarily ex-pressed in terms of the conception of the universe which prevailed in their own age; a fact which takes nothing whatever away from the properly theological basis of their commentaries upon the Biblical narrative of the creation. The theology of the Orthodox Church, con-stantly soteriological in its emphasis, has never entered into alliance with philosophy in any attempt at a doc-trinal synthesis: despite all its richness, the religious thought of the East has never had a scholasticism. If it does contain certain elements of Christian gnosis, as in the writings of St. Gregory of Nyssa, St. Maximus, or in the *Physical and theological chapters* of St. Gregory Palamas, the speculation is always dominated by the central idea of union with God and never acquires the character of a system. Having no philosophical preferences, the Church always freely makes use of philosophy and the sciences for apologetic purposes, but she never has any cause to defend these relative and changing truths as she defends the un-changeable truth of her doctrines. This is why ancient or more modern cosmological theories cannot affect in any way the more fundamental truth which is revealed to the Church: 'the truth of Holy Scripture is far deeper than

[1] 'De anima et resurrectione', ibid., 76–7.

the limits of our understanding', as Philaret of Moscow says.[1] In the face of the vision of the universe which the human race has gained since the period of the renaissance, in which the earth is represented as an atom lost in infinite space amid innumerable other worlds, there is no need for theology to change anything whatever in the narrative of Genesis; any more than it is its business to be concerned over the question of the salvation of the inhabitants of Mars. Revelation remains for theology essentially geocentric, for it is addressed to men and confers upon them the truth as it is relative to their salvation under the conditions which belong to the reality of life on earth. The Fathers saw in the parable of the Good Shepherd, coming down to seek one erring sheep from the mountains where he has left the remaining ninety-nine of his flock, an allusion to the smallness of the fallen world compared with the cosmos as a whole, and with the angelic aeons in particular.[2]

It is the mystery of our salvation that is revealed to us by the Church, and not the secrets of the universe in general which, quite possibly, does not stand in need of salvation; this is the reason why the cosmology of revelation is necessarily geocentric. It also enables us to see why copernican cosmology, from a psychological or rather spiritual point of view, corresponds to a state of religious dispersion or off-centredness, a relaxation of the soteriological attitude, such as is found in the gnostics or the occult religions. The spirit of the insatiable thirst for knowledge, the restless spirit of Faust, turning to the cosmos breaks through the constricting limits of the heavenly spheres to launch out into infinite space; where it becomes lost in the search for some synthetic

---

[1] See Fr. G. Florovsky, op. cit., p. 178.

[2] St. Cyril of Jerusalem, 'Catech., XV, 24', *P.G.*, XXXIII, 904; St. Cyril of Alexandria, 'Oratio pasch., XII, 2', *P.G.*, LXXVII, 673; St. John Chrysostom, 'Contra anom., II, 3', *P.G.*, XLVIII, 714.

understanding of the universe, for its own understanding, external and limited to the domain of becoming, can only grasp the whole under the aspect of disintegration which corresponds to the condition of our nature since the fall. The Christian mystic, on the other hand, entering into himself, and enclosing himself in the 'inner chamber' of his heart, finds there, deeper even than sin,[1] the beginning of an ascent in the course of which the universe appears more and more unified, more and more coherent, penetrated with spiritual forces and forming one whole within the hand of God. One may quote, by way of interest, the suggestion of a modern Russian theologian, who was also a great mathematician, Fr. Paul Florensky, that it would be possible to return to a geocentric cosmology on the basis of the scientific theories of our own time. It is hardly necessary to add that such a bold and, possibly, scientifically defensible synthesis has no real value for Christian theology, which is able to accommodate itself very easily to any scientific theory of the universe, provided that this does not attempt to go beyond its own boundaries and begin impertinently to deny things which are outside its own field of vision.

The cosmology, or rather cosmologies, of the Fathers, have only been mentioned here in order to single out from them certain theological ideas which have their place in the doctrine of union with God. The six days labour signifies—according to St. Basil in the Hexeameron as also to St. Gregory of Nyssa who completed this work—a successive distinction of elements which were created simultaneously on the first day. St. Basil envisages this first day, 'the beginning', the first moment of created being, as if it was 'outside the seven days', as is also the 'eighth day' which we celebrate on Sundays and which was also to be the beginning of eternity, the day of the resurrection.[2] In

---

[1] The expression is that of St. Isaac the Syrian: see Wensinck, p. 8.

[2] St. Basil, 'In Hexaemeron, homil. II, 8', *P.G.*, XXIX, 49–52.

Created Being

the five days which follow the creation of the intelligible and sensible elements, of the heavens and the earth, the visible universe becomes progressively organized; but this successive ordinance, according to St. Gregory of Nyssa, only exists from the point of view of creation, which is governed by a 'luminous force' which God has introduced into matter and which is His word (the 'logoi or willings' of St. Maximus), His ordination of created things which is spoken of in Genesis.[1] For the word of God, as Philaret of Moscow says, 'is not like the words of men, which cease and disappear into air as soon as they are spoken. In God there is nothing which ceases, nothing which has an end. His word proceeds forth but does not pass away. He has not created for a certain time, but for ever; He has brought the creation into existence by means of His creative word. *For He hath stablished the world, so that it cannot be moved.*' (Ps. xciii, 1.)[2]

St. Isaac the Syrian remarks that there is a certain mysterious scale of difference in creation, different modes of the divine activity: . . . If, after the creation of the heavens and the earth, it was by His successive ordinances that God created the multiplicity of beings out of matter, He created the world of the angelic spirits 'in silence'.[3] In the same way, the creation of man was not, as with the rest of living creatures, the result of an ordinance given to the earth: in this case God did not ordain, but said in His eternal Counsel 'let us make man in our image, after our likeness'. It is by His ordinances that God arranges the universe and organizes its parts; but men and angels, as personal beings, are not strictly speaking parts: for a per-

[1] St. Gregory of Nyssa, 'In Hexaemeron', *P.G.*, XLIV, 72–3.

[2] *Sermons and Discourses*, by Mgr Philaret, Moscow, 1877 (in Russian).

[3] A. J. Wensinck, Mystic treatises by Isaac of Nineveh, translated from Bedjan's syriac text. *Verhandelingen der koninklijke Akademie van Wetenschappen te Amsterdam, Afdeeling letterkunde, Nieuwe reeks*, XXIII, 1, Amsterdam, 1923, p. 127.

son cannot be a part of a whole, since it contains the whole within itself. In this respect, the human being is the richer, more complete and possesses more potentialities than the angelic spirits. Situated as he is at the meeting-place of the intelligible and the sensible, He unites these two worlds within himself, and participates at large in all the spheres of the created universe. 'For all things which have been created by God, in their diverse natures, are brought together in man as in a melting-pot, and form in him one unique perfection—a harmony composed of many different notes.'[1]

According to St. Maximus,[2] the work of creation contains five divisions, from which are derived concentric spheres of being, at whose centre is man, virtually containing them all in himself. In the first place, it is necessary to distinguish uncreated nature and created nature, God and the totality of creatures. We can then divide created nature into the intelligible universe and the sensible universe (νοητὰ καὶ αἰσθετὰ). In the sensible universe the heavens are divided from the earth (οὐράνὸς καὶ γῆ); and from the whole surface of the earth we find paradise (οἰκουμένη καὶ παράδεισος), the place of man's habitation divided off. Finally, man is divided into two sexes, male and female, a division which becomes definitive after sin, in the state of fallen human nature. This latter division was made by God in prevision of sin, according to St. Maximus, who is here reproducing the thought of St. Gregory of Nyssa. 'Being, which has had its origin in change—says the latter—retains an affinity with change. This is why He who, as Scripture says, sees

---

[1] St. Maximus, text quoted by L. Karsavine, *The holy Fathers and Doctors of the Church* (in Russian), Paris, 1926, p. 238. We have not been able to find this passage in the works of St. Maximus; however, the same idea is found in many places, e.g. in 'De Ambiguis', *P.G.*, XCI, 1305 AB.

[2] 'De Ambiguis', *P.G.*, XCI, 1305.

all things before their coming to be, having regarded or rather having foreseen in advance by the power of His anticipatory knowledge in which direction the movement of man's free and independent choice would incline, having thus seen how it would come to pass, added to the image the division into male and female: a division which has no relation to the divine Archetype, but which, as we have said, is in agreement with irrational nature.'[1] There is here an inevitable confusion in theological reasoning, so that clear expression becomes impossible: the plane of creation and that of the fall are superimposed upon one another, and we are only able to conceive of the first in images which belong to the second, in terms of sexuality as it exists in our fallen nature. The true meaning of this last mysterious division can only be glimpsed in those places where sex is surpassed in a new plenitude- in mariology and ecclesiology as well as in the sacrament of marriage and the 'angelic way' of monasticism. And it must be remembered that the other divisions of the cosmos as well as this latter one have acquired as a result of sin a limited, a separated and fragmentary character.

It was the divinely appointed function of the first man, according to St. Maximus, to unite in himself the whole of created being; and at the same time to reach his perfect union with God and thus grant the state of deification to the whole creation. It was first necessary that he should suppress in his own nature the division into two sexes, in his following of the impassible life according to the divine archetype. He would then be in a position to reunite paradise with the rest of the earth, for, constantly bearing paradise within himself, being in ceaseless communion with God, he would be able to transform the whole earth into paradise. After this, he

---

[1] ' De hominis opificio, XVI', *P.G.*, XLIV, 181–5. Cf. Henri de Lubac, S.J., *Catholicisme*, Paris, 1938, app. I, p. 296.

must overcome spatial conditions not only in his spirit but also in the body, by reuniting the heavens and the earth, the totality of the sensible universe. Having surpassed the limits of the sensible, it would then be for him to penetrate into the intelligible universe by knowledge equal to that of the angelic spirits, in order to unite in himself the intelligible and the sensible worlds. Finally, there remaining nothing outside himself but God alone, man had only to give himself to Him in a complete abandonment of love, and thus return to Him the whole created universe gathered together in his own being. God Himself would then in His turn have given Himself to man, who would then, in virtue of this gift, that is to say by grace, possess all that God possesses by nature.[1] The deification of man and of the whole created universe would thus be accomplished. Since this task which was given to man was not fulfilled by Adam, it is in the work of Christ, the second Adam, that we can see what it was meant to be.

Such is the teaching of St. Maximus on the divisions of created being, which was borrowed, in part, by John Scotus Eriugena in his *De divisione naturae.* These divisions of St. Maximus express the limited character of the creation which is indeed the very condition of its existence; at the same time they are problems to be resolved, obstacles to be surmounted on the way towards union with God. Man is not a being isolated from the rest of creation; by his very nature he is bound up with the whole of the universe, and St. Paul bears witness that the whole creation awaits the future glory which will be revealed in the sons of God (Rom. viii, 18–22). This cosmic awareness has never been absent from Eastern spirituality, and is given expression in theology as well as in liturgical poetry, in iconography and, perhaps above all, in the ascetical writings of the masters of the spiritual life of the Eastern

[1] St. Maximus, 'De ambiguis', *P.G.*, XCI, 1308.

Church. 'What is a charitable heart?'—asks St. Isaac the Syrian—'It is a heart which is burning with charity for the whole of creation, for men, for the birds, for the beasts, for the demons—for all creatures. He who has such a heart cannot see or call to mind a creature without his eyes becoming filled with tears by reason of the immense compassion which seizes his heart; a heart which is softened and can no longer bear to see or learn from others of any suffering, even the smallest pain, being inflicted upon a creature. This is why such a man never ceases to pray also for the animals, for the enemies of Truth, and for those who do him evil, that they may be preserved and purified. He will pray even for the reptiles, moved by the infinite pity which reigns in the hearts of those who are becoming united to God.'[1] In his way to union with God, man in no way leaves creatures aside, but gathers together in his love the whole cosmos disordered by sin, that it may at last be transfigured by grace.

Man was created last, according to the Greek Fathers, in order that he might be introduced into the universe like a king into his palace. 'As a prophet and a high priest', added Philaret of Moscow,[2] giving an ecclesiological accent to the cosmology of the Bible. For this great theologian of the last century, the creation is already a preparation for the Church, which was to begin to exist in the earthly paradise, with the first men. The books of God's Revelation are for him a sacred history of the world, beginning with the creation of the heavens and the earth, and ending with the new heaven and the new earth of the Apocalypse. The history of the world is a history of the Church which is the mystical foundation of the world. The Orthodox theology of the last things is essentially ecclesiological; and it is the doctrine of the Church which today is the hidden determining force of the thought and

[1] *Mystic treatises*, ed. A. J. Wensinck, p. 341.
[2] G. Florovsky, op. cit., p. 179.

religious life of Orthodoxy. Without being modified or modernized, the whole of the Christian tradition comes before us today under this new aspect of ecclesiology, showing once more that tradition is no stagnant and inert deposit, but the very life of the Spirit of Truth who informs the Church. It is therefore not surprising that cosmology also should receive in our day an ecclesiological turn; a development in no way opposed, but on the contrary giving a new value to, the christological cosmology of St. Maximus and other ancient writers.

Even when it has strayed furthest from the line of tradition, even, indeed, in its very errors, the thought of Eastern Christians in recent centuries—and Russian religious thought in particular—reflects a tendency to envisage the Cosmos in ecclesiological terms. The motifs are prominent in the religious philosophy of Soloviev, for example, in which the mystical cosmology of Jacob Boehme, of Paracelsus and of the Kabbala are mixed up with the sociological ideas of Fourier and of Auguste Comte; they are present also in the eschatological utopianism of Fedorov, and in the millenarian aspirations of Russian Christian socialism; and they are to be found most recently in the sophiology of Fr. Bulgakov, which is an ecclesiology gone astray. In these thinkers the idea of the Church is confounded with that of the Cosmos, and the idea of the Cosmos is dechristianised. But error itself sometimes bears witness to the truth, if in an indirect and negative fashion. Nevertheless, if the idea of the Church— as the place where union with God is accomplished—is already implied in that of the Cosmos, this is not the same thing as to say that the Cosmos is the Church. It is not legitimate to accord to origins that which belongs to vocation, to accomplishment and the final end.

The world was created from nothing by the sole will of God—this is its origin. It was created in order to participate in the fullness of the divine life—this its vocation. It is called to make this union a reality in liberty, in the free harmony of the created will with the will of God—this is the mystery of the Church inherent in creation. Throughout all the vicissitudes which followed upon the fall of humanity and the destruction of the first Church—the Church of paradise—the creation preserved the idea of its vocation and with it the idea of the Church, which was at length to be fully realized after Golgotha and after Pentecost, as the Church properly so-called, the indestructible Church of Christ. From that time on, the created and contingent universe has borne within itself a new body, possessing an uncreated and limitless plenitude which the world cannot contain. This new body is the Church; the plenitude which it contains is grace, the profusion of the divine energies by which and for which the world was created. Outside of the Church they act as determining exterior causes, as the constant willing of God by which all being is created and preserved. It is only in the Church, within the unity of the body of Christ, that they are conferred, given to men by the Holy Spirit; it is in the Church that the energies appear as the grace in which created beings are called to union with God. The entire universe is called to enter within the Church, to become the Church of Christ, that it may be transformed after the consummation of the ages, into the eternal Kingdom of God. Created from nothing, the world finds its fulfilment in the Church, where the creation acquires an unshakable foundation in the accomplishment of its vocation.

CHAPTER SIX

Image and Likeness

If man contains within himself all the elements of which the universe is composed, it is not in this that his true perfection, his claim to glory lies. 'There is nothing remarkable', says St. Gregory of Nyssa, 'in wishing to make of man, the image and likeness of the universe, for the earth passes away, the sky changes and all that they contain is as transitory as that which contains them.' 'People said, Man is a microcosm . . . and thinking to elevate human nature with this grandiloquent title, they did not notice that they had honoured man with the characteristics of the mosquito and the mouse.'[1] The perfection of man does not consist in that which assimilates him to the whole of creation, but in that which distinguishes him from the created order and assimilates him to his Creator. Revelation teaches us that man was made in the image and likeness of God.

All the Fathers of the Church, both of East and of West, are agreed in seeing a certain co-ordination, a primordial correspondence between the being of man and the being of God in the fact of the creation of man in the image and likeness of God. However, the theological expressions of this revealed truth, though they are not in any way contradictory one of another, often differ even within the traditions of East and West. St. Augustine

[1] 'De hominis opificio, XVI', *P.G.*, t. 44, 177 D–180 A.

takes as his starting point the image of God in man, and attempts to work out an idea of God, by trying to discover in Him that which we find in the soul created in His image. The method he employs is one of psychological analogies applied to the knowledge of God, to theology. On the other hand, St. Gregory of Nyssa, for instance, starts with what revelation tells us of God in order to discover what it is in man which corresponds to the divine image. This is a theological method applied to the knowledge of man, to anthropology. The first way seeks to know God by starting from man created in His image; the second wishes to define the true nature of man by starting from the idea of God in whose image man has been created.

If we try to find in the Fathers a clear definition of what it is in man which corresponds to the divine image, we run the risk of losing ourselves amidst varying assertions, which though not contradictory, cannot be applied to any one part of human nature. Sometimes the image of God is sought in the sovereign dignity of man, in his lordship over the terrestrial world; sometimes it is sought in his spiritual nature, in the soul, or in the principle, ruling (ἡγεμονικόν) part of his being, in the mind (νοῦς), in the higher faculties such as the intellect, the reason (λόγος), or in the freedom proper to man, the faculty of inner determination (ἀυτεξουσία), by virtue of which man is the true author of his actions. Sometimes the image of God is identified with a particular quality of the soul, its simplicity or its immortality, or else it is described as the ability of knowing God, of living in communion with Him, with the possibility of sharing the divine being or with the indwelling of the Holy Spirit in the soul. Sometimes, as in the Spiritual Homilies attributed to St. Macarius of Egypt, the image of God is presented in two ways. First it is the formal condition of liberty, free will, the faculty of choice which cannot be destroyed by sin; secondly, it is the 'heavenly image', the positive content of the image, which is that communion with God, whereby before the fall man was clothed with the Word and the Holy Spirit.[1] Finally, as in St. Ireneus, St. Gregory of Nyssa, and St. Gregory Palamas, not only the soul, but also the body of man shares in the character of the image, being created in the image of God. 'The word Man, says St. Gregory Palamas, is not applied to either soul or body separately, but to both together, since together they have been created in the image of God.'[2] Man according to Palamas is 'more in the image of God'' than the angels, because His spirit being joined to a body, possesses a life-giving energy, by which the bodily nature is quickened and controlled. The angels being bodyless spirits do not possess this faculty, though at the same time by reason of the simplicity of their spiritual nature they are nearer to God.[3]

The number of these definitions and their variety show us that the Fathers refrain from confining the image of God to any one part of man. In fact, the Biblical narrative gives no precise account of the nature of the image; but it does present the whole creation of man as an act apart, different from the creation of other beings. Like the angels, who, as St. Isaac the Syrian puts it, were created 'in silence',[4] man was not formed by a divine command addressed to the earth. Rather God Himself fashioned him from the dust of the earth with His own hands; that is to say, according to St. Ireneus, with the Word and the Holy Spirit,[5] and breathed the breath of life into him.

[1] 'Hom. Spirit, XII, 1, 6, 7, etc.', *P.G.*, t. 34, 557–61.

[2] 'Prosopopeiae', *P.G.*, t. 150, 1361 C. A work attributed to Palamas.

[3] 'Capita physica, theologica, etc.' (38 and 39), ibid., 1145–8.

[4] See above, p. 107, n. 3.

[5] 'Contra Haereses, IV, Praefatio, 4', *P.G.*, t. 7, 975 B. Also IV, 20, 1 (1032); V, 1, 3 (1123); V, 5, 1 (1134–5); V, 6, 1 (1136–7); V, 28, 3 (1200).

Image and Likeness

St. Gregory Nazianzen interprets the passage in Genesis in the following way: 'The Word of God taking a portion of the newly created earth, has with his own immortal hands fashioned our frame, and imparted life to it; since the spirit which he breathed into it, is an effluence (ἀπορροή) of the invisible Divinity. Thus out of the dust, and out of the breath, man was created in the image of the Immortal, for in both the spiritual nature reigns supreme. That is why being but dust, I am bound to the life here below; having also a divine part (θείαν μοίραν) I carry in my breast the longing for eternal life.'[1] And in the same poem on the soul, he says: 'The soul is a breath of God, and though heavenly, it allows itself to mingle with the earth. It is the light shut up in a cave, but it is none the less a light divine and inextinguishable.'[2] Taken literally, we ought apparently to deduce from these two passages the uncreated character of the soul, and see in man a God weighed down by his bodily nature, or at least a mixture of God and animal. Understood in this way, creation in the image of God would contradict the Christian teaching that man is a creature called to *attain* to union with God, to *become* god by grace, but in no way god by virtue of his origin. Without mentioning other outrageous consequences, the problem of evil would be inconceivable in these conditions. Either Adam could not sin, since by reason of his soul, a part of divinity, he was God, or else original sin would involve the divine nature —God Himself would sin in Adam. St. Gregory Nazianzen could not hold such a view. In his work on human nature, he addresses his soul thus: 'If you are truly the breath of God, and of divine origin, as you suppose, put away all iniquity that I may believe it. . . . How comes it that you are so troubled by the suggestions of the adver-

---

[1] 'Poemata dogmatica, VIII, περὶ ψυχῆς, vv. 70–7', *P.G.*, t. 37, 452.

[2] Ibid., vv. 1–3, 446–7.

sary, if you are one with the heavenly Spirit? If despite such assistance you still fall to the ground—alas, how powerful your sin must be.'[1] Mingled (κιρναμένη) with 'the heavenly Spirit', the soul is *helped* by something greater than itself. It is the presence of this divine power in it, which causes it to be called 'a portion of the Deity', for it originates in an infused 'effluence of deity', which is grace. The 'divine breath' points to a mode of creation, by virtue of which the human spirit is intimately connected with grace, and is produced by it in the same way as a movement of air is produced by the breath, contains this breath and is inseparable from it. It is a participation in the divine energy proper to the soul, which is meant by the phrase 'part of the deity'. Indeed, St. Gregory Nazianzen in one of his homilies speaks of this participation in connection with the 'three lights', of which the first is God, the supreme Light, unspeakable and unapproachable; the second the angels, 'a certain effluence (ἀπορροὴ τις) or participation (μετουσία) of the first, and the third, man also called light because his mind is enlightened by the 'archetypal Light', which is God.[2] Thus creation in the image and likeness of God implies the idea of participation in the divine Being, of communion with God. That is to say, it presupposes grace.

The image of God in man, in so far as it is perfect, is necessarily unknowable, according to St. Gregory of Nyssa; for as it reflects the fullness of its archetype, it must also possess the unknowable character of the divine Being. This is the reason why it is impossible to define what constitutes the divine image in man. We can only conceive it through the idea of participation in the infinite goodness of God. According to St. Gregory of Nyssa, 'God is, by His very nature, all the good it is possible to conceive;

---

[1] 'Poemata moralia, XIV, περι τῆς ἀνθρωπίνης φύσεως, vv. 76–84; ibid., 761–2.

[2] 'In sanctum baptisma, or XL, 5', *P.G.*, t. 36, 364 BC.

or rather He surpasses in goodness all that it is possible for our minds to understand or grasp. And His reason for creating human life is simply this—because He is good. Such being the nature of God, and such the one reason why He undertook the creation of man, there were to be no half measures when He set about to show forth the power of His goodness. He would not give a mere part of what was His own, and grudge to share the rest. The very perfection of goodness is displayed in the fact that He brought man into being from nothing and showered all that is good on him. Now so many are the benefits bestowed on every man that it would not be easy to enumerate them. For this reason all are briefly summed up in this one phrase, that man was made in the image of God. For this is equivalent to saying that God made human nature a sharer in all that is good. . . . But if the image resembles in all respects the excellence of tĥe Prototype, it would no longer be the image, but would itself be the Prototype, there being no means of distinguishing them. Wherein, then, lies the distinction between the Divine and that which resembles it? In this: that the one is uncreated and the other exists through creation.'[1] Clearly, St. Gregory of Nyssa here means by the image of God the final perfection of man, the state of deification sharing in the divine pleroma, in the fullness of blessings. And therefore, when he speaks of the image that is limited to the sharing of certain benefits that is to the image in the state of becoming, he sees the proper character of man created in the image of God, primarily in 'the fact that he is freed from necessity, and not subject to the domination of nature, but able freely to follow his own judgement. For virtue is independent and her own mistress.'[2] Freedom is, so to speak, the 'formal' image, the necessary condition

[1] 'De hominis opificio, XVI', *P.G.*, t. 44, 184 AC. Cf. de Lubac, *Catholicism* (Eng. trans.), p. 209.
[2] Ibid., 184 B.

for the attainment of perfect assimilation to God. Because created in the image of God, man is to be seen as a personal being, a person who is not to be controlled by nature, but who can himself control nature in assimilating it to its divine Archetype.

The human person is not a part of humanity, any more than the persons of the Trinity are parts of God. That is why the character of the image of God does not belong to any one part of the human make-up, but refers to the whole man in his entirety. The first man who contained in himself the whole of human nature was also the unique person. 'For the name Adam', says St. Gregory of Nyssa, 'is not yet given to the man, as in the subsequent narratives. The man created has no particular name, but is universal man. Therefore by this general term for human nature, we are meant to understand that God by His providence and power, included all mankind in this first creation. . . . For the image is not in a part of the nature, nor is grace in one individual among those it regards; this power extends to the whole human race. . . . In this respect there is no difference between the man made in the first creation of the world, and he who shall be made at the end of all things; both bear the same divine image.'[1] 'Thus man is made in the image of God, that is to say the whole human nature; it is that which bears the divine likeness.'[2] The divine image proper to the person of Adam is applied to the whole of mankind, to universal man. That is why the multiplication of persons in the race of Adam, each one of whom is in the image of God—one could say, the multiplication of the divine image in the plurality of human hypostases—is in no sort of contradiction with the ontological unity of the nature which is common to all men. Quite the reverse: a human person cannot realise the fullness to which he is called, that is to

[1] Ibid., 185 BC.
[2] Ibid., 204 D.

120

become the perfect image, if he claims for himself a part of the nature, regarding it as his own particular good. For the image reaches its perfection when the human nature becomes like the divine, in attaining a complete participation in God's uncreated bounty. Now there is only one nature common to all men, even though it now appears to us split up by sin, parcelled out among many individuals. This original unity of nature, re-established in the Church, seemed of so absolute a character to St. Paul that he called it the *body* of Christ.

Men have therefore a common nature, one single nature in many human persons. This distinction of nature and person in man is no less difficult to grasp than the analogous distinction of the one nature and three persons in God. Above all, we must remember that we do not know the person, the human hypostasis in its true condition, free from alloy. We commonly use the words 'persons' or 'personal' to mean individuals, or individual. We are in the habit of thinking of these two terms, person and individual, almost as though they were synonyms. We employ them indifferently to express the same thing. But, in a certain sense, individual and person mean opposite things, the word individual expressing a certain mixture of the person with elements which belong to the common nature, while person, on the other hand, means that which distinguishes it from nature. In our present condition we know persons only through individuals, and as individuals. When we wish to define, 'to characterize' a person, we gather together individual characteristics, 'traits of character' which are to be met with elsewhere in other individuals, and which because they belong to nature are never absolutely 'personal'. Finally, we admit that what is most dear to us in someone, what makes him himself, remains indefinable, for there is nothing in nature which properly pertains to the person, which is always unique and incomparable. The man who is governed by his nature and acts in the strength of his natural qualities, of his 'character', is the least personal. He sets himself up as an individual, proprietor of his own nature, which he pits against the natures of others and regards as his 'me', thereby confusing person and nature. This confusion, proper to fallen humanity, has a special name in the ascetic writings of the Eastern Church—αὐτότης, φιλαντία or, in Russian, *samost*, which can perhaps be best translated by the word egoism, or rather if we may create a Latin barbarism 'ipseity'.

A difficulty is met with in reference to the Christological dogma which would see the will as a function of the nature; for us it is easier to envisage the person as willing, asserting and imposing himself through his will. However, the idea of the person implies freedom *vis-à-vis* the nature. The person is free from its nature, is not determined by it. The human hypostasis can only realize itself by the renunciation of its own will, of all that governs us, and makes us subject to natural necessity. The individual, i.e. that assertion of self in which person is confused with nature and loses its true liberty, must be broken. This is the root principle of asceticism; a free renunciation of one's own will, of the mere simulacrum of individual liberty, in order to recover the true liberty, that of the person which is the image of God in each one. For this reason, Evagrius says that a perfect monk 'will after God, count all men as God Himself'.[1] The person of another will appear as the image of God to him who can detach himself from his individual limitations, in order to rediscover the nature common to all, and to realize by so doing his own person.

It is not, then, a part of our nature which corresponds to the image of God in us, but the person which includes the nature in itself. Leontius of Byzantium, a sixth-century theologian, uses a special term ἐνυπόστατον, 'enhypostasized', for the nature which is included in a person or

---

[1] 'Περὶ προσευχῆς, c. 123', *P.G.*, t. 79, 1193 C.

hypostasis. According to Leontius all nature is found in an hypostasis, such being the nature of a hypostasis which cannot otherwise exist.[1] But on the lower degrees of being, hypostases are only individuals, individual beings: they only receive the character of persons when it becomes a question of spiritual beings, man, the angels or God. In so far as it is person and not individual, the hypostasis does not divide the nature, giving place to many distinct natures. The Trinity is not three Gods, but one God. If in fact the multiplication of human persons does divide the nature, splitting it up into many individuals, it is only because we know of no other generation than that which takes place after sin, in human nature which has lost its likeness to the divine nature. As we have already seen, St. Gregory of Nyssa, and St. Maximus, regard the creation of Eve as itself an act wrought by God in His foresight of sin and its consequences for mankind. However, Eve taken from Adam's nature, 'bone of his bone, and flesh of his flesh', the new human person, completed the nature of Adam, was one nature, 'one flesh' with him. It was only as a consequence of sin that these two first human persons became two separate natures; two individuals, with exterior relationships between them—the desire of the woman being to her husband, and he exercising rule over her (Gen. iii, 16). After original sin human nature became divided, split up, broken into many individuals. Man now has a double character: as an individual nature, he is a part of a whole, one of the elements which make up the universe; but as a person, he is in no sense a part: he contains all in himself. The nature is the content of the person, the person the existence of the nature. A person who asserts himself as an individual, and shuts himself up in the limits of his particular nature, far

[1] 'Contra Nestorium et Eutychium', *P.G.*, t. 86, 1277 CD. The same ideas are developed by St. Maximus (*P.G.*, t. 91, 557–60) and St. John Damascene, *De fide orth.*, I, ix, 531.

from realizing himself fully becomes impoverished. It is only in renouncing its own possession and giving itself freely, in ceasing to exist for itself that the person finds full expression in the one nature common to all. In giving up its own special good, it expands infinitely, and is enriched by everything which belongs to all. The person becomes the perfect image of God by acquiring that likeness which is the perfection of the nature common to all men. The distinction between persons and nature reproduces the order of the divine life expressed by the doctrine of the Trinity, in mankind. It is the foundation of all Christian anthropology, of all evangelical living, for, as St. Gregory of Nyssa says, Christianity is an 'imitation of the nature of God'.[1]

Made in the image of God, man is a personal being confronted with a personal God. God speaks to him as to a person, and man responds. Man, according to St. Basil, is a creature who has received a commandment to become God.[2] But this commandment is addressed to human freedom, and does not overrule it. As a personal being man can accept the will of God; he can also reject it. Even when he removes himself as far as possible from God, and becomes unlike Him in His nature, he remains a person. The image of God in man is indestructible. In the same way, he remains a personal being when he fulfils the will of God and in his nature realizes perfect likeness with Him. For according to St. Gregory Nazianzen, 'God honoured man in giving him freedom, in order that goodness should properly belong to him who chooses it, no less than to Him who placed the first fruits of goodness in his nature.'[3] Thus, whether he chooses good or evil, whether he tends to likeness or unlikeness, man possesses

---

[1] 'De professione christiana', *P.G.*, t. 46, 224 C.

[2] Words of St. Basil reported by St. Gregory Nazianzen in 'In laudem Basilli Magni', of. XLIII, 48', *P.G.*, t. 36, 560 A.

[3] 'In sanctum Pascha, or. XLV, 8', *P.G.*, t. 36, 632 C.

his nature freely, because he is a person created in the image of God. All the same, since the person cannot be separated from the nature which exists in it, every imperfection, every 'unlikeness' in the nature limits the person, and obscures 'the image of God'. Indeed, if freedom belongs to us as persons, the will by which we act is a faculty of our nature. According to St. Maximus, the will is 'a natural force which tends towards that which is conformed to nature, a power which embraces all the essential properties of nature'.[1] St. Maximus distinguishes this natural will (θέλημα φυσικόν) which is the desire for good to which every reasonable nature tends, from the choosing will (θέλημά γνωμικόν) which is a characteristic of the person.[2] The nature wills and acts, the person chooses, accepting or rejecting that which the nature wills. However, according to St. Maximus, this freedom of choice is already a sign of imperfection, a limitation of our true freedom. A perfect nature has no need of choice, for it knows naturally what is good. Its freedom is based on this knowledge. Our free choice (γνώμη) indicates the imperfection of fallen human nature, the loss of the divine likeness. Our nature being overclouded by sin no longer knows its true good, and usually turns to what is 'against nature'; and so the human person is always faced with the necessity of choice; it goes forward gropingly. This hesitation in our ascent towards the good, we call 'free will'. The person called to union with God, called to realize by grace the perfect assimilation of its nature to the divine nature, is bound to a mutilated nature, defaced by sin and torn apart by conflicting desires. It knows and wills by means of this imperfect nature, and is in practice blind and powerless. It can no longer choose

[1] 'Opuscula theologica et polemica, Ad Marinum', *P.G.*, t. 19, 45 D–48 A.
[2] Ibid., 48 A–49 A, 192 BC. In St. John Damascene, 'De fide orth', III, 14', *P.G.*, t. 94, 1036–7; 1044–5.

well, and too often yields to the impulses of a nature which has become a slave to sin. So it is, that that in us which is made in the image of God is dragged into the abyss, though always retaining its freedom of choice, and the possibility of turning anew to God.

Man was created perfect. That, however, does not mean that his first state is identical with his last, or that he was united with God from the moment of his creation. Before the fall, Adam was neither a 'pure nature' nor a deified man. As we have said before, both the cosmology and the anthropology of the Eastern Church are dynamic in character, and resolutely exclude the possibility of juxtaposing the ideas of nature and grace. Nature and grace do not exist side by side, rather there is a mutual interpenetration of one another, the one exists in the other. St. John Damascene sees an unfathomable mystery in the fact that man was created 'for deification', moving towards union with God.[1] The perfection of our first nature lay above all in this capacity to communicate with God, to be united more and more with the fullness of the Godhead, which was to penetrate and transfigure created nature. St. Gregory Nazianzen refers to this highest faculty of the human spirit when he speaks of God breathing in 'the divine part', that is to say the grace which from the beginning is present in the soul able to receive and make its own the deifying energy of God. The human person was called, according to St. Maximus, 'to reunite by love created with uncreated nature, showing the two in unity and identity through the acquisition of grace'.[2] The unity and identity here refer to the person, to the human hypostasis. Man is thus to reunite by grace two natures in his created hypostasis, to become 'a created god', a 'god by grace', in contrast to Christ who being a divine person assumed human nature. To arrive at this

[1] 'De fide orth', II, 12', *P.G.*, t. 94, 924 A.
[2] 'De ambigius', *P.G.*, t. 91, 1308 B.

end the concurrence of two wills is necessary; on the one side there is the divine and deifying will granting grace through the presence of the Holy Spirit in the human person; on the other side there is the human will which submits to the will of God in receiving grace and making it its own, and allowing it to penetrate all its nature. As the will is an active power of rational nature, it acts by grace to the extent in which nature participates in grace, in which the likeness is restored by 'the transforming fire'.[1]

The Greek fathers sometimes describe human nature as threefold: consisting of spirit, soul and body (νοῦς, ψυχή, σῶμα), sometimes as the union of soul and body. The difference between the partisans of trichotomy and of dichotomy is in effect simply one of terminology. The dichotomists regard the νοῦς as a superior faculty of the reasonable soul, the faculty by which man enters into communion with God. The human person or hypostasis contains the parts of this natural complex, and finds expression in the totality of the human being which exists in and through it. It is the image of God, the constant principle in the nature which, being dynamic and changing, is always inclined by the will towards an external end. We may say that the image is a divine seal, imprinted on the nature and putting it into a personal relationship with God. This relationship is unique for every being. It is made effective and real by means of the will which orders the entire nature towards God, in whom man must find the fullness of his being. St. Tikhon Zadonsky, in the eighteenth century, writes: 'The human soul is a spirit created by God, and only in God, who has created it in His own image and likeness, can it find contentment and rest, peace, consolation and joy. Once separated from

---

[1] The expression πῦρ τῆς ἀλλαγῆς is from Diadochus of Photike, *Ascetic Treatise*, ch. LXVII, ed. *Sources chrétiennes*, 1955, p. 127.

Him, it seeks for satisfaction among created things, and feeds itself on passions, on husks, food for pigs; but finding not its true repose, nor its true satisfaction, it dies at length of hunger. For spiritual food is a necessity to the soul.'[1] The spirit must find its sustenance in God, must live from God; the soul must feed on the spirit; the body must live on the soul—such was the original ordering of our immortal nature. But turning back from God, the spirit, instead of providing food for the soul, begins to live at the expense of the soul, feeding itself on its substance (what we usually call 'spiritual values'); the soul in turn begins to live with the life of the body, and this is the origin of the passions; finally, the body is forced to seek its nourishment outside, in inanimate matter, and in the end comes on death. The human complex finally disintegrates.

Evil entered into the world through the will. It is not a nature (φύσις), but a condition (ἕξις). 'The nature of good is stronger than the habit of evil,' says Diadochus of Photike, 'for good exists, while evil does not exist, or rather it exists only at the moment in which it is practised.'[2] According to St. Gregory of Nyssa, sin is a disease of the will which is deceived, and takes a mere shadow of the good for the good itself. For this reason, the very desire to taste of the fruit of the knowledge of good and evil was itself a sin, for, according to St. Gregory, knowledge presupposes a certain disposition towards the object one wishes to know, and evil, being in itself non-existent, ought not to be known.[3] Evil becomes a reality only by means of the will, in which alone it subsists. It is the will which gives evil a certain being. That man, who was by

[1] *St. Tikhon Zadonsky*, Works, t. II, 192 (in Russian). Cf. also N. Gorodetzky, *St. Tikhon Zadonsky*, S.P.C.K., 1951.

[2] *Ascetic Treatise*, ch. III, *Sources chrét:*. p. 86. There is in Migne a Latin translation, 'Capita de perfectione spirituali', *P.G.* t. 65, 1168.

[3] 'De hominis opificio, XX', *P.G.*, t. 44, 197–200; 'De oratione dominica, IV', ibid., 1161 D–1164 A.

nature disposed towards the knowledge and love of God, could in his will incline towards a non-existent good, an illusory goal, can only be explained by some external influence, by the persuasion of some alien will to which the human will consented.[1] Before entering the earthly world through Adam's will, evil had already had its beginnings in the spiritual world. It was the will of the angelic spirits, eternally fixed in their enmity to God, which first gave birth to evil. And evil is nothing other than an attraction of the will towards nothing, a negation of being, of creation, and above all of God, a furious hatred of grace against which the rebellious will puts up an implacable resistance. Even though they have become spirits of darkness, the fallen angels remain creatures of God, and their rejection of the will of God represents a despairing intercourse with the nothingness which they will never find. Their eternal descent towards non-being will have no end. St. Seraphim of Sarov, a great Russian mystic of the last century, says of them: 'They are hideous; their conscious rejection of divine grace has transformed them into angels of darkness, and unimaginable horrors. Being angelic creatures, they possess enormous strength. The least among them could destroy the earth, did not divine grace render their hatred for God's creation powerless. Therefore they seek to destroy creation from within, by turning human freedom towards evil.'[2] The same saint, referring to an ascetic writing attributed to St. Antony,[3] distinguishes three different wills at work in man. First, there is the will of God, perfect and saving; secondly, the will of man, not necessarily pernicious, but certainly not in itself a saving will, and, thirdly, the demonic will, seeking our perdition.

[1] Ibid., 200 C.

[2] *Revelations of St. Seraphim of Sarov*, Paris, 1932 (in Russian).

[3] The passage about the three wills is to be found in 'Letter XX', published in Galland, *Vet. Patrum Bibl.*, Venice, 1788, IV, 696 ff.

E   129

The orthodox ascetic has special terms to denote the different activities of evil spirits in the soul. Λογισμοί are thoughts or images which rise out of the lower regions of soul, the 'subconscious'.[1] Προσβολή cannot be translated 'temptation'; it is rather the presence of some alien thought, introduced into our consciousness from outside by the will of the adversary. 'It is not a sin,' says St. Mark the Hermit, 'but a witness to our freedom.'[2] Sin begins where there is συγκάθατεσις,[3] the consent of the mind to some intruded thought or image, or still more a certain interest and attention which already indicates the beginning of an agreement with the enemy's will. For evil always presupposes freedom of consent, otherwise it would be no more than a violent and external possession.

Man sinned freely. But what constitutes original sin? The Fathers distinguish many moments in this decision of free will which separates man from God. The moral, and therefore personal, moment is for all of them, to be found in the disobedience to and transgression of the divine commandment. If man had received the commandment in a spirit of filial love, he would have responded to the will of God with a complete sacrifice; he would detach himself willingly, not only from the forbidden fruit, but from every external object, in order to live only for God, to aspire solely to union with Him. The commandment of God marks out for the human will the way which leads to deification, the way of detachment from all that is not God. Human will has chosen the opposite way, has become separated from God and has submitted to the tyranny of the devil. St. Gregory of Nyssa, and St. Maximus, pay special attention to the natural aspect of sin. Instead of

[1] For detailed analysis of these terms, V. Zarine, *The Foundations of Orthodox Ascetism*, St. Petersburg, 1902, which is still valuable. Unfortunately, this very useful book has never been translated.

[2] 'De baptismo', *P.G.*, t. 65, 1020 A.

[3] St. Mark the Hermit, 'Περὶ νόμου πνευματικοῦ, CXLII, *P.G.*, t. 65, 921-4.

following its natural disposition towards God, the human spirit has turned towards the world; instead of spiritualizing the body it has itself entered into the stream of animal and sensory life, and become subject to material conditions. St. Symeon the New Theologian,[1] sees a progressive development of sin in the fact that man, instead of repenting, tries to justify himself before God. Adam declines all responsibility for Eve, 'the woman whom thou gavest to be with me', and so makes God the root cause of his fall. Eve accuses the serpent. In this refusal to recognize that the unique origin of evil is in their own free will, men reject the possibility of freeing themselves from evil, and submit their freedom to external necessity. The will hardens, and shuts itself off from God. 'Man has closed up within himself the springs of divine grace,' says Philaret of Moscow.[2]

Is the deprivation of grace itself the cause of the decadence of our nature? The idea of supererogatory grace which is added to nature in order to order it towards God is foreign to the tradition of the Eastern Church. As the image of God, the ordering of the human person was towards its Archetype. Its nature tended spontaneously towards God by means of the will, a reasonable and spiritual power. 'Primitive righteousness' rested on the fact that since man was created in the image of God, he could not be other than a good nature, ordered towards goodness, towards communion with God, and the acquisition of uncreated grace. If this good nature has come into disharmony with its Creator, that can only be by reason of its power of determination from within, its αὐτεξουσία. It is this which confers on man the possibility of acting and willing not only in conformity with his natural dispositions, but also in opposition to his nature which he

---

[1] 'Homily 45' in the Smyrna edition; 'Homily 33' in the Latin translation in Migne, *P.G.*, t. 120, 499 AB.

[2] *Discours et sermons* (French translation), I, 5.

can pervert, and render 'against nature'. The decadence of human nature is the direct consequence of the free decision of man. He has willed it so, has deliberately placed himself in this position. A condition against nature must lead to the disintegration of the being of man, which dissolves finally in death, the last separation of nature, become unnatural and separate from God. There is no longer a place for uncreated grace in the perverted nature where, according to St. Gregory of Nyssa, the mind like a mirror turned about, instead of reflecting God, receives into itself the image of formless matter,[1] where the passions overthrow the original hierarchy of human being. The deprivation of grace is not the cause, but rather the consequence of the decadence of our nature. Man has obstructed the faculty in himself for communion with God, has closed up the way by which grace should have poured out through Him into the whole creation.

This 'physical' concept of sin and its consequences does not, in the teaching of the Eastern Church, exclude another element which must always be remembered, the personal, moral aspect, the aspect of fault and punishment. The two aspects are inseparably connected, because man is not only a nature, but also a person placed over against a personal God, and in a personal relationship with Him. If human nature disintegrates as a consequence of sin, if sin introduces death into the created universe, the reason for this is not only that human freedom has created a new state ($\xi\xi\iota\varsigma$), a new mode of existence in evil, but also that God has placed a limit to sin, allowing it to end in death. 'The wages of sin is death.'

'We are offspring of a tarnished line,' says St. Macarius of Egypt.[2] However, nothing in nature, not even the

---

[1] 'De hominis opificio, XII', *P.G.*, t. 44, 164.
[2] On the subject of the power of darkness invading the human race, see 'Homil Spirit', XXIV, 2, XLIII, 7–9 and *passim*; *P.G.*, t. 34, 664; 776–7.

demons, is essentially evil. But sin, this parasite of nature, rooted in the will, lives in it, makes it a prisoner of the devil, himself a prisoner of his own will frozen for ever in evil. A new pole is created in the world opposite to the image of God, in itself illusory, but real in the will; and here is the paradox of its having existence in non-existence, as St. Gregory of Nyssa puts it. By way of the human will, evil has become a power infecting the whole creation; 'cursed is the ground for thy sake' (Gen. iii, 17). The universe which still reflects the majesty of God, has at the same time acquired a sinister character, 'the nocturnal side of creatures', in the phrase of the Russian theologian and philosopher, Prince E. Troubetskoy.[1] Sin has been introduced where grace should reign, and instead of the divine plenitude, a gaping abyss has opened in God's creation, the gates of hell opened by the free will of man.

Adam did not fulfil his vocation. He was unable to attain to union with God, and the deification of the created order. That which he failed to realize when he used the fullness of his liberty became impossible to him from the moment at which he willingly became the slave of an external power. From the fall until the day of Pentecost, the divine energy, deifying and uncreated grace, was foreign to our human nature, acting on it only from outside and producing created effects in the soul. The prophets and righteous men of the Old Testament were the instruments of grace. Grace acted by them, but did not become their own, as their personal strength. Deification, union with God by grace, had become impossible. But the plan of God was not destroyed by the sin of man; the vocation of the first Adam was fulfilled by Christ, the

[1] Prince E. Troubetskoy, who died at the beginning of the revolution and was the author of *The Meaning of Life* (Moscow, 1917), is unknown in the West. He alone of the sophiological school remained perfectly orthodox in his theological thought.

second Adam. God became man in order that man might become god, to use the words of Ireneus and Athanasius, echoed by the Fathers and theologians of every age.[1] However, this work, finished by the incarnate Word, is seen primarily by fallen humanity in its most immediate aspect, as the work of salvation, the redemption of a world captive to sin and death. Fascinated by the *felix culpa*, we often forget that in breaking the tyranny of sin, our Saviour opens to us anew the way of deification, which is the final end of man. The work of Christ calls out to the work of the Holy Spirit (Luke xii, 49).

[1] St. Ireneus, 'Adv. Haereses, V, pref., *P.G.*, t. 7, 1120; St. Athanasius, 'De incarnatione Verbi, cap. 54', *P.G.*, t. 25, 192 B; St. Gregory Nazianzen, 'Poem. dogma, X, 5-9', *P.G.*, t. 37, 465; St. Gregory of Nyssa, 'Oratio Catechetica, XXV', *P.G.*, t. 45, 65 D.

CHAPTER SEVEN

The Economy of the Son

economy of salvation

In our examination of the elements of theology which form the basis of the doctrine of union with God in the tradition of the Eastern Church, we have indicated the main outline of the teaching on uncreated being and created being, on God and the creature which are the two terms of the union. We have come to the extreme limits of created being where man is separated from God not only by nature but also by will, creating thus a new existential mode of being, that of sin. For according to St. Gregory of Nyssa sin is an invention of the created will. The infinite distance between the created and uncreated, the natural separation of man from God which ought to have been overcome by deification, became an impassable abyss for man after he had willed himself into a new state, that of sin and death, which was near a state of non-being. In order to reach that union with God, to which the creature is called, it was then necessary to break through a triple barrier of sin, death and nature.

The way to deification, which was planned for the first man, will be impossible until human nature triumphs over sin and death. The way to union will henceforth be presented to fallen humanity as *salvation*. This negative term stands for the removal of an obstacle: one is saved from something—from death, and from sin—its root. The divine plan was not fulfilled by Adam; instead of the

135

straight line of ascent towards God, the will of the first
man followed a path contrary to nature, and ending in
death. God alone can endow men with the possibility of
deification, by liberating him at one and the same time
from death and from captivity to sin. What man ought to
have attained by raising himself up to God, God achieved
by descending to man. That is why the triple barrier
which separates us from God—death, sin, nature—impassable for men, is broken through by God in the inverse
order, beginning with the union of the separated natures,
and ending with victory over death. Nicholas Cabasilas, a
Byzantine theologian of the fourteenth century, said on this
subject: 'The Lord allowed men, separated from God by
the triple barrier of nature, sin and death, to be fully
possessed of Him and to be directly united to Him by the
fact he has set aside each barrier in turn: that of nature by
His incarnation, of sin by His death, and of death by His
resurrection. This is the reason why St. Paul writes: 'The
last enemy that shall be destroyed is death' (I Cor. xv,
26).[1] For St. Maximus the incarnation (σάρκωσις) and
deification (θέωσις) correspond to one another; they
mutually imply each other. God descends to the world
and becomes man, and man is raised towards divine fullness and becomes god, because this union of two natures,
the divine and the human, has been determined in the
eternal counsel of God, and because it is the final end for
which the world has been created out of nothing.[2] One
would suppose from some modern critics that St. Maximus
held a doctrine similar to that of Duns Scotus: if original
sin had not taken place, Christ would have become incarnate anyhow, in order to unite created being and the
divine nature in Himself. However, as we have seen, when
examining the teaching of St. Maximus on creation, Adam

---

[1] 'De la vie en Christ, III', *P.G.*, t. 150, trans. Fr. in *Irenikôn*, IX,
1932, suppl., pp. 89–90.
[2] 'Quaestiones ad Thalassium (60)', *P.G.*, t. 90, 621 AB.

was destined to unite in his own being the different spheres of the cosmos, in order that deification might be conferred upon them, through union with God.[1] If these unions or successive 'syntheses' that surmount the natural divisions are brought about by Christ, it is because Adam failed in his vocation. Christ achieves them successively by following the order which was assigned to the first Adam.

By his birth of the Virgin, He suppressed the division of human nature into male and female. On the cross He unites paradise, the dwelling place of the first men before the fall, with the terrestrial reality where the fallen descendants of the first Adam now dwell; indeed, He says to the good thief, 'today thou shalt be with Me in paradise', yet he nevertheless continues to hold converse with His disciples during His sojourn on earth after the resurrection. At His ascension, first of all, He unites the earth to the heavenly spheres, that is to the sensible heaven; then He penetrates into the empyreum, passes through the angelic hierarchies and unites the spiritual heaven, the world of mind, with the sensible world. Finally, like a new cosmic Adam, He presents to the Father the totality of the universe restored to unity in Him, by uniting the created to the uncreated.[2] In this conception of Christ, as the new Adam, who unifies and sanctifies created being, redemption appears as one of the stages in his work, a stage conditioned by sin and the historic reality of the fallen world, in which the incarnation has taken place. Maximus does not raise the scotist question, that is, whether the Word would have had to become incarnate apart from the *felix culpa*.[3] Less soteriological as a theologian, and perhaps more metaphysical than the other Fathers, he does not swerve at all from their practical way of thought; unreal cases do not exist for him. God has foreseen the fall of

[1] 'De ambiguis', *P.G.*, t. 91, 1308.
[2] Ibid., 1309.
[3] H. U. von Balthasar, *Kosmische Liturgie*, pp. 267–8.

Adam and the Son of God was 'the Lamb slain before the ages' in the pre-existent will of the Trinity. That is why we cannot expect to understand anything whatsoever apart from the cross of Christ. 'The mystery of the incarnation of the Word—said St. Maximus—contains in itself the meaning of all the symbols and all the enigmas of Scripture, as well as the hidden meaning of all sensible and intelligible creation. But he who knows the mystery of the Cross and the Tomb, knows also the essential principles of all things. Finally, he who penetrates yet further and finds himself initiated into the mystery of the Resurrection, apprehends the end for which God created all things from the beginning.'[1]

The work of Christ is a 'dispensation of the mystery, which from all ages has been hidden in God',[2] as St. Paul said, an 'eternal purpose which was realized in Jesus Christ'. However, there is no necessity of nature in the incarnation and the passion. 'It is not a work of nature, but a mode of economic condescension,' according to St. John the Damascene;[3] it is the work of the will, the mystery of divine love. We have seen (Chapter V) that 'purposes', 'ideas' do not for the Greek Fathers belong to the essence, but to the will common to the Trinity. That is why the incarnation of the Son, which is a manifestation of love,[4] does not introduce any change or new reality into the internal being of the Trinity. If 'the Word was made flesh'—ὁ λόγος σὰρξ ἐγένετο—this 'becoming' in no way affects the divine nature. 'The Word, though remaining what It was, became what It was not', according to the phrase of St. Theophilus of Bulgaria (twelfth century).[5]

---

[1] 'Gnostic centuries', I, 66, *P.G.*, t. 90, 1108 AB.
[2] Eph. iii, 9.
[3] 'Contra Jacobitas, 52', *P.G.*, t. 94, 1464 A.
[4] 'God so loved the world that He gave His only-begotten Son,' John iii, 16.
[5] 'Enarratio in Evangelium Ioannis, I, 14', *P.G.*, t. 123, 1156 C.

138

The Economy of the Son

Dionysius applies to the incarnation and even to the humanity of the Son the word φιλάνθρωπία,[1] 'love for men', which is a word signifying 'providence' (πρόνοια). Indeed, providence stands for the purposes of the divine will in relation to the human will, which are based on the foresight of the free acts of the creature. It is a will that is always beneficial, that understands how to make men profit greatly from all the vicissitudes of their wanderings, provided that man understands how to recognize the will of God. With a certain excusable inexactitude, one could say that God in His providence condescends to the liberty of men. He acts as a result of this liberty, co-ordinating his actions with the acts of created beings, in order to govern the fallen universe by accomplishing His will without doing violence to the liberty of creatures. Therefore the mystery hidden before all ages in God and revealed to angels by the Church,[2] this eternal and immutable foredetermination of the incarnation has at the same time a kind of contingency; one could almost say that it was occasional, provided this expression does not imply any idea of the unforeseen.

Unceasingly God 'descends into the world' by the acts of his providence, by his economy, which literally means the 'construction' or 'administration of a house'. In the 'fullness of time' the Wisdom of God, already acting in the world as power, energy, providence, entered the historical process in person. The hypostatic Wisdom of the Father 'built Himself a house'—the most pure flesh of the Virgin assumed by the Word. Thus St. Philotheus of Constantinople (fourteenth century) interprets the text of 'Proverbs' (ix, 1): *Sapientia aeificavit sibi domum . . .*[3]

---

[1] 'De divin. nomin, II, 3; 10'; Epist. IV et passim; *P.G.*, t. 3, 640 C; 648 D; 1072 B.   [2] Eph. iii, 9–10.

[3] *Three Discourses on Wisdom* (MS. 431 of the Synodical Library of Moscow)), published by Mgr. Arsène, Gk. text and Russian translation, Novgorod, 1898.

According to St. John of Damascus, 'The name of the Mother of God (Θεοτόκος) contains the whole history of the divine economy in the world.'[1] 'One could ask'— said St. Dimitri of Rostov (seventeenth century)—'why the Word of God delayed His descent to the earth and His incarnation to save fallen humanity. But before the middle of the 6th Millennium since the fall of Adam, it was not possible to find a virgin pure in body as well as in spirit. There was only one such, unique by her spiritual and bodily purity who was worthy to become the Church and the temple of the Holy Spirit.'[2]

The whole development of the Old Testament with its successive elections—the election of Noah, the election of the stock of Abraham, the election of the people of Israel, the election of the tribe of Judah, the election of the House of David, the law which preserved the purity of the people of God, the blessing on the chosen descendants, the whole of this sacred history appears as a providential and Messianic process, as a preparation of the Body of Christ, of the Church—the very focal point of union with God, and above all as a preparation of Her who was to lend her human nature so that the mystery of the incarnation could be realized.

The dogma of the immaculate conception is foreign to the Eastern tradition, which does not wish to separate the Holy Virgin from the descendants of Adam upon whom the fault of the first parents weighs. Nevertheless, sin acting as a force in her nature, and as impurity could find no place in her. St. Gregory Palamas in his homily on the Presentation to the temple, explains this sanctity of the virgin by the successive purifications which have taken place in the nature of her ancestors, as well as in her own

[1] 'De fide orth., III, 12', *P.G.*, t. 94, 1029 and 1032.
[2] Works of S. Dimitri of Rostov, t. III, p. 101, *Christian Readings*, 1842, IV, 395 (in Russian).

nature from the moment of her conception.[1] She was not holy in virtue of a privilege, of an exemption from the destiny common to all humanity, but because she has been kept from all taint of sin though without any impairment of her liberty. On the contrary, it was above all an expression of her liberty, and of the human response to the will of God. Nicolas Cabasilas states this idea in his homily on the Annunciation: 'The incarnation', he said, 'was not only the work of the Father, by His power and by His spirit, but it was also the work of the will and faith of the Virgin. Without the consent of the Immaculate, without the agreement of her faith, the plan was as unrealizable as it would have been without the intervention of the three divine Persons Themselves. It was only after having instructed her and persuaded her that God took her for His Mother and borrowed from her the flesh, that She so greatly wished to lend Him. Just as He became incarnate voluntarily, so He wished that His Mother should bear Him freely and with her full consent.'[2] In the person of the Virgin, humanity has given its consent to the Word becoming flesh and coming to dwell amongst men, for, according to the patristic phrase 'if the Divine will alone was the creator of man, it could not save him without the concord of the human will'. The tragedy of liberty was resolved by the words *ecce ancilla Domini*.

According to St. John the Damascene, who sums up the Christological doctrines of the Fathers, the Incarnation was accomplished by the action of the Holy Spirit who caused the Virgin to be fit to receive in her the Deity of the Word, as well as through the Word Himself who formed in the Virginal flesh the first-fruits of His human-

[1] 'Homily on the presentation to the temple of the Holy Virgin,' in the collection of the sermons of S. Gr. Palamas published by Sophocles, Athens, 1861, p. 216.

[2] M. Jugie, 'Homélies mariales byzantines,' *Patrologia orientalis*, XIX, fasc., 3, Paris, 1925, p. 463.

ity.[1] Thus, in the one and the same act the Word assumed human nature, gave it its existence, and deified it. The humanity, assumed and appropriated by the Person of the Son, received its being in the Divine hypostasis: it did not exist before as a distinct nature, and has not entered into union with God, but from the beginning it appeared as the human nature of the Word. This humanity, according to St. Maximus, had the immortal and incorruptible character of the nature of Adam before he sinned, but Christ submitted it voluntarily to the condition of our fallen nature.[2] Christ assumes not only human nature but also that which was against nature, the consequences of sin, though He Himself remained outside original sin in virtue of His Virginal birth. He therefore embraced all that was really human, such as it was after the fall, excepting sin: He took an individual nature liable to suffering and death. Thus the Word has descended to the last outpost of being, corrupted by sin, even to death and to hell. Perfect God, He has not only become 'perfect man', but has assumed also all the imperfections, all the limitations that proceed from sin. 'We are astonished' said St. Maximus—'to see how the finite and the infinite—things which exclude one another and cannot be mixed—are found to be united in Him and are manifested mutually the one in the other. For the unlimited is limited in an ineffable manner, while the limited is stretched to the measure of the unlimited.'[3]

Hellenistic thought could not admit the union of two perfect principles—δύο τέλεια ἐν γενέσθαι οὐ δύναται 'two perfects cannot become one'. The struggle over Christological dogma lasted nearly four centuries before Christian foolishness had triumphed over Greek 'wisdom'. As in the dogma of the Trinity, it was a question of the

---

[1] 'De fide orth., III, 2', *P.G.*, t. 94, 985 BC–988 A.
[2] 'Quaestiones ad Thalassium (21)', *P.G.*, t. 90, 312–16.
[3] 'Epist. XXI', *P.G.*, t. 91, 604 BC.

distinction between the nature (φύσις) and hypostasis. But while in the Trinity there is one nature in three hypostases, in Christ there are two different natures in the one hypostasis. The hypostasis includes both natures; it remains one though it becomes the other; 'the Word became flesh'; but deity did not become humanity, nor was humanity transformed into deity. Such is the meaning of the Christological dogma formulated by the Council of Chalcedon: 'In conformity with the tradition of the Fathers, we unanimously proclaim that we should confess one and the same Son, our Lord Jesus Christ, perfect in deity and perfect in humanity, true God and true man, composed of a reasonable soul and body, being consubstantial with the Father through the Divinity and consubstantial with us through the humanity, alike to us in all, save sin, born of the Father before all the worlds in His deity, born in these last times of Mary the Virgin, Mother of God, in His humanity, for us and for our salvation; one and the same Christ, Son, Lord, only-Begotten, who was made known in two natures without being mingled, without change, indivisibly, inseparably, in such a way that the union does not destroy the difference of the two natures, but on the contrary the properties of each nature only remain the more firm since they are found united in one person or hypostasis which is neither separated nor divided into two persons, being the one and the same person of the Son, only-Begotten, God and Word, Lord Jesus Christ.'[1] What strikes one about this formula is its apophatic character; in fact the union of the two natures is expressed by four negative definitions: ἀσυγχύτως, ἀτρέπτως, ἀδιαιρέτως, ἀχωρίστως. We know the fact of the union of the two natures in one person, but the 'how' of this union remains for us a mystery based on the incomprehensible distinction—identity of the nature and

[1] Mansi, *Consil. coll.* XII, 116; Denzinger, *Enchiridion*, Wurtzburg, 1865, n. 134, pp. 44–6.

of the person. The Divine Person, Christ, has in Him two principles which are different and united at the same time. One could say that the Son of God has suffered, that He died on the cross—but only in that which could suffer and die, His humanity. One could equally say that though He was born as an infant in the crib at Bethlehem, or was hung on the cross, or rested in the tomb, He did not cease to govern all-powerfully the whole of the created world, in virtue of His Divinity which suffers no change.

As we have said many times, the perfection of the person consists in self-abandonment: the person expresses itself most truly in that it renounces to exist for itself. It is the self-emptying of the Person of the Son, the Divine κένωσις.

'The entire mystery of economy'—said St. Cyril of Alexandria—'consists in the self-emptying and abasement of the Son of God.'[1] It is the renunciation of His own will in order to accomplish the will of the Father by being obedient to Him unto death and unto the cross. Besides, this renunciation of His own will is not a choice, or an act, but is so to speak the very being of the Persons of the Trinity who have only one will proper to their common nature. The Divine will in Christ was then the will common to the Three: the will of the Father—the source of will, the will of the Son—in obedience, the will of the Holy Spirit—the accomplishment. 'For the Son'—said St. Cyril of Alexandria—'could do nothing that the Father did not do. In fact, since He shares with the Father one and the same substance, He is bound, so as to speak, by certain physical laws, to possess the same will and the same power. . . . Besides, the Father shows the Son what He Himself does, not by presenting Him with His actions

[1] The principal 'kenotic' passages of S. Cyril: 'Quod unus sit Christus', *P.G.*, t. 75, 1308, 1332; 'Apologeticus contra orientales', t. 76, 340–1; 'Apologet, contra Theodoretum', 417, 440ss; 'Adversus Nestorium', III, 4, 152ss; 'De recta fide, ad reginas', II, 19, 1357–9; 'Homil. pasch.', XVII, t. 77, 773 *et passim*.

written on tablets, not by teaching Him what He is ignorant of (the Son knows everything inasmuch as He is God), but by portraying Himself completely in the nature of the Begotten, and by revealing in Him everything that His Begetter is.'[1] That is why 'He who has seen the Son has seen the Father.' The κένωσις is the mode of existence of the Divine Person who was sent into the world, the Person in whom was accomplished the common will of the Trinity whose source is the Father. Christ's saying, 'the Father is greater than I', expresses this kenotic renunciation of His own will. That means that the work accomplished on the earth by the incarnate Son is the work of the Holy Trinity, from whom Christ cannot be separated, since He shares the same essence and the same will as the Father and the Holy Spirit. Thus the outpouring, self-emptying of Himself only produces the greater manifestation of the deity of the Son to all those who are able to recognize greatness in abasement, wealth in spoliation, liberty in obedience. For the eyes of faith are necessary to recognize not only the Divine Person, but also each human person who is created in the image of God. The two natures of Christ remain distinct and unmixed with one another. However, being united hypostatically without being transformed into one another, they permeate one another (περιχώρησις εἰς ἀλλήλας), according to St. Maximus who reproduces here, in the framework of the Christological dogma, the Eastern conception of energies or processions of the nature.[2] This perichoresis, or permeation, for St. John Damascene, is on the whole unilateral: comes from the divine side and not from the fleshly side.[3] However, the Divinity, having once penetrated the flesh, gives to it an ineffable faculty of pene-

---

[1] 'In Ioannem', II, t. 73, 361 D.
[2] 'Disputatio cum Pyrro', *P.G.*, t. 91, 344, 345 D–348 A. Cf. S. Jean Damascene, 'De fide orth., III, 3', *P.G.*, t. 94, 994–6.
[3] 'De fide orth., III, 8', *P.G.*, t. 94, 1013 B.

trating the Divinity. 'When adoring my King and my God, I adore at the same time the porphyry of His Body' —said the Damascene—'not as a garment or a fourth person, but as a body united to God, and abiding without change, as well as the divinity by which it has been anointed. For the corporal nature has not become God but, just as the Word did not change and remained what He was though becoming flesh, so also the flesh became the Word without having lost what it had, though it was identified with the Word in the hypostasis.'[1] The humanity of Christ is a deified nature that is permeated by the divine energies from the moment of the Incarnation. St. Maximus uses here the example of iron penetrated by fire, becoming fire, though remaining iron by nature—an example which the Greek Fathers habitually use in expressing the state of deified nature. In each act of Christ one can see two distinct operations, for Christ acts in conformity to both His natures, and by both His natures—as the sword reddened by the fire cuts and burns at the same time: 'as iron it cuts, as fire it burns'.[2]

Each nature acts according to its own properties: the human hand raises the young girl, the divine restores her to life; the human feet walk on the surface of the water, because the divinity has made it firm. 'It is not the human nature that raises Lazarus, it is not the divine power which sheds tears before his tomb,' said St. John the Damascene.[3]

The two wills proper to the two natures are different, but He who wills is one, though He wills in conformity with each of the two natures. The volition also has one object, because the two wills are united, the human will being

---

[1] Ibid., 1013 C–1016 A; IV, 3, 1105 AB.
[2] 'Disputatio cum Pyrrho', *P.G.*, t. 91, 337 C; 'De ambiguis', ibid., 1060 A; cf. S. John Damascene, 'De fide orth., III, 15', *P.G.*, t. 94, 1053 D–1056 A.
[3] 'De fide orth., III, 15', 1057 A.

freely subject to the divine will. However, this liberty is not our free will—γνωμή, that faculty of choice which belongs to the person. In fact, the divine person of the Word had no need to choose or to decide by deliberation. Choice is a limitation, characteristic of our debased liberty: if the humanity of Christ could will in a human way, His divine person did not choose, it did not exercise free will as do human persons.[1]

According to St. John the Damascene the divine will permits the human will to will, and to manifest fully what is proper to humanity.[2] It always 'prevents' the human will, in such a way that the humanity of Christ wills 'divinely' (θεικῶς) in accord with the divinity which allows it to expand. Thus His body experienced hunger or thirst, His soul loved, grieved (at the death of Lazarus), and was indignant; His human spirit had recourse to prayer, the nourishment of all created spirit. The two natural wills in the person of the God-Man could not enter into conflict. The prayer of Gethsemane was an expression of horror in face of death, a reaction proper to all human nature, especially to an incorrupt nature which should not submit to death, and for whom death could only be a voluntary rending contrary to nature. 'When His human will'—said St. John Damascene—'refused to accept death, and His divine will made way for this manifestation of His humanity, the Lord in conformity with His human nature, submitted to struggle and fear, and prayed to be spared from death. But since His divine will desired that His human will should accept death, the humanity of Christ voluntarily accepted the Passion.'[3] Also the last cry of mortal agony of Christ on the cross was a manifestation

[1] S. Maximus, 'Opuscula theologica et polemica, Ad Marinum', *P.G.*, t. 91, 48 A–49 A; S. John Damascene, 'De fide orth., III, 14', 1036–7, 1044–5.

[2] 'De fide orth., III, 15', 1060 BC.

[3] Ibid., III, 18, 1073 BC.

humanity which voluntarily submitted to
nal stripping, emptying, the culmination of
vωσις.

aximus,[1] the divine humiliation, the kenosis,
was not an impoverishment of the deity, but an ineffable
descent of the Son who is reduced to the 'form of a slave'
without ceasing to be fully God. It is in virtue of this
humiliation that Christ, the new Adam, incorruptible and
immortal in His human nature—a nature which was completely deified by the hypostatic union—submitted voluntarily to all the consequences of sin and became Isaiah's
'Man of sorrows' (liii, 3). Thus, by assimilating the historic reality in which the Incarnation had to take place
He introduced into His divine person all sin-scarred,
fallen human nature. That is why the earthly life of Christ
was a continual humiliation. His human will unceasingly
renounced what naturally belonged to it, and accepted
what was contrary to incorruptible and deified humanity:
hunger, thirst, weariness, grief, sufferings, and finally,
death on the cross. Thus, one could say that the person of
Christ, before the end of His redemptive work, before the
Resurrection, possessed in His humanity as it were two
different poles—the incorruptibility and impassibility
proper to a perfect and deified nature, as well as the corruptibility and passibility voluntarily assumed, under
which conditions His kenotic person submitted and continued to submit His sin-free humanity. That is why St.
Maximus distinguishes two assumptions of humanity by
the Word: the natural assumption and the relative or
economic assumption.[2] The first is, so to speak, concealed
by the second. It is only manifested once before the
Passion, when Christ appeared to the three Apostles in
His deified humanity, resplendent with the light of His

[1] 'De ambiguis', *P.G.*, t. 91, 1044 BC, 1048 C.
[2] 'Opuscula theologica et polemica', *P.G.*, t. 91, 156–7; 'De
ambiguis', ibid., 1040, 1049 D–1052, 1317 D–1321.

divinity. The hymn for the feast of the Transfiguration clearly expresses the two aspects of Christ's humanity— His natural state and His state of voluntary submission to conditions of fallen humanity: 'Thou wast transfigured on the mountain, O Christ our Lord, and the glory has so caught the wonder of Thy disciples, that when they see Thee crucified they will understand that Thy Passion is voluntary, and they will proclaim to the world that Thou art truly the Splendour of the Father.'[1]

The feast of the Transfiguration, so venerated by the Orthodox Church, serves as a key to the understanding of the humanity of Christ in the Eastern tradition. This never considers the humanity of Christ in abstraction, apart from His Godhead, whose fullness dwells in Him bodily (Col. ii, 9). Deified by the divine energies, the humanity of the Word had to appear to the sons of the Church, after the Resurrection and Pentecost, in that glorious way which before the advent of grace was hidden from human eyes. This humanity revealed the divinity which is the splendour of the Three Persons. The humanity of Christ provides the opportunity for the manifestation of the Trinity. That is why the Epiphany (the feast of the Baptism of Christ, according to the liturgical tradition of the East) and the Transfiguration are celebrated so solemnly: it is the revelation of the Trinity that is being celebrated—for the voice of the Father was made heard and the Holy Spirit was present the first time in the form of a dove, and the second time as the luminous cloud which covered the Apostles. This royal aspect of Christ— 'the One of the Holy Trinity'—who came into the world to conquer death is characteristic of Orthodox spirituality in every epoch and in every country. Even the

---

[1] This hymn, as well as the other liturgical texts which we cite lower down, are to be found in the *Menologia* (immovable feasts) and the *Lenten Triodion*. Some of these texts are translated into French by the Benedictine Fathers of Amay-sur-Meuse.

Passion, the death on the cross, and the laying in the tomb become triumphant acts by which the Divine Majesty of Christ illuminates the images of the fall and abandonment whilst accomplishing the mystery of our salvation. 'They stripped me of my raiment and arrayed me in purple, they placed a crown of thorns on my head and put a reed in my hand that I might break them as the potter's vessels.' Christ arrayed in a garment of mockery appears suddenly towards the end of this hymn as a king coming to judge the world, as the eschatological Christ of the last Judgement. 'He who covers Himself with light as with a garment, stood naked before the judges and His face was struck by the hands He had made. Lawless men nailed the Lord of Glory to the cross. At that time the veil of the Temple was rent, the sun darkened its rays for it could not bear the sight of God tormented, He before Whom every creature trembles.' Here Christ on the cross appears as the Creator of the cosmos in the midst of His creation which is overcome by terror before the mystery of His death. The same idea is expressed in another hymn for Good Friday: 'On this day, He who suspended the earth upon the waters, is hung on the tree. The King of Angels is crowned with a crown of thorns. He who adorned the heavens with clouds, is arrayed in the purple of mockery. He who freed Adam in the Jordan, bears to be struck. The Spouse of the Church is nailed to the tree. The Son of the Virgin is pierced with a lance. Glory to Thy Passion, O Christ, Glory to Thy Passion! Reveal to us Thy holy Resurrection.' Across the motifs of the Passion the hope of Easter becomes more and more felt. 'Behold, He who holds all creation in His hand, is held within the tomb. The Lord who covered the heavens with beauty is covered with a stone. Life sleeps and hell trembles with awe. Adam is freed from his bonds. Glory to Thy Passion by which Thou hast created eternal rest, O my God, revealing to us Thy all holy Resurrection.'

Lastly, the repose in the tomb, the final culmination of divine self-limitation, brings us suddenly into the mysterious repose of the Creator: the work of redemption is identified with the work of creation. 'The great Moses mysteriously foretells this day saying: *and God blessed the seventh day.* This is the blessed Sabbath, this is the day of repose. For on this day the only Son of God rested from all His works.' In this sacred hymn, chanted on Good Friday, the Church half reveals to us 'the mystery of God hidden before all ages'. Let us recall the words of St. Maximus which were cited at the beginning of this chapter: 'He who knows the mystery of the cross and tomb, also knows the essential principles of all things.'[1] But the mind remains dumb before this mystery and theological thought finds no words to express it.

The apophatic or negative outlook characteristic of Eastern theology is expressed in the great variety of images given us by the Greek Fathers so that our minds may be lifted up to contemplate the work of Christ, a work which, according to St. Paul, the angels do not understand. This work is more usually called the work of redemption, a term which implies the idea of a debt, or the payment of a ransom for the release of captives, and is borrowed from legal practice. All the Fathers use this figure of speech which originated from St. Paul. St. Paul also uses another legal term, that of the 'Mediator' who reconciles men to God by the cross on which He abolished enmity. Other figures have rather a warlike ring—such as struggle, victory, destruction of the opposing power. St. Gregory of Nyssa represents the economy of salvation as a divine ruse to baffle the evil spirit's cunning and so to free humanity. Figures of the physical order are also very frequent, such as fire destroying the impurity of nature, the incorruptibility which causes corruptibility to disappear, a medicine which cures weak nature, etc. . . . the desire

[1] See above on page 138.

to use any one of these images as an adequate expression of the mystery of our salvation involves the risk of substituting purely human and inappropriate conceptions for 'the mystery hidden in God before all ages'. St. Maximus brings together all the figures of the work of redemption in a powerful sentence rich in meaning: 'The death of Christ on the cross', he says, 'is a judgement of judgement.'[1]

St. Gregory of Nazianzen applies the apophatic or negative method to the theology of redemption. He thus distinguishes the unfathomable mystery of the victory over death by somewhat ironically rejecting as inappropriate the images by which one habitually tends to express the work of our salvation accomplished by Christ. 'We must now examine', said he, 'the question and the dogma so often passed over in silence, but which (I think) demands no less deep study. To whom was that blood offered that was shed for us, and why was it shed? I mean the precious and glorious blood of God, the blood of the High Priest and of the Sacrifice. We were in bondage to the devil and sold under sin, having become corrupt through our concupiscence. Now, since a ransom is paid to him who holds us in his power, I ask to whom such a price was offered and why? If to the devil it is outrageous! The robber receives the ransom, not only from God, but a ransom consisting of God Himself. He demands so exorbitant a payment for his tyranny that it would have been right for him to have freed us altogether. But if the price is offered to the Father, I ask first of all, how? For it was not the Father who held us captive. Why then should the blood of His only begotten Son please the Father, who would not even receive Isaac when he was offered as a whole burnt offering by Abraham, but replaced the human sacrifice with a ram? Is it not evident that

[1] 'Quaestiones ad Thalassium (43)', *P.G.*, t. 90, 408 D; (61) 633 D; (63) 684 A–685 B.

the Father accepts the sacrifice not because He demanded it or because He felt any need for it, but on account of economy: because man must be sanctified by the humanity of God, and God Himself must deliver us by overcoming the tyrant through His own power, and drawing us to Himself by the mediation of the Son who effects this all for the honour of God, to whom He was obedient in everything. . . . What remains to be said shall be covered with a reverent silence. . . .'[1] 'We needed an incarnate God, a God put to death that we might live.'[2] 'Nothing can equal the miracle of my salvation: a few drops of blood recreate the whole world.'[3]

This victory over death is first of all declared in the Resurrection of the Lord: 'on that day Christ was recalled from among the dead with whom He had been united. On that day He shattered the sting of death, He burst the lugubrious doors of gloomy hell, by delivering the souls therein. On that day, rising from the tomb, He appeared to the men for whose sake He was born, died and rose from the dead.'[4]

Christ assumed our nature; He voluntarily submitted to all the consequences of sin; He took on Himself the responsibility for our error, while remaining a stranger to sin, in order to resolve the tragedy of human liberty, and in order to bridge the gulf between God and man by leading him into the heart of His Person where there is no room for any division or interior conflict. According to St. Maximus, Christ healed all that belonged to man, but particularly the will which was the source of his sin. By His ineffable κένωσις the God-Man was integrated into corruptible reality, draining and emptying it from with-

---

[1] 'In sanctum Pascha, or. XLV, 22', *P.G.*, t. 36, 653 AB.

[2] Ibid., 28, 661 C.

[3] Ibid., 29, 664 A.

[4] 'Poemata de seipso', xxxviii: 'Hymnus ad Christum post silentium, in Paschate', *P.G.*, t. 37, 1328, vv. 39–44.

in by means of His incorruptible will. This voluntary in-
tegration into the condition of fallen humanity had to
end in the death on the cross, and the descent into hell.
Thus, the whole of our fallen nature—death included—
and all the existential consequences of sin, such as had the
character of penalty, chastisement and curse, have been
transformed by the Cross of Christ into the means of our
salvation. The cross which should stand for final decay,
became the unshakable foundation of the universe: 'The
life-giving Cross, the power of Kings, the constancy of the
righteous, the magnificence of priests.'[1] According to St.
Maximus, the work of salvation consists of three stages
which Christ successively re-establishes in nature: being,
well being (εὖ εἶναι), and eternal being (ἀεὶ εἶναι). The
first is attained by the Incarnation, the second by the
incorruptibility of the will in this earthly life ending in
the Cross, the third by the incorruptibility of nature as it
is revealed in the Resurrection.[2] Let us return again to
the passage in St. Maximus, where he says: 'He who
penetrates beyond the Cross and the Tomb and finds himself initiated into the mystery of the resurrection, learns
the end for which God has created all things.'[3]

The Fathers of the 'Christological centuries', though
they formulated a dogma of Christ the God-Man, never
lost sight of the question concerning *our* union with God.
The usual arguments they bring up against unorthodox
doctrines refer particularly to the fullness of our union,
our deification, which becomes impossible if one separates
the two natures of Christ, as Nestorius did, or if one only
ascribes to Him one divine nature, like the Monophysites,
or if one curtails one part of human nature, like Apollina-
rius, or if one only sees in Him a single divine will and
operation, like the Monothelites. 'What is not assumed,

[1] *Hymn for the Exaltation of the Cross.*
[2] 'De ambiguis', *P.G.*, t. 91, 1392.
[3] See earlier in this chapter on page 138.

cannot be deified'—this is the argument to which the Fathers continually return.[1] What is deified in Christ is His human nature assumed in its fullness by the divine person. What must be deified in us is our entire nature, belonging to our person which must enter into union with God, and become a person created in two natures: a human nature which is deified, and a nature or, rather, divine energy, that deifies. The work accomplished by Christ is related to our nature, it is no longer separated from Christ by our fault. It is a new nature, a restored creature which appears in the world. It is a new body, pure from all taint of sin, free from all external necessity, separated from our iniquity and from every alien will by the precious Blood of Christ. It is the pure and incorruptible realm of the Church where one attains union with God; it is also our nature in so far as it is incorporated in the Church, and is part of the Body of Christ, in which we were made an integral part through Baptism.

But if in our nature we are members, and parts of the humanity of Christ, our persons have not yet reached union with the Godhead. Redemption and purification of nature do not yet provide all the conditions necessary for deification. The Church is already the Body of Christ, but she is not yet 'the fullness of Him who filleth all in all' (Eph. i, 23). The work of Christ is consummated; the work of the Holy Spirit is waiting for accomplishment.[2]

[1] See, for example, S. Gregory Nazianzen, Epist. 101, *P.G.*, t. 37, 181.

[2] S. Gregory Nazianzen, 'In Pentecosten', or. XLI, 5, *P.G.*, t. 36, 436–7.

CHAPTER EIGHT

The Economy of the Holy Spirit

The Incarnation of the Word is a greater and more profound mystery than that of the creation of the world; yet the work of Christ is fulfilled in relation to what is contingent, as a divine action wrought in consequence of Adam's sin. This pre-existing consequence, this divine will of salvation which preceded the human will of the fall, this 'mystery which from all ages hath been hid in God' (Eph. iii, 9), disclosing itself in time as the mystery of the Cross of Christ, is not, properly speaking, occasional, in so far as human freedom was involved in the idea of creation. That is why this freedom was not able to break asunder the universe which God conceived. It found itself included in another and vaster existential design which was opened up by the cross and resurrection. A new reality came into the world, a body more perfect than the world—the Church, founded on a twofold divine economy: the work of Christ and the work of the Holy Spirit, the two persons of the Trinity sent into the world. The work of both persons forms the foundation of the Church. The work of both is requisite that we may attain to union with God.

If Christ is 'Head of the Church which is his body', the Holy Spirit is He 'that filleth all in all' (Eph. i, 23). Thus, the two definitions of the Church which St. Paul gives show two different poles within her which correspond to the two divine persons. The Church is *body* in so far as Christ is her head; she is *fullness* in so far as the Holy Spirit quickens her and fills her with divinity, for the Godhead dwells within her bodily as it dwelt in the deified humanity of Christ. We may say with Irenaeus: 'where the Church is, there is the Spirit; where the Spirit is, there is the Church.'[1]

Nevertheless, the Spirit who 'spake by the prophets' was never alien to the divine economy in the world in which the common will of the Holy Trinity was being revealed. He was no less present in the work of creation than in that of redemption. It is the Holy Spirit who accomplishes all things, according to St. Basil: 'Christ comes, the Spirit goes before. He is present in the flesh, and the Spirit is inseparable from Him. There are workings of miracles and gifts of healing, through the Holy Spirit. Demons are driven out by the Spirit of God. The Devil was stripped of his power in the presence of the Spirit. Sins are remitted by the grace of the Spirit. . . . Familiarity with God, through the Spirit . . . the resurrection from the dead, by the operation of the Spirit.'[2] And yet, the words of the Gospel are explicit: 'the Spirit was not yet given; because Jesus was not yet glorified' (John vii, 39). The operation of the Holy Spirit in the world before the Church and outside the Church is not, therefore, the same as His presence in the Church after Pentecost. As the Word, 'by whom all things were made', revealed the Wisdom of God in creation before He was sent into the world or entered its history through His Incarnation; so also the Holy Spirit (in whom the divine will—creator and upholder of the universe—was fulfilled from the moment of creation) was at a given moment sent into the world to be present there not only by His opera-

---

[1] 'Contra Haeres., III, 24, 1', *P.G.*, VII, 966 C.

[2] 'De Spiritu Sancto, XIX, 49', *P.G.*, XXXII, 157 AB. Cf. Greg. Naz., 'Or. XXXI, 29', *P.G.*, XXXVI, 165 B.

tion, common to all three Persons of the Trinity, but considered as Person.

Theologians have always insisted on the radical difference between the eternal procession of the Persons, which is, according to St. John Damascene, 'the work of nature' —the very being of the Holy Trinity—and the temporal mission of the Son and of the Holy Spirit in the world, the work of the will which is common to the three hypostases. In regard to the Holy Spirit the Greek Fathers habitually made use of the verb ἐκπορεύομαι to designate His eternal procession, while the verbs προΐημι and προχέομαι most often denote His mission in the world. On the eternal level the Persons of the Son and the Spirit proceed from the Father, 'the unique source of deity'. On the level of the temporal mission, which is a work of the will belonging to the substance of the Trinity, the Son is sent by the Father and is incarnate by the Holy Spirit. We may also say that He is sent by Himself in so far as He fulfills the will of being sent, not having His 'own will'. The same thing is true as to the mission of the Holy Spirit in the world. He performs the will which is common to the Three, being sent by the Father and imparted by the Son. According to St. Symeon the New Theologian, 'we say that the Holy Spirit is sent or given, but that in no wise implies that He remains a stranger to the will of His mission. In fact, the Holy Spirit, one of the Persons of the Holy Trinity, fulfils through the Son that which the Father desires as if it were His own will; for the Holy Trinity is indivisible as to its nature, substance and will.'[1]

Thus, just as the Son comes down to earth and accomplishes His work through the Spirit, so the Person of the

[1] 'Homily 62.' The works of St. Symeon the New Theologian were published at Smyrna in 1886. This edition is not to be come by: Krumbacher avows that he has never seen it (*Geschichte der byzantinischen Litteratur*, Munich, 2nd ed. 1897, p. 194). We quote Symeon from a Russian translation made by Bishop Theophanes of the

The Economy of the Spirit

Holy Spirit comes into the world, being sent by the Son: 'the Comforter . . . whom I will send unto you from the Father, even the Spirit of truth, which proceedeth from the Father, he shall bear witness of me' (John xv, 26). Intimately linked as they are in the common work upon earth, the Son and the Holy Spirit remain nevertheless in this same work two persons independent the one of the other as to their hypostatic being. It is for this reason that the personal advent of the Holy Spirit does not have the character of a work which is subordinate, and in some sort functional, in relation to that of the Son. Pentecost is not a 'continuation' of the Incarnation. It is its sequel, its result. The creature has become fit to receive the Holy Spirit and He descends into the world and fills with His presence the Church which has been redeemed, washed and purified by the blood of Christ.

One can say that in a certain sense the work of Christ was a preparation for that of the Holy Spirit: 'I came to cast fire upon the earth; and what will I, if it is already kindled?' (Luke xii, 49). Pentecost is thus the object, the final goal, of the divine economy upon earth. Christ returns to the Father that the Spirit may descend: 'It is expedient for you that I go away: for if I go not away, the Comforter will not come unto you; but if I go, I will send him unto you' (John xvi, 7). Yet in His personal coming the Holy Spirit does not manifest His Person. He comes, not in His own name but in the name of the Son, to bear witness to the Son—as the Son came in the name of the Father, to make known the Father. 'One does not think of the Father without the Son', says St. Gregory of Nyssa,

Russian monastery of St. Panteleimon on Mount Athos (Moscow, 2nd ed., 1892). The passage in question is to be found on p. 105 of Vol. 1. Migne published part of the works of St. Symeon in a Latin translation made in 1603 by Pontanus (*P.G.* 120, 321–694). A new edition by Father Basil Krivoshein and Dr. Joan Hussey is in preparation.

'one does not conceive of the Son without the Holy Spirit. For it is impossible to attain to the Father except by being raised by the Son, and it is impossible to call Jesus Lord save in the Holy Spirit.'[1]

The divine Persons do not themselves assert themselves, but one bears witness to another. It is for this reason that St. John Damascene said that 'the Son is the image of the Father, and the Spirit the image of the Son'.[2] It follows that the third Hypostasis of the Trinity is the only one not having His image in another Person. The Holy Spirit, as Person, remains unmanifested, hidden, concealing Himself in His very appearing. This is why St. Symeon the New Theologian was to praise Him, in his hymns to the divine love, under the apophatic lineaments of a Person at once unknowable and mysterious: 'Come, true light; come, eternal life; come, hidden mystery; come, treasure without name; come, unutterable thing; come, unknowable person; come, incessant joy! Come, light unfading; come, hope which will save all. Come, resurrection of the dead; come, O powerful one, who fulfillest, transformest and changest all things by thy will alone; come, invisible one, wholly intangible and inpalpable. Come, thou who restest always immovable and who, at all times, movest thyself and comest toward us who lie in hell. Thou standest higher than the heavens. Thy name so greatly desired and constantly proclaimed, none is able to say what it is. None can know how thou art, of what kind or species, for that is impossible. Come, garland never withered; come, thou whom my wretched soul has loved and whom it loves! Come alone to me alone. Come, thou who hast separated me from all and hast made me lonely in this world and who thyself art become desire in me, who hast willed that I should desire thee, thou, absolutely inaccess-

---

[1] 'Contra Macedonium, 12', *P.G.*, XLIV, 1316.
[2] 'De fide orth., I, 13', *P.G.*, XCIV, 856.

ible. Come, breath and my own life, consolation of my lowly heart.'[1]

The doctrine of the Holy Spirit (in contrast to the dazzling manifestation of the Son which the Church proclaims to the farthest confines of the universe), has the character of a secret, a partially revealed tradition. St. Gregory Nazianzen points to a mysterious economy in our knowledge of the truths which concern the person of the Holy Spirit: 'The Old Testament', he says, 'manifested the Father plainly, the Son obscurely. The New Testament revealed the Son and hinted at the divinity of the Holy Spirit. Today the Spirit dwells among us and makes Himself more clearly known. For it was not safe, when the Godhead of the Father was not yet acknowledged, plainly to proclaim the Son; nor when that of the Son was not yet received to burden us further (if I may use so bold an expression) with the Holy Spirit . . . but rather that by gradual additions, and, as David says, goings up and advances and progress from glory to glory, the light of the Trinity might shine upon the more illuminated. . . . You see lights breaking upon us gradually; and the order of Theology, which it is better for us to keep, neither proclaiming things too suddenly, nor yet keeping them hidden to the end. For the former course would be unreasonable; the latter impious; and the former would be calculated to startle outsiders, the latter to alienate our own people. . . . Our Saviour had some things which, He said, could not be borne at that time by His disciples (though they were filled with many teachings) . . . and again He said that all things should be taught us by the Spirit when He should come to dwell among us. Of these things one, I take it, was the Deity of the Spirit Himself, made clear later on when such knowledge should be opportune and capable of being received after our Saviour's restoration when the knowledge of His own Deity should be estab-

[1] *P.G.*, CXX, 507–9 (Latin trans.)

lished.'[1] The Godhead of the Son is established by the Church and preached throughout the whole universe. We confess, too, the Deity of the Holy Spirit in common with that of the Father and that of the Son: we confess the Holy Trinity. But the very Person of the Holy Spirit who reveals these truths to us and who renders them inwardly luminous, manifest, almost tangible to us, nevertheless remains Himself undisclosed and hidden, concealed by the deity which He reveals to us, by the gift which He imparts.

In the theology of the Eastern Church the Person of the Holy Spirit is distinguished from the gifts which He bestows upon men. The distinction is founded on the words of Christ: 'He shall glorify me: for he shall take of mine, and shall declare it unto you. All things whatsoever the Father hath are mine: therefore said I, that he taketh of mine' (John xvi, 14–15). That which is common to the Father and the Son is the divinity which the Holy Spirit communicates to men within the Church, in making them 'partakers of the divine nature', in conferring the fire of deity, uncreated grace, upon those who become members of the Body of Christ. As we sing in an antiphon of the Eastern rite: 'The Holy Spirit giveth life to souls; He exalteth them in purity; He causeth the sole nature of the Trinity to shine in them mysteriously.'[2]

The gifts of the Holy Spirit are often described by the names of the seven spirits which are found in a passage from Isaiah: 'The spirit of wisdom and understanding, the spirit of counsel and might, the spirit of knowledge and of the fear of the Lord' (Is. xi, 2). Orthodox theology, however, makes no special distinction between these gifts and deifying grace. In the tradition of the Eastern Church grace usually signifies all the abundance of the divine nature, in so far as it is communicated to men; the deity

[1] 'Or. XXXI (Theol. V), 26–7', *P.G.*, XXXVI, 161–4.
[2] Antiphon in the 4th tone from the Sunday Office.

162

The Economy of the Holy Spirit

which operates outside the essence and gives itself, the divine nature of which we partake through the uncreated energies.

The Holy Spirit, source of these uncreated and infinite gifts, while Himself remaining anonymous and unrevealed yet receives all the multiplicity of names which can be attributed to grace. 'I am seized with dread', says St. Gregory Nazianzen, 'when I think of the abundance of titles. . . . He is called the Spirit of God, the Spirit of Christ, the Mind of Christ, the Spirit of the Lord, and Himself the Lord, the Spirit of Adoption, of Truth, of Liberty. . . . The Creator-Spirit, who by baptism and by resurrection creates anew; the Spirit who knoweth all things, who teacheth, who bloweth where and to what extent He listeth . . . who revealeth, giveth light, quickeneth, or rather is the very Light and Life; who maketh temples, who deifieth; who perfecteth so as even to anticipate baptism, yet after baptism to be sought as a separate gift; who doeth all things that God doeth; divided into fiery tongues; dividing gifts; making Apostles, Prophets, Evangelists, Pastors and Teachers . . . another Paraclete in the sense of another God.'[1] According to St. Basil, there is no gift conferred upon the creature in which the Holy Spirit is not present.[2] He is 'the Spirit of truth, the gift of adoption, the pledge of future inheritance, the firstfruits of eternal blessings, the life-giving power, the source of sanctification'.[3] St. John Damascene calls Him: 'Spirit of God, direct, authoritative, the fountain of wisdom, and life, and holiness; God existing and addressed along with the Father and Son: uncreated, full, creative, all-ruling, all-effecting, all-powerful, of infinite power, Lord of all creation and not subject to any lord: deifying, not deified: filling, not filled: shared in, not sharing in: sanctifying,

[1] 'Or. XXXI (Theol. V), 29–30', *P.G.*, XXXVI, 159 BC.
[2] 'De Spiritu Sancto XVI, 37', *P.G.*, XXXII, 133 C.
[3] Secret prayer from the Liturgy of St. Basil.

163

not sanctified.'[1] All this infinite multitude of titles relates, as we have said, primarily to grace, to the natural abundance of God which the Holy Spirit imparts to those in whom He is present. Now, He is present in His divinity, which He causes to be perceived while Himself remaining unknown and unmanifested: an unrevealed hypostasis not having His image in another divine Person.

The Holy Spirit was sent into the world (or, rather, to the Church), in the name of the Son: 'the Comforter, even the Holy Spirit, whom the Father will send in my name' (John xiv, 26). It is needful, therefore, to bear the name of the Son, to be a member of His body, in order to receive the Holy Spirit. Christ, according to a favourite expression of St. Irenaeus, recapitulated humanity in Himself. He became the Head, the principle, the hypostasis, of the renewed human nature which is His body. This is why the same Irenaeus attributes to the Church the title of *Son of God*.[2] It is the unity of the 'new man' to which we have access in 'putting on Christ', in becoming members of His body through baptism. This nature is one and undivided: 'the unique man'. Clement of Alexandria sees in the Church Christ in His entirety, the whole Christ who is not divided: 'There is neither barbarian nor Jew, nor Greek; neither man nor woman; but the new man, refashioned by the Holy Spirit of God.'[3] 'Men, women and children', says St. Maximus, 'profoundly divided as to race, nation, language, manner of life, work, knowledge, honour, fortune . . . the Church recreates all of them in the Spirit. To all equally she communicates a divine aspect. All receive from her a unique nature which cannot be broken asunder, a nature which no longer permits one henceforth to take into consideration the many

[1] 'De fide orth., I, 8', *P.G.*, XCIV, 821 BC.
[2] 'Adv. Haeres., IV, 33, 14', *P.G.*, VII, 1082.
[3] 'Protreptic XI, 112, 3', *P.G.*, VIII, 229 B. Ed. Mondésert (*Sources chrétiennes*, II, 2nd ed., Paris, 1949), p. 180.

and profound differences which are their lot. In that way all are raised up and united in a manner which is truly catholic. In her none is in the least degree separated from the community, all are grounded, so to speak, in one another by the simple and indivisible power of faith. . . . Christ, too, is all in all, He who contains all in Himself according to the unique, infinite and all-wise power of His goodness—as a centre upon which all lines converge— that the creatures of the one God may not live as strangers or enemies one with another, having no place in common, where they may display their love and their peace.'[1] St. John Chrysostom, faced with this unity of nature in the Church, asks: 'What does this mean? It means that Christ makes all and sundry into one body. Thus, he who dwells at Rome looks upon the Indians as his own members. Is there any union comparable to this? Christ is the head of all.'[2] This is indeed the meaning of the 'recapitulation' of the universe, of all nature, in the man Adam who was to unite the created world to God. Christ, the second Adam, now fulfils this recapitulation. Head of His body, He becomes the hypostasis of this body gathered together from the confines of the universe. In Him the sons of the Church are His members, and, as such, are included in His hypostasis. This 'unique man' in Christ, however, while he is one through His renewed nature is nevertheless multiple in persons: he exists in many persons. If human nature finds itself reunited in the hypostasis of Christ, if it is an 'enhypostasized' nature—one existing in an hypostasis—the human persons who form the hypostases of this unified nature are not suppressed. They are not mingled or one with the divine Person of

---

[1] 'Mystagogy, I', *P.G.*, XCI, 665–8. De Lubac, op. cit., p. 27. See the whole of the second chapter of this remarkable work in which the author develops the idea of the unity of human nature in the Church, basing himself in the main upon the Greek Fathers.

[2] 'Hom. 61, I', *P.G.*, LIX, 361–2.

Christ. For one hypostasis cannot be identified with another hypostasis without ceasing to exist as a personal being: that would mean the annihilation of human persons in the unique Christ, an impersonal deification, a blessedness in which there would be no blessed. The Church, the new body of humanity, while it is one nature in Christ, yet includes many human hypostases. As St. Cyril of Alexandria says: 'divided in some sort in well-defined personalities in virtue of which such a one is Peter, or John, or Thomas, or Matthew, we are rooted in one body in Christ, feeding on one flesh.'[1]

The work of Christ concerns human nature which He recapitulates in His hypostasis. The work of the Holy Spirit, on the other hand, concerns persons, being applied to each one singly. Within the Church the Holy Spirit imparts to human hypostases the fullness of deity after a manner which is unique, 'personal', appropriate to every man as a person created in the image of God. St. Basil says that the Holy Spirit is 'the source of sanctification which never fails by reason of the multitude of those who share in it', who 'is wholly present to every being, and wholly everywhere; impassibly divided, and shared without division, like a sunbeam, whose gracious influence is as much his who enjoys it as though he were alone in the world, but which also blends with the air, and shines over land and sea. Thus, too, the Spirit is present with everyone who receives Him as if there were but one receiver, but bestows sufficient and complete grace on all; whom all things that partake of Him enjoy according to the capacity of their nature, not according to the extent of His power.'[2]

Christ becomes the sole image appropriate to the common nature of humanity. The Holy Spirit grants to each person created in the image of God the possibility of ful-

[1] 'In Ioannem XI, II', *P.G.*, LXXIV, 560.
[2] 'De Spiritu Sancto., IX, 22', *P.G.*, XXXII, 108-9.

filling the likeness in the common nature. The one lends His hypostasis to the nature, the other gives His divinity to the persons. Thus, the work of Christ unifies; the work of the Holy Spirit diversifies. Yet, the one is impossible without the other. The unity of nature is realized in persons; and persons can only attain to perfection—become fully *personal*—within that unity of nature, in ceasing to be 'individuals' living for themselves, having their separate individual nature and will. The work of Christ and the work of the Holy Spirit are therefore inseparable. Christ creates the unity of His mystical body through the Holy Spirit; the Holy Spirit communicates Himself to human persons through Christ. Indeed, it is possible to distinguish two communications of the Holy Spirit to the Church: one was effected by the breath of Christ when He appeared to His apostles on the evening of the day of His resurrection (John xx, 19–23); the other by the personal coming of the Holy Spirit on the day of Pentecost (Acts ii, 1–5).

The first communication of the Holy Spirit was made to the whole Church, to the Church as a body; or, rather, the Spirit was given to the college of the apostles, on whom, at the same time, Christ bestowed the priestly power of binding and loosening. This is a presence of the Holy Spirit which is not so much personal as functional in relation to Christ, by whom the Spirit is given—the bond of unity in the Church, according to St. Gregory of Nyssa.[1] Here the Spirit is bestowed upon all in common as a bond of unity and as sacerdotal power: He remains unknown to persons and imparts to them no personal holiness. This is the last perfection which Christ grants to His Church before He leaves the earth. Nicholas Cabasilas draws an analogy between the creation of man and the reconstitution of our nature by Christ in the creation of His Church: 'He does not create anew,' says Cabasilas,

[1] 'In Cant., Hom. XV', *P.G.* XLIV, 1116–7.

'out of the same matter with which He created in the beginning. Then, He made use of the dust of the earth, today He calls upon His own flesh. He restores life to us not by forming anew a vital principle which He formerly maintained in the natural order, but by shedding His blood in the hearts of communicants that He may cause life to spring up in Him. Of old He breathed a breath of life, now He imparts to us His own Spirit.'[1] This is a work of Christ which relates to nature, to the Church in as much as it is His body.

Quite distinct is the communication of the Holy Spirit at the time of His personal coming, when He appeared as a Person of the Trinity, independent of the Son as to His hypostatic origin, though sent into the world 'in the name of the Son'. Then He appeared under the form of divided tongues of fire which rested upon *each one* of those who were present: upon each member of the body of Christ. This is no longer a communication of the Spirit to the Church considered corporately. This communication is far from being a function of unity. The Holy Spirit communicates Himself *to persons*, marking each member of the Church with a seal of personal and unique relationship to the Trinity, becoming present in each person. How does this come about? That remains a mystery—the mystery of the self-emptying, of the κένωσις of the Holy Spirit's coming into the world. If in the κένωσις. of the Son the Person appeared to men while the Godhead remained hidden under the form of a servant, the Holy Spirit in His coming, while He manifests the common nature of the Trinity, leaves His own Person concealed beneath His Godhead. He remains unrevealed, hidden, so to speak, by the gift in order that this gift which He imparts may be fully ours, adapted to our persons. In one of his hymns, St. Symeon the New Theologian glorifies the Holy Spirit who mysteriously unites Himself with us in bestowing upon us the

[1] 'De Vita in Christo IV', *P.G.*, CL, 617 AB.

divine fullness: 'I give thanks to Thee for this, that Thou, divine Being above all things, makest Thyself a single spirit with me—without confusion, without change—and that Thou didst become all in all for me: ineffable nourishment, freely distributed, which falls from the lips of my soul, which flows abundantly from the source of my heart; the resplendent vesture which covers me and protects me and which destroys the demons; the purification which washes me from every stain through these holy and perpetual tears that Thy presence accords to those whom Thou visitest. I give thanks to Thee for Thy being which was revealed to me as the day without twilight, as the sun which does not set; O Thou who hast no place where Thou hidest Thyself, for Thou dost never shun us, never hast Thou disdained anyone; it is we, on the contrary, who hide ourselves, not wishing to go towards Thee.'[1]

The personal coming of the Holy Spirit—'sovereignly free', to use an expression from a hymn for Pentecost[2]—could not be conceived as a plenitude, as an infinite treasure suddenly disclosed within each person, did not the Eastern Church acknowledge the independence (as to His eternal origin) of the Hypostasis of the Holy Spirit in relation to the Son. Were it otherwise, Pentecost—the source of sanctification—would not be distinct from the breath which Christ communicated to His apostles, the Holy Spirit acting as a helper in the work of Christ, creating the unity of His mystical body. If the Holy Spirit, as a divine Person, were to be considered as dependent upon the Son, He would appear—even in His personal advent—as a bond which connects us with the Son. The mystical life would then unfold as a way towards the

[1] 'Introduction to the Hymns of Divine Love', *P.G.*, CXX, 509.
[2] αὐτεξούσιον. The expression is taken from St. Gregory Nazianzen's 'Sermon for Pentecost' (Or. XLI, 9, *P.G.*, XXXVI, 441) which has provided matter for some of the most beautiful of the liturgical texts for the Feast.

union of the soul with Christ through the medium of the Holy Spirit. This raises again the question of the place of human persons in this union: either they would be annihilated in being united to the Person of Christ, or else the Person of Christ would be imposed upon them from without. In this latter case grace would be conceived as external in relation to freedom, instead of as being its inward flowering. But it is in this freedom that we acknowledge the Deity of the Son, made manifest to our understanding through the Holy Spirit dwelling in us.

For the mystical tradition of Eastern Christendom, Pentecost, which confers the presence of the Holy Spirit and the first-fruits of sanctification upon human persons, signifies both the end and final goal, and, at the same time, marks the commencement of the spiritual life. As He descended upon the disciples in tongues of fire, so the Holy Spirit descends invisibly upon the newly-baptized in the sacrament of the holy chrism. In the Eastern rite confirmation follows immediately upon baptism. The Holy Spirit is operative in both sacraments. He recreates our nature by purifying it and uniting it to the body of Christ. He also bestows deity—the common energy of the Holy Trinity which is divine grace—upon human persons. It is on account of this intimate connection between the two sacraments of baptism and confirmation that the uncreated and deifying gift, which the descent of the Holy Spirit confers upon the members of the Church, is frequently referred to as 'baptismal grace'. Thus St. Seraphim of Sarov says of the grace of Pentecost: 'This enkindled breath which we faithful Christians all receive in the sacrament of holy baptism is sealed with the sacred seals of holy chrism affixed to the principal parts of our body according to the directions of the Church; for from this moment onwards our body becomes a tabernacle of grace for all eternity. . . . This baptismal grace is so great, this source of life so necessary to man, that it is not withdrawn from a heretic until the hour of his death, until that day which Providence assigned to man to prove him during his life upon earth. For God proves men in assigning to them the time within which they must accomplish their work, in turning to good account the power of the grace which has been given to them.' Baptismal grace, the presence within us of the Holy Spirit—inalienable and personal to each one of us—is the foundation of all Christian life. It is, according to the same St. Seraphim, the Kingdom of God which the Holy Spirit prepares within us.

The Holy Spirit, in coming to dwell in us, makes of our being the throne of the Holy Trinity, for the Father and the Son are inseparable from the deity of the Spirit. 'We receive the naked fire of the Godhead,' says St. Symeon the New Theologian, 'the fire of which our Lord said: *I am come to cast fire upon the earth* (Luke xii, 49). What is this fire if not the Holy Spirit, consubstantial with the Son by His deity, the Holy Spirit with whom the Father and the Son enter into us and can be contemplated?'[1] Through the coming of the Holy Spirit the Trinity dwells within us and deifies us; confers upon us the uncreated energies, Its glory, and Its deity which is the eternal light of which we must partake. This is why, according to St. Symeon, grace cannot remain hidden within us: the habitation of the Holy Trinity cannot remain undisclosed. 'If anyone claims', says this great mystic, 'that all believers have received and possessed the Holy Spirit without having consciousness or experience of Him, he blasphemes by treating as a falsehood the words of Christ who says that the Spirit is *a well of water springing up into eternal life* (John iv, 14), and again, *He that believeth on me . . . out of his belly shall flow rivers of living water* (John vii, 38). If the spring gushes up within us, the stream which flows from it must of necessity be visible to those who have eyes to see. But if all this happens within us without our having

[1] 'Hom. XLV', 9.

any experience or consciousness of it, then it is certain that we shall not know the eternal life which comes thence, that we shall not see the light of the Holy Spirit; that we shall remain as dead, blind and insensible in the life of eternity as we are in this present life. Our hope will thus be vain and our life useless if we rest always in death, if we remain dead after the spirit, deprived of the knowledge of eternal life. But it is not thus in truth, it is not thus. That which I have said many times I will say again, and will not cease to repeat: the Father is light, the Son is light, the Holy Spirit is light. The Three are one single light, untemporal, indivisible, without confusion, eternal, uncreated, inexhaustible, without bounds, invisible—because beyond and above all things—a light which none has ever been able to see before he has been purified, nor to receive before he has seen it. For it is necessary first to have seen it in order afterwards to attain to it with pains and manifold labours. . . .'[1]

In the theology of the Eastern Church, as we have already remarked, the Person of the Holy Spirit, the Giver of grace, is always distinguished from the uncreated grace which He confers. Grace is uncreated and by its nature divine. It is the energy or procession of the one nature: the divinity ($\theta\epsilon\acute{o}\tau\eta s$) in so far as it is ineffably distinct from the essence and communicates itself to created beings, deifying them. It is, accordingly, no longer as in the Old Testament an effect produced in the soul by the divine will acting externally upon the person. Now it is the divine life which is opened up within us in the Holy Spirit. For He mysteriously identifies Himself with human persons whilst remaining incommunicable. He substitutes Himself, so to speak, for ourselves; for it is He who cries in our hearts *Abba, Father!* as St. Paul puts it. We should say, rather, that the Holy Spirit effaces Himself, as Person, before the created persons to whom He appropriates grace. In Him the will

[1] 'Hom. LVII', 4.

of God is no longer external to ourselves: it confers grace inwardly, manifesting itself within our very person in so far as our human will remains in accord with the divine will and co-operates with it in acquiring grace, in making it *ours*. This is the way of deification leading to the Kingdom of God which is introduced into our hearts by the Holy Spirit, even in this present life. For the Holy Spirit is the sovereign unction resting upon the Christ and upon all the Christians called to reign with Him in the age to come. It is then that this divine Person, now unknown, not having His image in another Hypostasis, will manifest Himself in deified persons: for the multitude of the saints will be His image.

CHAPTER NINE

Two Aspects of the Church

Although the Son and the Holy Spirit accomplish the same work upon earth, in creating the Church within which union with God will be brought about, the role of the two divine Persons sent into the world is not the same. The Church, as we have said, is at once the body of Christ and the fullness of the Holy Spirit, 'filling all in all'. The unity of the body relates to the nature, which appears as the 'unique man' in Christ; the fullness of the Spirit to persons, to the multiplicity of human hypostases each one of whom represents not merely a part but a whole. Thus, man is at one and the same time a part, a member of the body of Christ by his nature, but also (considered as a person) a being who contains all within himself. The Holy Spirit who rests like a royal unction upon the humanity of the Son, Head of the Church, communicating Himself to each member of this body, creates, so to speak, many Christs, many of the Lord's anointed: persons in the way of deification by the side of the divine Person. Since the Church is the work of Christ and of the Holy Spirit, the doctrine of the Church has a double foundation—it is rooted both in Christology and in pneumatology. Father Congar, in his book *Divided Christendom*, asserts that 'from the first, eastern ecclesiological thought envisaged the divine realities at the heart of the mystery of the Church rather than its earthly

aspect and human implications. It saw the inward unity
of faith and love more clearly than the concrete demands
of ecclesiastical communion. The relatively feeble development of ecclesiology by the Greek Fathers has', he says,
'often been remarked, the fact being that their emphasis
was rather on Christology and still more on pneumatology; seeing the Church in Christ and in the Holy Spirit
rather than in its ecclesiastical being as such.'[1] There is a
sense in which Father Congar is right: Eastern theology
never thinks of the Church apart from Christ and from
the Holy Spirit. And yet this is in no way due to a feeble
development of the doctrine of the Church. It signifies,
rather, that for Eastern ecclesiology 'the ecclesiastical
being as such' is something extremely complex; it is not
of this world, though taken from the midst of this world;
it exists in the world and for the world. The Church
cannot, therefore, be reduced purely and simply to its
'earthly aspect' and to its 'human implications' without
abandoning its true nature which distinguishes it from
every other human society. Father Congar looks in vain
for a sociology of the Church in the dogmatic tradition of
the East: he leaves on one side and fails to notice the
prodigious wealth of the canonical tradition of the Orthodox Church: the various collections of canons, the admir-
able work of Byzantine commentators such as Aristinus,
Balsamon or Zonaras, and modern canonical literature.
The canons which regulate the life of the Church in its
'earthly aspect' are inseparable from Christian dogma.
They are not, properly speaking, juridical statutes, but the
applications of the dogmas of the Church, of her revealed
tradition, to every sphere of the practical life of Christian
society. In the light of the canons this society would appear
as a 'totalitarian collectivity' in which 'individual rights'
do not exist; but, at the same time, each person in this
body is its end and cannot be regarded as a means. This

[1] Op. cit., p. 14. Eng. trans., p. 12.

is the only society in which the reconciliation of individual interests with those of the society as a whole does not present an insoluble problem, for the ultimate aspirations of each one are in accord with the supreme end of all, and the latter cannot be realized at the expense of the interest of any.

In truth, we are not here concerned with *individuals* and with *collectivity* but with human *persons* who can only attain to perfection within the unity of *nature*. The Incarnation is the foundation of this unity of nature, Pentecost is the affirmation of the multiplicity of persons within the Church.

In the realm of ecclesiology we find ourselves confronted anew by the distinction between nature and persons, a mysterious distinction of which we first caught a glimpse when examining the dogma of the Trinity in the Eastern tradition. This is hardly surprising since, as St. Gregory of Nyssa puts it: 'Christianity is an imitation of the divine nature.'[1] The Church is an image of the Holy Trinity. The Fathers repeat this continually, the canons assert it—the celebrated canon 34 of the *Apostolic Canons*, for example, which institutes the synodical administration of metropolitan provinces 'that the Father, the Son and the Holy Spirit may be glorified', in the very ordering of ecclesiastical life. It is in the light of the dogma of the Holy Trinity that the most wonderful attribute of the Church—that of catholicity—is disclosed in its true and properly Christian sense, which cannot be translated by the abstract term of universality. For the highly concrete sense of the word 'catholicity' comprehends not only unity but also multiplicity. It points to a harmony between the two or, rather, to a certain identity of unity with multiplicity which makes the Church catholic in its wholeness as well as in each of its parts. The fullness of the whole is not the total of the parts, for each part possesses the same fullness as the whole. The miracle of catholicity

[1] 'De professione christiana', *P.G.*, XLVI, 244 C.

176

reveals in the very life of the Church that order of life proper to the Holy Trinity. The pre-eminently 'catholic' dogma of the Trinity is the model, the *canon*, for all the canons of the Church, the foundation of the whole ecclesiastical economy. We shall leave on one side questions of canonical order, despite the interest which a study of the intimate bond between trinitarian dogma and the administrative structure of the Orthodox Church could have. That would lead us too far from our subject, which concerns those elements of theology which relate to the question of our union with God. It is solely from this point of view that we intend to examine Eastern ecclesiology: the Church regarded as the sphere wherein the union of human persons with God is accomplished.

The Church, according to St. Cyril of Alexandria, is 'the holy city which has not been sanctified by observing the law—*for the law made nothing perfect* (Heb. vii, 19)—but by becoming conformed to Christ: participating in the divine nature through the communication of the Holy Spirit, who stamped us with His seal in the day of our deliverance when we were washed from every stain and freed from all iniquity.'[1] It is in the body of Christ, according to St. Irenaeus, that we have access to the fount of the Holy Spirit.[2] It is therefore necessary to be united to the body of Christ in order to receive the grace of the Holy Spirit. Yet the one and the other—the union with Christ and the giving of grace—are wrought through the same Spirit. St. Maximus distinguishes different modes of the Holy Spirit's presence in the world. 'The Holy Spirit', he says, 'is present in all men, without exception, as preserver of all things and quickener of natural seed; but He is particularly present in all those who have the law, calling attention to the transgressions of the commandments and bearing witness to the Person of Christ. As for Christians,

[1] 'In Isaiam V, I, c. 52, I', *P.G.*, LXX, 1144 CD.
[2] 'Adv. Haeres., V, 24, I', *P.G.*, VII, 966.

the Holy Spirit is present in each one of them, making them sons of God; but as giver of wisdom He is hardly present in them all but only in those who have understanding, that is to say, in those who by their struggles and labours in God have become worthy of the deifying indwelling of the Holy Spirit. For all those who do not fulfil the will of God have not an understanding heart.'[1] Thus, in relation to union with God, the universe is arranged in concentric circles about a centre which is occupied by the Church, the members of which become sons of God. Nevertheless, this adoption is not the final goal, for there is a yet narrower circle within the Church itself—that of the saints, of 'those who have understanding' τῶν συνιέντων, according to the passage quoted above —who enter into union with God.

The Church is the centre of the universe, the sphere in which its destinies are determined. All are called to enter into the Church, for if man is a microcosm, the Church is a *macro-anthropos*, as St. Maximus says.[2] It increases and is compounded in history, bringing the elect into its bosom and uniting them to God. The world grows old and falls into decay, while the Church is constantly rejuvenated and renewed by the Holy Spirit who is the source of its life. At a given moment, when the Church has attained to the fullness of growth determined by the will of God, the external world, having used up its vital resources, will perish. As for the Church, it will appear in its eternal glory as the Kingdom of God. It will then stand revealed as the true foundation of the creatures raised up in incorruptibility to be united to God who will be all in all. But some will be united by grace (κατὰ χάριν), others apart from grace (πάρὰ τὴν χάριν), according to St. Maximus.[3]

---

[1] 'Capita theologica et oeconimica, cent. I, 73', *P.G.*, XC, 1209 A.
[2] 'Mystagogy, cap. II-IV', *P.G.*, XCI, 668–72.
[3] 'Quaestiones ad Thalassium, LIX', *P.G.*, XC, 609 B. 'Cap. Theol. and oecon., cent. IV, 20', ibid., 1312 C.

Some will be deified by the energies which they have acquired in the interior of their being; others will remain without, and for them the deifying fire of the Spirit will be an external flame, intolerable to all those whose will is opposed to God. The Church, then, is the sphere within which union with God takes place in this present life, the union which will be consummated in the age to come, after the resurrection of the dead.

All the conditions which are necessary that we may attain to union with God are given in the Church. This is why the Greek Fathers frequently liken it to the earthly paradise in which the first men were to have gained access to the state of deification. Assuredly, human nature no longer possesses its primitive immortality and incorruptibility: but death and corruption are become the way toward eternal life, for Christ 'united to Himself all through which death reaches'[1] and through death has overthrown death. We enter into eternal life, says St. Gregory of Nyssa, through baptism and resurrection. Baptism—image of the death of Christ—is already the beginning of our resurrection, 'a way out from the labyrinth of death'.[2] The body of Christ, to which Christians are united through baptism, becomes, according to St. Athanasius, 'the root of our resurrection and of our salvation'.[3]

The Church surpasses the earthly paradise. The state of Christians is better than the condition of the first men. We no longer run the risk of losing irremediably our communion with God, for we are included in one body in which the blood of Christ circulates, purifying us from all sin and from every stain. The Word took flesh that we might receive the Holy Spirit.[4] This presence of the Holy

---

[1] Greg. Naź., 'Or. XXX (Theol. IV), 21', *P.G.*, XXXIV, 132 B.

[2] 'Or. catechetica magna, cap. 35', *P.G.*, XLV, 88 ff.

[3] 'Or. III contra Arianos, 13', *P.G.*, XXV, 393–6.

[4] Αὐτὸς ἐστι θεὸς σαρκοφόρος, καὶ ἡμεῖς ἄνθρωποι πνευματοφόροι.
Athanasius: 'De incarn. and contra Arianos, VIII', *P.G.*, XXVI, 996 C

Spirit in us, which is the condition of our deification, cannot be lost. The notion of a state of grace of which the members of the Church can be deprived, as well as the distinction between venial and mortal sins, are foreign to Eastern tradition. All sin, even the most trifling—that of the inward state of the heart no less than that of an outward act—can render our nature opaque and impenetrable to grace. Grace will remain inactive, though always present, united to the person who has received the Holy Spirit. The sacramental life—'the life in Christ'[1]—is thus. seen to be an unceasing struggle for the acquisition of that grace which must transfigure nature; a struggle in which victories alternate with falls, without man ever being deprived of the objective conditions of salvation. In Eastern spirituality 'a state of grace' has no absolute or static sense. It is a dynamic and shifting reality which varies according to the fluctuations of the infirmities of the human will. All members of the Church who aspire to union with God are more or less in grace; all are more or less deprived of grace. As Ephrem the Syrian says: 'the whole Church is the Church of the penitent; the whole Church is the Church of those who are perishing.'[2]

To be freed from every touch of sin and to grow continually in grace, it is necessary to be rooted more and more in the unity of nature which has Christ Himself for its hypostasis. The sacrament of the body and the blood is a realization of the unity of our nature both with Christ and, at the same time, with all the members of the Church. It is necessary, says St. John Chrysostom,[3] to understand the wonder of this sacrament, 'what it is,

[1] So Nicolas Cabasilas entitles his treatise on the sacraments.

[2] Quoted by Fr. G. Florovsky, *The Eastern Fathers of the fourth century* (in Russian), Paris, 1931, p. 232. Cf. *Paraenetica* XXXVIII ed. Assemani, Vol. iii, 493 f.; *Testam.* II, 241; *De Poenitentia* iii, 167–8; Th. J. Lamy, *S. Ephraemi Syri hymni et sermones*, Mechliniae, 1882, I, 358.

[3] '*In Ioannem, homil. XLVI*', P.G., LIX, 260.

why it was given, and what is the profit of the action.
We become one body; members, as it is said, of His flesh
and of His bones. . . . This is effected by the food which
He has freely given us. . . . He has mingled His body with
ours that we may be one, as body joined to head.' Or as
St. John Damascene puts it: 'If union is in truth with
Christ and with one another, we are assuredly voluntarily
united also with all those who partake with us.'[1] In the
eucharist the Church appears as a single nature united to
Christ. 'Thou hast vouchsafed me, O Lord, that this corruptible temple—my human flesh—should be united to
Thy holy flesh, that my blood should be mingled with
Thine; and henceforth I am Thy transparent and trans-
lucent member. . . . I am transported out of myself, I see
myself—O marvel—such as I am become. Fearful and at
the same time ashamed of myself I venerate Thee and
fear Thee, and I know not where to shelter nor how to use
these new, dreadful and deified members.'[2] Thus St.
Symeon the New Theologian extols in one of his hymns
the eucharistic union in which our character as members
of Christ is fulfilled. It introduces into the depth of our
being 'the fire of deity' which is inseparable from the body
and blood of Christ: 'I, who am but straw, receive the
Fire, and—unheard of wonder!—am inflamed without
being consumed, as of old the burning bush of Moses.'[3]

In the Church and through the sacraments our nature
enters into union with the divine nature in the hypostasis
of the Son, the Head of His mystical body. Our humanity
becomes consubstantial with the deified humanity, united
with the person of Christ; but our person has not yet
attained its perfection, whence the hesitation of St.
Symeon who, face to face with himself, feels full of shame

[1] 'De fide orth., IV, 13', P.G., CXIV, 1153 B.
[2] St. Symeon the New Theologian (Fr. trans. in La Vie spirituelle
XXVII, 3, 1931, pp. 309–10).
[3] Ibid., p. 304.

and dread, not knowing what to do with his 'dreadful' and 'deified' limbs. Our nature is united with Christ in the Church which is His body, and this union is fulfilled in the sacramental life, but it is necessary that every person of this one nature should become conformed to Christ—χριστοειδός; it is necessary that these human hypostases also should become 'two-natured', should unite in themselves a created nature with the fullness of uncreated grace, with the divinity, adapted to each member of the body of Christ, which the Holy Spirit confers. For the Church is not only one nature in the hypostasis of Christ: it consists also of multiple hypostases in the grace of the Holy Spirit.

This multiplicity, however, cannot be realized save in unity. The Christian life—the life in Christ—is a way which leads from the multiplicity of corruption (that of the individuals which divide up humanity), towards the unity of the one pure nature in which there is disclosed a new multiplicity: that of persons united to God in the Holy Spirit. That which was divided in the nature portioned out among many individuals, must be united in a single foundation in Christ, to be divided in the persons of the saints who have assimilated the deifying flames of the Holy Spirit.

We are not to seek after what is personal, for the perfection of each person is fulfilled in total abandonment and in the renunciation of self. Every person who seeks his own self-assertion comes in the end only to the disintegration of his nature: to a particular and individual existence accomplishing a work which is contrary to that of Christ: 'He that gathereth not with me, scattereth' (Matt. xii, 30). Now it is necessary to scatter with Christ, to abandon one's own nature (which is in reality the common nature), in order to gather, to acquire the grace which must be *appropriated* to each person and become his own. 'If ye have not been faithful in that which was another's, who will give you that which is your own?' (Luke xvi, 12). Our nature is another's: Christ has secured it by His most precious blood; uncreated grace is our own—it has been conferred upon us by the Holy Spirit. This is the unfathomable mystery of the Church, the work of Christ and of the Holy Spirit; one in Christ, multiple through the Spirit, *a single human nature* in the hypostasis of Christ, *many human hypostases* in the grace of the Holy Spirit. Yet, one Church because a single body: a single nature united with God in the person of Christ; for our personal union, the perfect union with God in *our* persons, will be fulfilled only in the age to come. The sacramental unions which the Church offers us—even the eucharistic union, the most perfect of them all—relate to our nature in so far as it is received into the person of Christ. The sacraments, in relation to our persons, are means, gifts which must be realized, acquired and become fully ours, in the course of constant struggles wherein our wills are conformed to the will of God in the Holy Spirit present in us. The sacraments of the Church, freely given to our nature, render us apt for the spiritual life in which the union of our persons with God is accomplished. In the Church our nature receives all the objective conditions of this union. The subjective conditions depend only upon ourselves.

As we have frequently observed, the Church has two aspects which have been pointed out by St. Paul in his epistle to the Ephesians—an epistle which is pre-eminently ecclesiological. These two aspects, or, rather, these two fundamental characteristics of the Church, are so intimately bound up the one with the other that St. Paul brings them together in a single verse (Eph. i, 23). The Church is here portrayed (vv. 17–23) as the fulfilment of the trinitarian economy; as a revelation of the Father in the work of the Son and of the Holy Spirit. The Father of glory gives to the faithful the Spirit of wisdom and of revelation (πνεῦμα σοφίας καί ἀποκαλύψεως) that they may know their calling (κλῆσις): personal union for each one, the riches of the glory of His inheritance (κληρονομία) which will be made manifest in the saints, in the union fulfilled by the multitude of human persons. The same Spirit makes known to us the divine work which the Father has wrought in Christ; this is the testimony borne to the deity of Christ. The Christological aspect of the Church is thus revealed to us through the pneumatological: the Spirit manifests to all the Christ whom the Father raised from the dead and made Him to sit at His right hand, above every dominion and power and every name that can be named, not only in this world but in that which is to come; and put all things in subjection under His feet by establishing Him head of the Church. Then follows the definition of the Church (v. 23), in which the two aspects—the two principles, Christological and pneumatological—are presented simultaneously, almost blended together in one supreme synthesis: 'the Church which is His body, the fullness of Him that filleth all in all' (ἥτις ἐστὶ τὸ σῶμα αὐτοῦ, τὸ πλήρωμα τοῦ τὰ πάντα ἐν πᾶσι πληρουμένου). The Church is our nature recapitulated by Christ and contained within His hypostasis. It is a theandric organism, both divine and human. Yet if our nature finds itself brought into the body of Christ, human persons are in no way caught up in a blind physical process of deification, abolishing freedom and annihilating the persons themselves. Once freed from the determinism of sin, we do not fall under the sway of a divine determinism. Grace does not destroy freedom, for it is not a unitive force proceeding from the Son, the hypostatic Head of our nature; it has a different hypostatic principle, a different source, independent of the Son—the Holy Spirit who proceeds from the Father. The Church thus has a character which is at one and the same time organic and personal; an accent both of necessity and of freedom, of objectivity and of subjectivity; it is

184

a stable and definite reality, but also a reality in becoming. United to Christ—'enhypostasized'—it is a theandric being having two natures and two wills inseparably united; a union of the creature with God, fulfilled in the person of Christ. In the human persons who are the multiple hypostases of its nature, on the other hand, the Church has only virtually attained its perfection. The Holy Spirit communicates Himself to each person. He opens to each member of the body of Christ the fullness of the divine inheritance; but human persons, the created hypostases of the Church, cannot become 'two-natured' if they do not rise up freely toward the perfect union with God; if they do not realize that union in themselves through the Holy Spirit and their own will. The divine hypostasis of the Son descended to us and reunited in Himself created nature and uncreated nature in order that it might be possible for human hypostases to rise to God, reuniting in themselves, in their turn, uncreated grace and created nature, in the Holy Spirit.

We are called to fulfil and to build up our persons in the grace of the Holy Spirit. According to St. Paul, however, we build upon a foundation that is already laid, upon an immovable rock which is Christ (I Cor. iii, 11). Founded upon Christ, who contains our nature in His divine Person, we may attain to union with God in our created persons; may become, after the image of Christ, persons having two natures. In other words (to use a daring saying of St. Maximus), it is necessary for us to reunite 'the created nature to the uncreated nature through love, causing them to appear in unity and identity through the acquisition of grace'.[1] The union which is accomplished in the Person of Christ must be fulfilled in our persons by the Holy Spirit and our own freedom. Hence the two aspects of the Church: that of fulfilment and that of be-

---

[1] 'De ambiguis', *P.G.*, XCI, 1308 B.

coming. The latter is grounded in the former which is its objective condition.

The Church, in its Christological aspect, appears as an organism having two natures, two operations and two wills. In the history of Christian dogma all the Christological heresies come to life anew and reappear with reference to the Church. Thus, there arises a Nestorian ecclesiology, the error of those who would divide the Church into distinct beings: on the one hand the heavenly and invisible Church, alone true and absolute; on the other, the earthly Church (or rather 'the churches') imperfect and relative, wandering in the shadows, human societies seeking to draw near, so far as is possible for them, to that transcendent perfection. A monophysite ecclesiology, on the contrary, manifests itself in a desire to see the Church as essentially a divine being whose every detail is sacred, wherein everything is imposed with a character of divine necessity, wherein nothing can be changed or modified, because human freedom, *synergy*, the co-operation of man with God, have no place within this hieratic organism from which the human side is excluded; this is a magic of salvation operative through sacraments and rites faithfully carried out. These two ecclesiological heresies of opposite tendency appeared, almost at the same time, during the course of the seventeenth century. The first (the Eastern protestantism of Cyril Loukaris) arose within the jurisdiction of the patriarchate of Constantinople; the second developed in Russia, in the form of the schism (*raskol*) known as that of the 'Old Believers'. The two ecclesiological errors were crushed by the great councils of Jerusalem and of Moscow. Monothelitism in ecclesiology is expressed above all in a negation of the economy of the Church in regard to the external world, for the salvation of which the Church was founded. The contrary error (which could not have a precedent in the Christological heresies, unless it be in a semi-Nestorianism) consists in an attitude of compromise which is ready to sacrifice the truth to the exigencies of ecclesiastical economy in relation to the world. This is the ecclesiological relativism, a danger proper to the 'oecumenical' movement and to other similar trends. The Appollinarian heresy, which denied the human understanding in the manhood of Christ, shows itself in the realm of ecclesiology in the refusal to acknowledge the full human consciousness—as, for example, in the doctrinal ministry of the Church, when the truth is regarded as being revealed to the councils like a *deus ex machina*, independently of those who were present.

Thus, all that can be asserted or denied about Christ can equally well be applied to the Church, inasmuch as it is a theandric organism, or, more exactly, a created nature inseparably united to God in the hypostasis of the Son, a being which has—as He has—two natures, two wills and two operations which are at once inseparable and yet distinct. This Christological structure determines a permanent and necessary operation of the Holy Spirit in the Church; an operation which is functional in relation to Christ, who conferred the Spirit upon the college of the Apostles under the outward form of breath. This impersonal union with the Holy Spirit, this conditional sanctity of the ecclesiastical hierarchy, bestows upon the theurgic acts of the clergy an objective character which is independent of persons, and, above all, of intentions. The sacraments and sacred rites which are carried out within the Church thus admit of two wills and of two operations taking place simultaneously: the priest who consecrates the bread and wine upon the altar invokes the Holy Spirit, and the Spirit effects the eucharistic sacrament; the confessor pronounces the words of absolution, and the transgressions are remitted by the will of God; the bishop lays his hands upon the ordinand, and the Holy Spirit confers sacerdotal grace. . . . The same concurrence of the two wills takes place in the exercise of episcopal power, though with a certain difference. The acts which emanate from the episcopal power have a binding character, for the bishop acts by divine authority: in submitting to the will of the bishop one is submitting to the will of God. Here, however, a personal element is inevitably involved; the bishop, if he has not himself acquired grace, and if his understanding is not enlightened by the Holy Spirit, can act according to human motives, he can err in the exercise of the divine power which is conferred upon him. He will assuredly be responsible for his actions before God; they will have, nevertheless, an objective and binding character, save only in the case of a bishop who acts contrary to the canons—in other words, at variance with the common will of the Church. In such a case he becomes the promoter of schism and places himself outside the unity of the Church. The definitions of the councils also express the harmony of the two wills in the Church. That is why the first council—that of the Apostles—which is the pattern for all the councils of the Church, caused its definitions to be preceded by the formula: 'For it seemed good to the Holy Ghost, and to us' (Acts xv, 28). Although the councils bear witness to tradition by their binding and objective decisions, the truth itself which they declare is never subjected to canonical forms. Tradition, in fact, has a pneumatological character: it is the life of the Church in the Holy Spirit. Truth can have no external criterion for it is manifest of itself and made inwardly plain; it is given in greater or lesser degree to all the members of the Church; for all are called to know, to preserve and to defend the truths of the faith. Here the Christological and pneumatological aspects are in accord in the catholic character of the Church. By the power which it holds from Christ the Church proclaims that which the Spirit reveals. But the function of defining, of stating, of causing mysteries which are unfathomable to human understanding to be contained in exact dogmas, this belongs to the

Two Aspects of the Church

Christological aspect of the Church, that aspect which is grounded upon the Incarnation of the Word.

The same principle lies at the root of the cult of the holy images which express things in themselves invisible, and render them really present, visible and active. An icon or a cross does not exist simply to direct our imagination during our prayers. It is a material centre in which there reposes an energy, a divine force, which unites itself to human art.

Likewise, the sign of the cross, holy water, the words of Scripture read in the course of the divine office, the ecclesiastical chant, the ornaments of the church, incense and lighted candles are all symbols in the realistic sense of the word: material signs of the presence of the spiritual world. Ritual symbolism is more than a representation addressed to the senses in order to remind us of spiritual realities. The word ἀνάμνησις does not mean commemoration simply; rather does it denote an initiation into a mystery, the revelation of a reality which is always present in the Church. It is in this sense that St. Maximus speaks of liturgical symbols. For him the eucharistic office manifests the whole of God's saving providence. The lesser entry during the synaxis represents the first coming of the Saviour. The ascent of the presiding bishop to the altar and to his throne is an image of the Ascension. The entry of the assistant ministers symbolizes the entrance of the Gentiles into the Church; the forgiveness of sins represents the judgement of God revealing to each one severally the divine will as it concerns himself. The liturgical chants express the joy encompassing the pure hearts which it lifts up towards God. The invocations of peace recall the serene life of contemplation to which the fearful battles of asceticism give place. The reading of the Gospel, the descent of the presiding bishop from his throne, the expulsion of the catechumens and the penitents, and the closing of the doors of the church, symbolize the events of the

Last Judgement, the second coming of the Lord, the separation of the elect from the damned, and the passing away of the visible world. Then the entry with the holy gifts represents the revelation of eternity; the kiss of peace —the union of all souls with God, gradually being accomplished. The confession of faith is the great thanksgiving of the elect. The Sanctus is the lifting up of human souls toward the choirs of angels who, in the immobility of eternal motion in God, bless and hymn the one and only Trinity. The Lord's Prayer represents our sonship in Christ, and the final chant *One is Holy, One is Lord*, brings to mind the supreme entry of the creation into the abyss of the divine union.[1] The Church's festivals make us participants in the events of Christ's earthly life on a deeper level than that of mere historical fact; for in the Church we are no more spectators who watch from without, but witnesses enlightened by the Holy Spirit.

We have considered the Christological aspect of the Church; the objective and unchangeable features which are grounded in the fact that Christ is the Head of His mystical body and that our nature is contained in His hyspostasis; whence it is that the Church is an organism with two natures. But, as we have said, the Church is incomplete if we leave out of account another aspect, which, more intimate, less evident, is yet the more important in that it concerns the very end of the Church; it affects that union with God which must be brought about in every human person. This is the pneumatological aspect of the Church, rooted in the mystery of Pentecost. The difference between these two aspects of the Church will become clear to us if we compare the mode according to which grace is present in the sacraments, in theurgic actions, the hierarchy and the power that it wields, the Church's worship, the sacred symbols—in all of which it

[1] 'Mystagogy, cap. 8–21', *P.G.*, XCI, 688–97. H. von Balthasar, *Kosmische Liturgie*, pp. 326–7.

has a certain character of predetermined necessity—with
another order of grace in the Church, with a more inward,
not merely external and functional presence of grace,
wherein grace is made one with the very being that bears
it, wherein grace is acquired, appropriated by the person,
becoming *personal*. If, in the first instance, the presence of
grace has an objective character, one would like to say of
the second that it is subjective, did not this word suggest a
somewhat unfortunate notion of uncertainty. Rather
would we say that the first presence is based on a pre-
determination, while the second is founded upon an election. Such are the manifestations of grace in relics, in
places sanctified by appearances of the Virgin or by the
prayer of saints, in holy wells, in wonder-working images,
charismatic gifts and miracles; finally, in the saints, in
those human persons who have made the presence their
own. This is the grace which works in persons and through
persons as though it were their own strength—the divine
and uncreated power *appropriated* by human persons in
whom union with God is brought to pass. For the Holy
Spirit bestows divinity upon human persons called to
realize in themselves this deifying union. This mystery
will be revealed in the age to come but its first-fruits show
themselves even now in those who give themselves to God.

Thus, we may say that, in its Christological aspect, the
Church appears as a perfect stability: as the immovable
foundation of which St. Paul speaks—'Ye are . . . built
upon the foundation of the apostles and prophets, Jesus
Christ himself being the chief corner-stone; in whom all
the building fitly framed together groweth unto an holy
temple in the Lord: in whom ye also are builded together
for an habitation of God through the Spirit' (Eph. ii,
20–2). In its pneumatological aspect—that of the economy
of the Holy Spirit towards human persons, to which St.
Paul refers in the passage just quoted—the Church has a
dynamic character, it reaches out towards its final goal,

towards the union of each human person with God. In its first aspect the Church appears as the body of Christ; in its second, as a flame having one single base but forking into many divided tongues. The two aspects are inseparable, and yet, in the first the Church exists in the hypostasis of Christ, while in the second we can catch a glimpse of its own being, distinct from that of its Head.

If we consider St. Paul's image of the union of Christ and His Church—the image of the union of the bride and bridegroom—it would appear that Christ is the head of His body, head of the Church, in the same sense in which the husband is the head of the single, unique body of the man and the woman in marriage—οἱ δύο εἰς σάρκα μίαν (Eph. v, 31). In this mysterious union—τὸ μυστήριον τοῦτο μέγα ἐστίν, says St. Paul—the one body, the nature common to two persons, receives the hypostasis of the Bridegroom: the Church is 'the Church of Christ'. But it does not cease to be the other person in this union, subjected to the Bridegroom, distinct from Him as bride. In the Song of Songs, as in other passages of the Old Testament which, according to the Fathers, express the union of Christ and His Church under the image of fleshly union, the bride necessarily possesses personal characteristics; she is a person, loved by the Bridegroom and reciprocating His love. The question must needs arise—who is this other person, this person of the Church, distinct from the person of her Head? Who is the bride in this union 'in one flesh'—εἰς σάρκα μίαν? What is the Church's own *hypostasis*? Certainly not the hypostasis of the Holy Spirit. As we saw in the last chapter, the Holy Spirit—unlike the Son—does not in His personal coming bestow upon the Church His hypostasis: He remains hidden, unrevealed. He hides Himself, identifying Himself, so to speak, with the human persons upon whom He confers a second nature—deity, the deifying energies. He becomes the source of personal deification, of the uncreated treasure in each person. He brings to each person its ultimate perfection, but He does not become the *person* of the Church. The Holy Spirit does not contain within Himself the human hypostases—as Christ contains the nature —but gives Himself separately to each person. The Church, then, in its own being, considered as the bride of Christ, would thus appear as a multitude of created hypostases. The hypostases of the one nature of the Church are human persons. That is why, in their commentaries on the Song of Songs, the Fathers see in the figure of the Bride not only the Church but also every person entering into union with God. But, as St. Paul says: τό μυστήριον τοῦτο μέγα ἐστίν—'this is a great mystery'. It belongs to the age to come, when the Church will be perfected in the Holy Spirit, when created nature and uncreated fullness will be united in human persons who will become deified human hypostases, in the face of Christ, the incarnate divine Hypostasis.

Thus it would seem that until the consummation of the ages, until the resurrection of the dead and the Last Judgement, the Church will have no hypostasis of her own, no created hypostasis, no human person having attained to perfect union with God. And yet, to say this would be to fail to perceive the very heart of the Church, one of her most secret mysteries, her mystical centre, her perfection already realized in a human person fully united to God, finding herself beyond the resurrection and the judgement. This person is Mary, the Mother of God. She who gave human nature to the Word and brought forth God become man, gave herself freely to become the instrument of the incarnation which was brought to pass in her nature purified by the Holy Spirit. But the Holy Spirit descended once more upon the Virgin, on the day of Pentecost; not this time to avail Himself of her nature as an instrument, but to give Himself to her, to become the means of her deification. So the most pure nature which itself contained the Word, entered into perfect union with the deity in the person of the Mother of God. If she still remained in the world; if she submitted to the conditions of human life, even to the acceptance of death; it was by virtue of the perfect will whereby she reproduced the voluntary κένωσις of her Son. But death had no more dominion over her. Like her Son, she was raised from the dead and borne up to heaven—the first human hypostasis in whom was fulfilled the final end for which the world was created. Thenceforth the Church and the entire universe have their crown, their personal achievement which throws open the way of deification to the whole creation.

St. Gregory Palamas, in one of his homilies treating of the Virgin Mary, would see in the Mother of God a created person bringing together in herself all perfections, both created and uncreated, the complete realization of the beauty of creation. 'Wishing to create', he says, 'an image of all beauty, and to manifest clearly to men and to angels the power of His art, God truly created Mary all-beautiful. In her He has brought together all the partial beauties which he distributed amongst other creatures, and has made her the ornament of all beings, visible and invisible; or, rather, He has made her a blending of all perfections—divine, angelic, and human; a sublime beauty adorning two worlds, lifted up from earth to heaven, and even transcending that.'[1] The Mother of God, in the words of the same doctor, 'is the boundary of created and uncreated nature.'[2] She has crossed the frontier which separates us from the age to come. This is why, freed from the limitations of time, Mary can be the cause of that which is before her; can preside over that which comes after her. She obtains eternal benefits. It is through her that men and angels receive grace. No gift is received

[1] 'In Dormitionem', *P.G.*, CLI, 468 AB.
[2] Ibid., 472 B.

in the Church without the assistance of the Mother of God, who is herself the first-fruits of the glorified Church.[1] Thus, having attained to the limits of becoming, she necessarily watches over the destinies of the Church and of the universe, still unfolding in time.

In one of the hymns of the Eastern Church the Mother of God is extolled as a human person who has attained to the fullness of the divine being: 'Let us hymn the Glory of the universe, Flower of the human race, who gave birth to the Master, Gate of heaven, the Virgin Mary; Song of the bodiless powers and Adornment of the faithful; she who appears as Heaven and as Temple of the Godhead; she who has overthrown the middle-wall of enmity; she who has brought in peace and has thrown open the Kingdom; She in whom we have an anchor of faith. In Him who is born of her, the Lord, have we a champion. Be bold, therefore, O people of God, be bold, for He will war against your enemies, He who is almighty.'[2]

In the two perfect persons the divine person of Christ and the human person of the Mother of God—is contained the mystery of the Church.

---

[1] Ibid., 472 D–473 A. 'In praesentationem', ed. Sophocles, ii, 158–9, 162.

[2] Dogmatic of Great Vespers of the 1st tone.

CHAPTER TEN

The Way of Union

The deification or θέωσις of the creature will be realized in its fullness only in the age to come, after the resurrection of the dead. This deifying union has, nevertheless, to be fulfilled ever more and more even in this present life, through the transformation of our corruptible and depraved nature and by its adaptation to eternal life. If God has given us in the Church all the objective conditions, all the means that we need for the attainment of this end, we, on our side, must produce the necessary subjective conditions: for it is in this synergy, in this co-operation of man with God, that the union is fulfilled. This subjective aspect of our union with God constitutes the way of union which is the Christian life.

Early in the last century, St. Seraphim of Sarov sought, in the course of a conversation, to define the object of the Christian life. This definition, though it may at first sight appear over-simplified, sums up the whole spiritual tradition of the Orthodox Church. 'Prayer, fasting, vigils, and all other Christian practices,' he says, 'although wholly good in themselves, certainly do not in themselves constitute the end of our Christian life: they are but the indispensable means for the attainment of that end. For the true end of the Christian life is the acquiring of the Holy Spirit. As for fasts, vigils, prayers, alms, and other good works done in the name of Christ—these are the means whereby we acquire the Holy Spirit. Note well that it is only those good works which are done in the name of Christ that bring us the fruits of the Holy Spirit. Other actions, even good ones, not done in the name of Christ, can neither procure us a reward in the life of the age to come, nor win us the grace of God in this present life. That is why our Lord Jesus Christ has said: 'He that gathereth not with me, scattereth' (Matt. xii, 30). In other words, there is for the Christian no such thing as an autonomous good: a work is good in so far as it furthers our union with God, in so far as it makes grace *ours*. The virtues are not the end but the means, or, rather, the symptoms, the outward manifestations of the Christian life, the sole end of which is the acquisition of grace.

The notion of merit is foreign to the Eastern tradition. The word is seldom encountered in the spiritual writings of the Eastern Church, and has not the same meaning as in the West. The explanation is to be sought in the general attitude of Eastern theology towards grace and free will. In the East, this question has never had the urgency which it assumed in the West from the time of St. Augustine onwards. The Eastern tradition never separates these two elements: grace and human freedom are manifested simultaneously and cannot be conceived apart from each other. St. Gregory of Nyssa describes very clearly the reciprocal bond that makes of grace and free will two poles of one and the same reality: 'As the grace of God cannot descend upon souls which flee from their salvation, so the power of human virtue is not of itself sufficient to raise to perfection souls which have no share in grace . . . the righteousness of works and the grace of the Spirit, coming together to the same place (προελθοῦσαι εἰς ταυτόν), fill the soul in which they are united with the life of the blessed.'[1]

Thus, grace is not a reward for the merit of the human

[1] 'De Instituto Christiano', *P.G.*, XLVI, 289 C.

will, as Pelagianism would have it; but no more is it the cause of the 'meritorious acts' of our free will. For it is not a question of merits but of a co-operation, of a synergy of the two wills, divine and human, a harmony in which grace bears ever more and more fruit, and is appropriated —'acquired'—by the human person. Grace is a presence of God within us which demands constant effort on our part; these efforts, however, in no way determine grace, nor does grace act upon our liberty as if it were external or foreign to it. This doctrine, faithful to the apophatic spirit of the Eastern tradition, expresses the mystery of the coincidence of grace and human freedom in good works, without recourse to positive and rational terms. The fundamental error of Pelagius was that of transposing the mystery of grace on to a rational plane, by which process grace and liberty, realities of the spiritual order, are transformed into two mutually exclusive concepts which then have to be reconciled, as if they were two objects exterior to one another. St. Augustine, in his attack on Pelaganianism, followed the example of his adversary in taking his stand on the same rational ground, where there was no possibility of the question ever being resolved. It is not, in the circumstances, surprising that a representative of the Eastern tradition—St. John Cassian—who took part in this debate and was opposed both to the Pelagians and to St. Augustine, was not able to make himself correctly understood. His position of seeming to stand 'above' the conflict, was interpreted, on the rational plane, as a semi-pelagianism, and was condemned in the West. The Eastern Church, on the other hand, has always considered him as a witness to tradition.[1] As a master of Christian asceticism, St. John Cassian of Marseilles was the father of Western

[1] He was, moreover, for long venerated as a saint in the West also: St. Gregory the Great refers to him as such, and even in the fourteenth century, Pope Urban V calls him 'St. John Cassian' in one of his bulls.

monasticism before St. Benedict, who in great part bases himself upon his writings; and St. Bernard and the whole Cistercian school are extensively indebted to him. But the disharmony between the spirituality of Eastern inspiration springing from St. John Cassian, and the Augustinian doctrine about the relationship between grace and free will which developed and spread throughout the West, became more and more accentuated as living contact with the Eastern tradition was lost. Eastern tradition has always asserted simultaneity in the synergy of divine grace and human freedom. As St. Macarius of Egypt says: 'The will of man is an essential condition, for without it God does nothing.'[1] In the nineteenth century, Bishop Theophanes, a great Russian ascetic writer, asserted that 'the Holy Ghost, acting within us, accomplishes with us our salvation', but he says at the same time that 'being assisted by grace, man accomplishes the work of his salvation.'[2] Grace, which according to St. Macarius, permeates the human personality like the yeast in the making of bread, 'becomes fixed in a man like a natural endowment, as though it were one substance with him.'[3] It is this that St. Seraphim calls 'the acquisition of grace'—the subjective aspect of union with God.

The beginning of the spiritual life is conversion (ἐπιστροφή), an attitude of the will turning towards God and renouncing the world. 'The world' has here a particular ascetical connotation. 'The world is said by speculative examination to be the extension of a common name to distinct passions,' says St. Isaac the Syrian. For this great ascetic and mystic, the 'passions are part of the usual current of the world. Where they have ceased, there the world's current has ceased. . . . Where their current

---

[1] 'Spiritual Homilies, XXXVII, 10', *P.G.*, XXXIV, 757 A.

[2] Mgr Theophanes, *Letters on the Spiritual Life*, pub. Mount Athos, pp. 19, 65, 67, 83 (in Russian).

[3] 'Spiritual Homilies, VIII, 2', *P.G.*, 528 D, 529 A.

has been dammed, there the world after their example has to some extent ceased to be maintained and to exist.'[1] 'The world' signifies here a dispersion, the soul's wandering outside itself, a treason against its real nature. For the soul is not in itself subject to passions, but becomes so when it leaves its interior simplicity and exteriorizes itself. Renunciation of the world is thus a re-entering of the soul into itself, a concentration, a reintegration of the spiritual being in its return to communion with God. This conversion is a free act, just as sin also is a voluntary separation from God; and conversion in this sense may be defined as a constant effort of the will turned towards God. Monasticism is simply the highest degree of this attitude of will. St. John Climacus has formulated this in a lapidary definition: 'The monk is constraint of nature continuous, and guarding of senses unintermittent.'[2] 'Who then is that faithful and wise monk who has kept his fervour unquenched, and up to his exodus has not ceased adding fire to fire, fervour to fervour, longing to longing, and zeal to zeal.'[3]

But, if the heart must always be ardent, the spirit must remain calm, for it is the spirit which is the guardian of the heart. For the ascetic tradition of the Christian East, the heart (ἡ καρδία) is the centre of the human being, the root of the 'active' faculties, of the intellect and of the will, and the point from which the whole of the

---

[1] Wensinck, op. cit., p. 13. The Syriac text of the works of St. Isaac was published for the first time by P. Bedjan, *Mar Issacus Ninevita, De perfectione religiosa* (Paris, 1909); English translation from this edition by A. J. Wensinck, *Mystic treatises by Isaac of Nineveh*; Greek text (translation of the ninth century, the only one known before the edition of Bedjan), ed. N. Theotoki (Leipzig, 1770). We shall refer mainly to Wensinck and sometimes to the Theotoki Edition.

[2] 'Scala Paradisi, I', *P.G.*, LXXXVIII, 633 C. The translation is that of the Rev. D. J. Chitty, whose edition of this classic of Greek spirituality is in preparation.

[3] Ibid., 644 A.

spiritual life proceeds, and upon which it converges. Source of all intellectual and spiritual activity, the heart, according to St. Macarius of Egypt, is 'a workshop of justice and injustice'.[1] It is a vessel which contains all the vices, but where at the same time, 'God, the angels, life and the Kingdom, light and the apostles, and the treasures of grace are to be found'.[2] 'Where grace fills the pastures of the heart, it reigns over all the parts and the thoughts: for there inhabit the intelligence (νοῦς) and all the thoughts of the soul.'[3] In this way grace passes by way of the heart into the whole of man's nature. The spirit (νοῦς, πνεῦμα), the highest part of the human creature, is that contemplative faculty by which man is able to seek God. The most personal part of man, the principle of his conscience and of his freedom, the spirit (νοῦς) in human nature corresponds most nearly to the person; it might be said that it is the seat of the person, of the human hypostasis which contains in itself the whole of man's nature— spirit, soul and body. This is why the Greek Fathers are often ready to identify the νοῦς with the image of God in man.[4] Man must live according to the spirit; the whole human complex must become 'spiritual' (πνευματικός), must acquire the 'likeness'. It is in fact the spirit which becomes united with baptismal grace, and through which grace enters into the heart, the centre of that total human nature which is to be deified. 'The uniting of the spirit with the heart', 'the descent of the spirit into the heart', 'the guarding of the heart by the spirit'—these expressions constantly recur in the ascetic writings of the Eastern Church. Without the heart, which is the centre of all activity, the spirit is powerless. Without the spirit, the heart remains blind, destitute of direction. It is therefore

[1] 'Hom. Spirit., XV, 32', *P.G.*, XXXIV, 597 B.
[2] Ibid., XLIII, 7, 776 D.
[3] Ibid., XV, 20, 589 B.
[4] See above, the chapter 'Image and Likeness'.

necessary to attain to a harmonious relationship between
the spirit and the heart, in order to develop and build up
the personality in the life of grace—for the way of union
is not a mere unconscious process, and it presupposes an
unceasing vigilance of spirit and a constant effort of the
will. 'This world is an arena and a running place. . . .
And this is a time of struggle,' says St. Isaac the Syrian.
In order to overcome in this struggle our attention must
be constantly directed towards God: for the Lord, says
the same writer, is 'the omnipotent, the almighty, the
victorious at all times, whenever he descends into the body
of mortals to fight for them. But it is manifest that those
who are defeated . . . are those whose will is stripped of
Him because of their injustice.'[1] When ardour slackens,
resolution falters and grace remains inactive. The evangelical precept to watch, not to allow oneself to be
weighed down by sleep, is a constant theme of Eastern
asceticism, which demands the full consciousness of the
human person in all the degrees of its ascent towards
perfect union.

This ascent is composed of two stages, or, more exactly,
it is achieved simultaneously on two different but closely
interrelated levels: that of action ($\pi\rho\acute{a}\xi\iota\varsigma$) and that of
contemplation ($\theta\epsilon\omega\rho\acute{\iota}a$). The two are inseparable in
Christian knowledge, which is the personal and conscious
experience of spiritual realities—$\acute{\eta}$ $\gamma\nu\hat{\omega}\sigma\iota\varsigma$—'gnosis'.[2]
According to St. Maximus, contemplation without action,
theory which is not applied in practice, differs in no way
from imagination, from fantasy without any real sub-
stance—$\acute{a}\nu\upsilon\pi\acute{o}\sigma\tau\alpha\tau\sigma\varsigma$ $\phi\alpha\nu\tau\alpha\sigma\acute{\iota}a$; similarly, action, if it is

[1] Ed. Wensinck, 'Hom. LXIII', p. 340, and 'Hom. XXXVI', p.
187; ed. Theotoki, 'Hom. L and LIV'; Russian trans., 3rd ed., 1911,
pp. 204 and 331.

[2] It should be unnecessary to point out that this term, signifying
that knowledge of the divine which the human person acquires by
the Holy Spirit, has nothing in common with the speculations of the
gnostics.

The Way of Union

not inspired by contemplation, is as sterile and rigid as a statue.[1] 'The very life of the spirit being the work of the heart', says St. Isaac the Syrian, 'it is purity of heart which gives integrity to the contemplation of the spirit.'[2] Thus the active life consists in the purifying of the heart, and this activity is conscious, being directed by the spirit (νοῦς), the contemplative faculty which enters into and unites itself with the heart, co-ordinating and uniting the human being in grace.

By means of action (πρᾶξις), according to Evagrius Ponticus, man may attain finally to a state of impassability (ἀπάθεια), to the freedom of his nature no longer subject to passions, nor affected by anything.[3] But this ἀπάθεια or impassability is not a passive condition. On the level of the spiritual life, where it is operative, the opposition between active and passive no longer has any meaning: these two contrary dispositions belong to the domain of fallen nature, which is subject to sin. The spirit, which thus regains its integrity, is no longer affected by anything whatever, it no longer 'suffers'; but, on the other hand, it is not 'active' in the usual sense of the word. The ascetical and mystical tradition of the Eastern Church makes no very clear distinction between active and passive states in the higher levels of the spiritual life. The human spirit, in its normal condition, is neither active nor passive: it is vigilant. This is the 'sobriety' (νῆψις), 'the attention of the heart' (ἡ καρδιακή προσοχή), the faculty of discernment and of the judgement in spiritual matters (διάκρισις), which are characteristic of human nature in its state of wholeness. The active and passive states, on the contrary, are the signs of an inner disintegration, for

---

[1] 'Capita theologica et oeconomica, Centuria IV, cap. 88', P.G., XC, 1341-4.

[2] Theotoki ed., XVII, pp. 87-8; Wensinck, XL, p. 202. Cf. Ibid., I, p. 20.

[3] 'Capita practica, LXXI', P.G., XL, 1244 AB. Cf. ibid., 1221 D.

ɔnsequences of sin. To introduce them into
fe would be to falsify its perspectives and
n.

... the Syrian distinguishes three stages in the way
of union: penitence, purification and perfection—that is
to say, conversion of the will, liberation from the passions,
and the acquisition of that perfect love which is the fullness of grace. If it is true that penitence is the beginning
of this way, 'the gateway of grace',[1] this is not to say that
it is a passing moment, a stage to be left behind. It is in
fact not a stage but a condition which must continue per-
manently, the constant attitude of those who truly aspire
to union with God. The word 'penitence' does not properly
express the idea of this fundamental attitude of every
Christian soul which turns to God. The word 'repentance'
would perhaps be less inadequate, despite its almost
wholly negative connotation. The Greek μετάνοια
means literally 'change of mind' or 'transformation of
spirit'. It is a 'second regeneration' granted by God after
baptism; a possibility of return to the Father; a continuous exodus from ourselves; a power which brings about
the transformation of our nature. It is the opposite state
of soul to self-sufficiency, to the spiritual complacency of
the pharisee, of the 'just man' who considers himself to be
in a 'state of grace' because he is without self-knowledge.
Repentance, like the way of ascent towards God, can
have no end. 'Repentance', says St. Isaac the Syrian, 'is
fitting at all times and for all persons. To sinners as well
as to the righteous who look for salvation. There are no
bounds to perfection, for even the perfection of the most
perfect is nought but imperfection. Hence, until the
moment of death neither the time nor the works of repentance can ever be complete.'[2] This conception of repentance corresponds to the apophatic attitude towards God:

[1] Wensinck, p. 210.
[2] Theotoki ed., LV, p. 325.

the more one is united to Him, the more one becomes aware of His unknowability, and, in the same way, the more perfect one becomes, the more one is aware of one's own imperfection.

The soul which is not transformed by repentance does not know grace; and thus ceases to make progress in the way of ascent. This is the 'insensibility of a heart of stone', and the symptom of spiritual death. Repentance, according to St. John Climacus, is a renewal of baptism, 'the fount (πηγή) of tears after baptism has become greater than baptism, though this be a bold saying'.[1] This judgement may appear paradoxical or even scandalous, if it be forgotten that repentance is the fruit of baptismal grace; it is indeed that same grace when it has been acquired, appropriated by the human person, and become in it 'the gift of tears'—the infallible sign that the heart has been overwhelmed by the love of God.[2] 'When our soul departs from life', says St. John Climacus, 'we shall not be accused because we have not worked miracles, or have not been theologians, or have not seen visions, but we shall all certainly have to give account before God because we have not wept unceasingly for our sins.'[3] These charismatic tears, which are the consummation of repentance are at the same time the first-fruits of infinite joy: 'Blessed are ye that weep now: for ye shall laugh.' Tears purify our nature, for repentance is not merely *our* effort, *our* anguish, but is also the resplendent gift of the Holy Spirit, penetrating and transforming our hearts. St. John Damascene describes penitence as the return to God, the healing of our sick nature: 'repentance is a return, accompanied by trial and toil, from that which is contrary to nature to

---

[1] 'Scala paradisi, gr. VII', *P.G.*, LXXXVIII, 804 AB.

[2] On the gift of tears, see the article of Mme Lot-Borodine, 'Le Mystère du don des larmes dans l'Orient chrétien,' in *La Vie Spirituelle*, XLVIII, n. 3 (1936); *Etudes et documents*, pp. 65–110.

[3] Ibid., 816 D.

that which is in accordance with nature: a return from the devil to God.'[1] Such efforts are required at every stage of the ascent, for even to the end we must constantly mistrust the possibilities of our own freedom, according to St. Isaac the Syrian.[2] The prayer of the publican—'Lord, have mercy on me a sinner,' will accompany the just even to the gates of the Kingdom, for the Christian in the way of salvation must be constantly 'between hope and fear', to quote the *starets* Ambrose of Optina, one of the great spiritual directors of the last century. St. Isaac the Syrian has expressed the same thought in a particularly arresting phrase: 'Repentance is the trembling of the soul before the gates of paradise.'[3]

Unless man turns towards God of his own free will and with all his longing, unless he cries to Him in prayer with complete faith, he cannot be cured.[4] Tears and contrition are the beginning of prayer, but this weapon against the passions must not itself become a passion, as says Evagrius.[5] There is active prayer, that of words; this leads to that passionlessness which is the frontier of prayer— ὅρος τῆς ἀπάθεις. Here wordless, contemplative prayer begins; the prayer in which the heart lays itself open in silence before God. Prayer is the motive power behind all human efforts, and behind the whole of the spiritual life. It is the 'converse with God which takes place in secret', and is also 'every thought of God, every meditation on spiritual things', says St. Isaac the Syrian, giving the word 'prayer' its widest sense.[6]

Union with God cannot take place outside of prayer, for prayer is a personal relationship with God. Now this

[1] 'De fide orth., II, 30', *P.G.*, XCIV, 976 A.

[2] Wensinck, p. 338.

[3] Ibid., p. 310; cf. p. 210.

[4] St. Macarius of Egypt, 'Hom. Spir., XXXIII', *P.G.*, XXXIV, 741s.

[5] 'De oratione, c. 8', *P.G.*, LXXIX, 1169 AB.

Wensinck, pp. 294-5, Theotoki ed., hom. XXXV.

The Way of Union

union must be fulfilled in human persons; it must be personal, conscious and voluntary. 'The power of prayer . . . fulfils the sacrament of our union with God', says St. Gregory Palamas, 'because it is a bond connecting rational creatures with their Creator.'[1] It is more perfect than the practice of the virtues, for it is 'the leader of the choir of the virtues' (κορυφαῖος τις τοῦ χοροῦ τῶν ἀρετῶν).[2] All the virtues together subserve perfection in prayer; while the virtues cannot possibly be assured if the spirit is not constantly turned towards prayer. Moreover, the greatest of the virtues, charity, that love of God in which the mystical union is accomplished, is itself the fruit of prayer—ἡ ἀγάπη ἐκ τῆς εὐχῆς, as St. Isaac the Syrian says.[3] For in prayer man meets with God *personally*—he knows Him and he loves Him. Knowledge (*gnosis*) and love are closely inter-connected in Eastern asceticism.

The beginning of prayer is petition—'the prayer of supplication', in the words of St. Isaac the Syrian—which is anxious, and weighed down with preoccupations and fears.[4] This is no more than a preparation for true prayer —'spiritual' prayer—and consists in a gradual ascent towards God in seeking and effort. Little by little the soul reintegrates itself, regains its unity, and particular petitions begin to disappear and seem superfluous, as God answers prayer by making manifest His all-embracing providence. There is an end of petition when the soul entrusts itself wholly to the will of God. This state is called 'pure prayer' (προσευχή καθαρά). It is the end of πρᾶξις, since nothing inconsistent with prayer can any longer gain access to the mind, nor turn aside the will which is now directed towards God, and united to the divine will. The synergy, the harmony of two co-operating wills, continues

---

[1] 'Περὶ προσευχῆς', P.G., CL, 1117 B.
[2] St. Gregory of Nyssa, 'De instituto christiano', P.G., XLVI, 301 D.
[3] Theotoki ed., XXXV, p. 229; LXIX, p. 402; Wensinck, p. 318s.
[4] Wensinck, p. 113.

throughout all the stages of the ascent towards God; but at a certain level when one leaves the psychic realm, in which the spirit is active, all movement is at an end, and even prayer itself ceases. This is the perfecting of prayer, and is called spiritual prayer or contemplation. 'The mind has ascended here above prayer, and, having found what is more excellent, it desists from prayer.'[1] It is absolute peace and rest—ἡσυχία. 'The movements of the soul', says St. Isaac the Syrian, 'partake of the influence of the Holy Spirit, on account of their complete purity.' 'Nature remains without motion, without action, without the memory of earthly things.'[2] It is the 'spiritual silence' which is above prayer. It is that state which belongs to the kingdom of Heaven. 'As the saints in the world to come no longer pray, their minds having been engulfed in the Divine Spirit, but dwell in ecstasy in that excellent glory; so the mind, when it has been made worthy of perceiving the blessedness of the age to come, will forget itself and all that is here, and will no longer be moved by the thought of anything.'[3]

This 'astonishment', 'wonder', 'ravishing' of the spirit in a condition of silence or tranquillity (ἡσυχία) is sometimes called 'ecstasy' (ἔκστασις), for in it a man leaves his own being and is no longer conscious whether he is in this life or in the world to come; he belongs to God and no longer to himself; he is his own master no more but is guided by the Holy Spirit. According to St. Isaac the Syrian, his very liberty is taken away from him.[4] But ecstatic states of this nature, with their characteristic passivity, loss of liberty and of self-consciousness, are particularly typical of the early stages of the mystical life.

---

[1] St. Isaac the Syrian, Theotoki ed., XXXII, pp. 206–7; Wensinck, p. 118.

[2] Theotoki ed., LXXXV, p. 511; Wensinck, p. 174.

[3] Theotoki ed., XXXII, p. 202; Wensinck, p. 115.

[4] Ibid., continuation of the passage quoted.

The Way of Union

According to St. Symeon the New Theologian, such ecstasies and ravishment are appropriate only to beginners and novices—whose nature has not yet gained experience of the uncreated. St. Symeon compares ecstasy to the condition of a man born in a dark prison feebly lit by a single lamp, who can thus have no conception of the light of the sun or of the beauty of the outside world, who suddenly catches a glimpse of a landscape bathed in sunlight through a crack in the wall of his prison. Such a man would be carried away, and would be 'in ecstasy'; little by little, however, his senses would become accustomed to the light of the sun, and adapted to the new experience. In the same way, the soul which progresses in the spiritual life no longer knows ecstasies: instead it has the constant experience of the divine reality in which it lives.[1]

The mystical experience which is inseparable from the way towards union can only be gained in prayer and by prayer. In the most general sense, every presence of man before the face of God is a prayer; but this presence must become a constant and conscious attitude—prayer must become perpetual, as uninterrupted as breathing or the beating of the heart. For this a special mastery is needed, a technique of prayer which is a complete spiritual science, and to which monks are entirely dedicated. The method of interior or spiritual prayer which is known by the name of 'hesychasm', is a part of the ascetic tradition of the Eastern Church, and is undoubtedly of great antiquity. Transmitted from master to disciple by word of mouth, by example and by spiritual direction, this discipline of interior prayer was only committed to paper at the beginning of the eleventh century in a treatise attributed to St. Symeon the New Theologian. Later, it was the subject of special treatises by Nicephorus the Monk (thirteenth century), and above all by St. Gregory of Sinai, who at the

[1] Smyrna edition of 1886, 'Hom. XLV', 10; Russian ed. of Mount Athos, I, 414–16.

beginning of the fourteenth century re-established its practice on Mount Athos. Less explicit references to the same ascetic tradition are to be found in St. John Climacus (seventh century), St. Hesychius of Sinai (eighth century), and other masters of the spiritual life in the Christian East. Hesychasm is chiefly known in the West through the works of Jugie and Hausherr, both very learned writers, but both unfortunately possessed of a curious zeal for the disparagement of the object of their studies. Fixing their attention primarily on the external technique of spiritual prayer, these modern critics set out in their writings to ridicule a way of living the spiritual life which is unfamiliar to them. They represent the hesychasts as ignorant monks of a grossly materialist turn of mind, who imagined that the seat of the soul is the navel, and who thought that the Holy Spirit of God was contained in our physical breathing; it was then necessary to hold one's breath and fix the gaze upon the navel while constantly repeating the same formula, in order to induce a state of ecstasy. In other words, this would be a purely mechanical technique to achieve a certain spiritual condition. But, in fact, mental prayer as it is conceived of in the ascetic tradition of the East has nothing in common with this caricature. There is, it is true, a physical aspect involved—certain procedures in regard to the control of breathing, the position of the body during prayer, the rhythm of prayer— but this exterior discipline has only one object in view: that of assisting concentration. The whole of the attention must be given to the words of the short prayer: 'O Lord Jesus Christ, Son of God, have mercy on me a sinner.' This prayer, continually repeated at each drawing of breath, becomes to a monk as it were second nature. Far from rendering the interior life mechanical, it has the effect, on the contrary, of freeing it and turning it towards contemplation by constantly driving away from the region of the heart all contagion of sin, and every external thought or image; and this by the power of the most holy Name of Jesus. Bishop Theophanes, the great ascetical writer and master of the spiritual life of the last century, writes thus about the object of spiritual prayer: 'The object of our search', he says, 'is the fire of grace which enters into the heart. . . . When the spark of God Himself —grace—appears in the heart, it is the prayer of Jesus which quickens it and fans it into flame. But it does not itself create the spark—it gives only the possibility that it may be received, by recollecting the thoughts and making ready the soul before the face of the Lord. The essential thing is to hold oneself ready before God, calling out to Him from the depths of one's heart. This is what all those who seek the fire of grace must do; as to words or positions of the body during prayer, these have only a secondary importance. God is concerned with the heart.'[1] Thus, in contrast to what some have said, the practice of spiritual prayer in the tradition of the Christian East consists in making the heart ready for the indwelling of grace by constantly guarding its interior purity.

Far from seeking ecstasy or a state of excitement, the spirit must constantly be on its guard against giving any particular image to the Godhead. 'In your longing to see the face of the Father in heaven,' says Evagrius, 'never try to see any shape or form when you are praying.' 'Do not wish to see angels or powers or Christ with your senses or in the end you will become unbalanced, taking the wolf for the shepherd, and worshipping evil spirits.' 'The beginning of error is the vanity of mind . . . which tries to circumscribe the divine in forms and shapes.'[2] On the contrary, in freeing itself completely from all conceptualization of the Godhead, 'the spirit receives into itself the characteristics of a deiform image, and becomes clothed

[1] Theophanes, known as 'the Recluse', *Correspondence*, vol. *v*, n. 911 (in Russian).

[2] 'De oratione, ch. 114-16', *P.G.*, LXXIX, 1192-3. Cf. ibid. 1181-4, etc, *passim*.

with the ineffable beauty of the likeness of the Lord'—
according to St. Mark the Hermit.[1] Diadochus of Photike
sees this image in the Name of Jesus, fixed in our heart by
constant remembrance and perpetual prayer. 'This glorious Name, so greatly desired,' he says, 'being long treas-
ured in the fervour of the heart and retained in the memory, produces in us the habit of loving God perfectly and
without hindrance. It is the pearl of great price that can
be gained by selling all that one has to secure joy unspeakable and without end.'[2]

The fruit of prayer is divine love, which is simply grace,
appropriated in the depths of our being. For love, according to Diadochus, is not simply a movement of the soul, but
is also an uncreated gift—'a divine energy'—which continually inflames the soul and unites it to God by the
power of the Holy Spirit.[3] Love is not of this world, for it
is the name of God Himself. That is why it is ineffable,
according to St. John Climacus: 'the word of love is
known to the angels,' he says, 'and even to them only
according to the energy of their illumination.'[4] 'Thou hast
ravished my soul, and I cannot contain thy flame, so I go
forward praising Thee.'[5] 'O holy Love,' says St. Symeon,
the New Theologian, 'he who knows thee not has never
tasted the sweetness of thy mercies which only living experience can give us. But he who has known thee, or who
has been known by thee, can never again have even the
smallest doubt. For thou art the fulfilment of the law,
thou who fillest, burnest, enkindlest, embracest my heart
with a measureless charity. Thou art the teacher of the
Prophets, the offspring of the Apostles, the strength of the
Martyrs, the inspiration of Fathers and Doctors, the per-

[1] 'Ad Nicolaum praecepta', *P.G.*, LXV, 1040 C.
[2] *Ascetical Discourse*, 59, ed. *Sources Chrétiennes* (1955), p. 119.
[3] Ibid., p. 93.
[4] 'Scala paradisi, XXX', *P.G.*, LXXXVII, 1156 A.
[5] Ibid., 1160 B.

fecting of all the Saints. And thou, O Love, preparest even me, for the true service of God.'[1]

As we have already remarked, Eastern theology always distinguishes between the gift and the Giver, between uncreated grace and the Person of the Holy Spirit who communicates it. We have also noted that the third Person of the Godhead is never thought of as the mutual love of the Father and the Son, as the *nexus amoris* uniting the first two Persons of the Trinity. This follows from the fact that the doctrinal tradition of the Eastern Church sees the Father as the sole hypostatic source of the Holy Spirit; the word 'love' (ἀγάπη), when it is used of the Holy Spirit by the Eastern mystics, does not describe His 'hypostatic character', His position in the Trinity, but always His nature as the giver of love, as the source of love within us, as He who enables us to participate in that supreme perfection of the common nature of the Holy Trinity. For love is 'the very life of the divine nature', in the words of St. Gregory of Nyssa.[2]

The doctrine of Peter Lombard, according to which 'we love God by means of the love of God', that is to say by the Holy Spirit, who is for Western theologians the mutual love of the Father and the Son, is inadmissible for Eastern theology, according to which love belongs to the common nature of the Trinity, in which the Holy Spirit is distinguished as Person. Moreover, the Thomist conception —radically opposed to that of the Master of the Sentences —is no more acceptable for the mystical theology of the Eastern Church. In fact, the power of love communicated to the soul by the Holy Spirit, although distinct from His divine hypostasis, is not a created effect, an accidental quality whose existence would depend upon our created substance, but an uncreated gift, a divine and deifying energy in which we really participate in the nature of the

---

[1] *Homily LIII*, 2, Russian ed. of Mt. Athos, II, 7.
[2] 'De anima et resurrectione', *P.G.*, XLDI, 96 C.

Holy Trinity, by becoming partakers of the divine nature. Love is of God—ἡ ἀγάπη ἐκ τοῦ θεοῦ ἐστιν—says St. John. But this divine gift of love presupposes, according to St. Basil, a corresponding disposition in created nature, a germ or potentiality for love (ἡ ἀγαπητική δύναμις) in the human being called to attain his own perfection in love.[1]

'Love, the divine gift, perfects human nature until it makes it appear in unity and identity by grace with the divine nature', as St. Maximus puts it.[2] Love of one's neighbour is the sign of having acquired the true love of God. The certain test by which one may recognize those who have arrived at this perfection is simply that—according to St. Isaac the Syrian: 'if they were cast into fire ten times a day for the sake of their love of mankind, even this would seem to them too little'.[3] 'I know a man', says St. Symeon the New Theologian, 'who desired the salvation of his brethren so fervently that he often besought God with burning tears and with his whole heart, in an excess of zeal worthy of Moses, that either his brethren might be saved with him, or that he might be condemned with them. For he was bound to them in the Holy Spirit by such a bond of love that he did not even wish to enter the kingdom of heaven if to do so meant being separated from them.'[4] In love directed towards God each human person finds his perfection; nevertheless, individual persons cannot arrive at perfection without the realization of the fundamental unity of human nature. Love of God is necessarily bound up with love of one's fellow-man. This perfect love will make a man like Christ, for, in his created nature he will be united to the whole of humanity,

[1] 'Regulae fusius tractatae', *P.G.*, XXXI, 908 CD.
[2] 'De ambiguis', *P.G.*, XCL, 1308.
[3] Wensinck, p. 342.
[4] *Book of the divine love*, Homily LIV, 1, Russian ed. of Mt. Athos, II, p. 11; Latin trans., *P.G.*, CXX, 425.

while in his person he will unite the created and the uncreated, the human complex and deifying grace.

The elect—those united to God—come to the condition of the perfect man, the measure of the stature of the fullness of Christ, as St. Paul says. If, however, this conformity to Christ is the final state to which we come, the way which leads to it, as we have already seen, is not that of the imitation of Christ. The way which Christ, the divine Person, took, was that of a descent towards created being, a taking upon Himself of our nature; the way of created persons, on the other hand, must be that of ascent, a rising up towards the divine nature by means of union with uncreated grace communicated by the Holy Spirit. The spirituality of the imitation of Christ which is sometimes found in the West is foreign to Eastern spirituality, which may rather be defined as a *life in Christ.* Such a life in the unity of the body of Christ provides human beings with all the conditions necessary for the acquisition of the grace of the Holy Spirit, and thus for participation in the very life of the Holy Trinity, in that supreme perfection which is love.

Love is inseparable from knowledge—'gnosis'. There is an element of personal awareness necessary, without which the way towards union would be blind, and without any certain object, 'an illusory discipline' (ἄσκησις φαινομένη), according to St. Macarius of Egypt.[1] The ascetic life, 'apart from gnosis' (οὐκ ἐν τῇ γνώσει), has no value, according to St. Dorotheos;[2] only a spiritual life that is fully aware—ἐν γνώσει—a life in constant communion with God, is able to transfigure our nature by making it like the divine nature, by making it participate in the uncreated light of grace, after the example of the humanity of Christ who appeared to the disciples on Mount Tabor clothed in uncreated glory. Gnosis, or per-

---

[1] 'Spiritual homilies, XL, 1', *P.G.*, XXXIV, 761.
[2] 'Doctrina, XIV, 3', *P.G.*, LXXXVIII, 1776–80.

sonal awareness, grows in the measure in which nature becomes transformed by entering into an ever-closer union with deifying grace. In one who is perfect, there will remain no further room for the 'unconscious', for the instinctive or the involuntary; all will be illumined with divine light, appropriated to the human person which has acquired its proper character by the gift of the Holy Spirit. For 'the righteous shall shine forth as the sun' in the kingdom of God (Matt. xiii, 43).

All the conditions necessary for attaining this final end are given to Christians in the Church. But union with God is not the result of an organic or unconscious process: it is accomplished in persons by the co-operation of the Holy Spirit and our freedom.

When St. Seraphim of Sarov was asked if the Christians of his own day lacked any of the conditions necessary to produce the same fruits of sanctity which had been so abundant in the past, he replied: there is one condition only lacking—a firm resolve.[1]

Cf. William Law, *A Serious Call to a Devout and Holy Life*. C.2.

CHAPTER ELEVEN

The Divine Light

Union with God is a mystery which is worked out in human persons.

The personal character of a human being who has entered on the way of union is never impaired, even though he renounces his own will and his natural inclinations. It is just by this free renunciation of all which by nature belongs to it that the human personality comes to its full realization in grace. What is not free and definitely conscious has no personal value. Deprivation and suffering cannot become a way towards union unless they are freely accepted. One who has reached perfection is fully conscious in all his acts of will; he is freed from all constraint and from all natural necessity. The further a person advances in the way of union, the greater is his growth in consciousness. This awareness in the ways of the spiritual life is called knowledge (γνῶσις) by Eastern ascetical writers. In the higher stages of the mystical way, it is fully revealed as perfect knowledge of the Trinity. That is why Evagrius Ponticus identifies the Kingdom of God with knowledge of the Holy Trinity—awareness of the object of union. On the other hand, lack of awareness (ἄγνοια), pushed to its furthest limits, would be nothing other than hell, the final destruction of the person.[1] Spiritual life—the growth of the human person in grace—always has this

[1] 'Capita practica, XXXIII, 25', P.G., XL, 1268 A.

quality of awareness; the absence of this quality is a mark of sin, 'the sleep of the soul'. The soul must therefore be constantly on guard, we must 'walk as children of light', in the words of St. Paul: 'Awake, thou that sleepest and arise from the dead, and Christ shall give thee light.'[1]

The Bible is full of expressions relating to light, to the divine illumination, to God who is called Light. In the mystical theology of the Eastern Church, these expressions are not used as metaphors or as figures of speech, but as expressions for a real aspect of the Godhead. If God is called Light, it is because He cannot remain foreign to our experience. *Gnosis*, the highest stage of awareness of the divine, is an experience of uncreated light, the experience itself being light: 'in Thy light, we shall see light'. It is both that which one perceives, and that by which one perceives in mystical experience. For St. Symeon the New Theologian, the experience of light, which is conscious spiritual life, or gnosis, reveals the presence of the grace which a person has acquired. 'We do not speak of things of which we are ignorant,' he says, 'but we bear witness to that which we know. For the light already shines in the darkness, in the night and in the day, in our hearts and minds. This light without change, without decline and never extinguished enlightens us; it speaks, it acts, it lives and gives life, it transforms into light those whom it illumines. God is Light, and those whom He makes worthy to see Him, see Him as Light; those who receive Him, receive Him as Light. For the light of His glory goes before His face, and it is impossible that He should appear otherwise than as light. Those who have not seen this light, have not seen God: for God is Light. Those who have not received this light, have not yet received grace, for in receiving grace, one receives the divine light, and God Himself. . . . Those who have not yet received, who have not yet participated in this light, find them-

[1] Eph. v, 8 and 14.

selves always under the yoke of the law, in the region of shadows and fantasies; they are still the children of the bondwoman. Kings or patriarchs, bishops or priests, princes or servants, seculars or monks, all are equally in the shadows and walk in darkness, unless they are willing to repent as they ought to do. For repentance is the gate which leads from the realm of darkness into that of light. Those therefore who are not yet in the light, have not truly crossed the threshold of repentance. . . . The servants of sin hate the light, fearing that it will reveal their hidden works.'[1] Whereas the life of sin is sometimes wilfully unconscious (we shut our eyes in order not to see God), the life of grace is an increasing progress in knowledge, a growing experience of the divine light.

According to St. Macarius of Egypt, the fire of grace kindled in the hearts of Christians by the Holy Spirit makes them shine like tapers before the Son of God. Sometimes this divine fire, bestowed in proportion to the response of the human will, burns brightly and with an increasing light; sometimes it decreases and shines no more in a heart troubled by passions. 'The immaterial and divine fire enlightens and tests souls. This fire descended on the apostles in the form of fiery tongues; this fire shone upon St. Paul, it spoke to him, it enlightened his mind, and at the same time it blinded his eyes, for flesh cannot bear the brightness of this light. This fire Moses saw in the burning bush; this fire in the form of a chariot caught up Elijah from the earth. . . . Angels and spirits in the service of God participate in the brightness of this fire. . . . This fire expels demons and destroys sin. It is the power of the resurrection, the reality of eternal life, the enlightenment of holy souls, the strengthening of the rational powers.'[2]

---

[1] *Homily LXXIX*, 2 (Russian ed. from Mt. Athos, II, pp. 318–19).
[2] 'Spiritual Homilies, V, 8; XII, 14; and XXV, 9–10', *P.G.*, XXXII, 513 B, 565 AB and 673.

These are the divine energies, the 'rays of divinity' of which Dionysius the Areopagite speaks: the creative powers which penetrate throughout the universe, and make themselves known, not through any created being, as the unapproachable light wherein the Holy Trinity dwells. The energies, bestowed upon Christians by the Holy Spirit, no longer appear as exterior causes, but as grace, an interior light, which transforms nature in deifying it. 'God is called Light,' says St. Gregory Palamas, 'not with reference to His essence, but to His energy.'[1] In so far as God reveals Himself, communicates Himself and is able to be known, He is Light. It is not only by analogy with physical light that God is called Light. The divine light is not an allegorical or abstract thing; it is given in mystical experience. 'This experience of the divine is given to each according to his capacity, and can be greater or less according to the worthiness of him who experiences it.'[2] Perfect vision of the deity, perceptible in its uncreated light, is 'the mystery of the eighth day'; it belongs to the age to come. But those who are worthy attain to the vision of 'the Kingdom of God come with power' even in this life, a vision such as the three apostles saw on Mount Tabor.

The theological controversies about the nature of the light of the Transfiguration of Christ—controversies which, about the middle of the fourteenth century, divided the upholders of the doctrinal traditions of the Eastern Church from certain rationalizing theologians, related basically to a religious problem of the first importance. It concerned the reality of mystical experience, the possi-

[1] 'Contra Akindynum', *P.G.*, CL, 823.
[2] St. Gregory Palamas, 'Homily on the Transfiguration', *P.G.*, CLI, 448 B. See Father Basil Krivosheine's excellent study of the ascetic and theological teaching of St. Gregory Palamas in *The Eastern Churches Quarterly*, Vol. III (1938–9), pp. 26 ff., 71 ff., 138 ff., and 192 ff.

bility of conscious communion with God, and the nature of grace—whether it is created or uncreated. The questions of man's ultimate destiny, his beatitude and deification, were at stake. It was a conflict between mystical theology and a religious philosophy, or, rather, a theology of concepts which refused to admit what seemed to it to be an absurdity, foolishness. The God of revelation and of religious experience was confronted with the God of the philosophers, on the battlefield of mysticism, and, once again, the foolishness of God put to nought the wisdom of men. Finding themselves obliged to define their position, to formulate concepts of realities utterly transcending philosophical speculation, the philosophers had finally to give a judgement which in its turn appeared 'foolishness' to Eastern tradition: they asserted the created nature of deifying grace. We shall not discuss again the question (treated in Chapter IV) of the distinction between the essence and the energies of God. At the end of our study we must think of another aspect of the divine energies: that of the uncreated light in which God reveals and communicates Himself to those who enter into union with Him.

This light (φῶς) or effulgence (ἐλλάμψις) can be defined as the visible quality of the divinity, of the energies or grace in which God makes Himself known. It is not a reality of the intellectual order, as the illumination of the intellect, taken in its allegorical and abstract sense, sometimes is. Nor is it a reality of the sensible order. This light is a light which fills at the same time both intellect and senses, revealing itself to the whole man, and not only to one of his faculties. The divine light, being given in mystical experience, surpasses at the same time both sense and intellect. It is immaterial and is not apprehended by the senses; that is why St. Symeon the New Theologian while affirming its visibility yet calls it 'invisible fire':

Mystical Theology of the Eastern Church

Ἔστι πῦρ τὸ θεῖον ὄντως
Ἄκτιστον ἀορὰτόν γε
Ἄναρχον καὶ ἀΰλόν τε . . . .[1]

But neither is it an intellectual light. The *Hagioritic Tome* (an apologia edited by the monks of Mount Athos during the theological disputes about the light of the Transfiguration), distinguishes between light apprehended by the senses, the light of the intellect, and the uncreated light which transcends both. 'The light of the intellect is different from that which is perceived by the senses. Physical light shows us objects perceptible by the senses, while intellectual light makes clear the truth in our thinking. Thus, the sight of the eye and the sight of the mind do not perceive one and the same light, but it is the property of each of these faculties to act according to its own nature and limitations. Since, however, those who are worthy of it receive spiritual and supernatural grace and strength, they perceive, both by the senses and by the intellect, that which is altogether above both sense and intellect . . . but this light is known only to God and to those who have had experience of His grace.'[2]

Most of the Fathers who speak of the Transfiguration witness to the divine and uncreated nature of the light which appeared to the apostles. St. Gregory Nazianzen, St. Cyril of Alexandria, St. Maximus, St. Andrew of Crete, St. John Damascene, St. Symeon the New Theologian, Euthymius Zigabenus, all speak of it in this way, and it would be perverse in the extreme to interpret all the passages in question as mere figures of speech. St. Gregory Palamas develops this teaching in relation to the question of mystical experience. The light seen by the apostles on Mount Tabor is proper to God by His nature: eternal, infinite, existing outside space and time, it ap-

[1] *Works of St. Symeon*, Smyrna ed. of 1886, pt. II, p. 1.
[2] *P.G.*, CL, 1833 D.

peared in the theophanies of the Old Testament as the glory of God—a terrifying and unbearable apparition to created beings, because foreign and external to human nature as it was before Christ and outside the Church. That is why—according to St. Symeon the New Theologian—Paul on the road to Damascus, not yet having faith in Christ, was blinded and struck down by the apparition of the divine light.[1] Mary Magdalene, on the other hand, according to St. Gregory Palamas, was able to see the light of the resurrection, which filled the tomb and rendered visible everything that she found there despite the darkness of the night: 'physical day' having not yet illumined the earth, it was this light that enabled her to see the angels and to talk with them.[2] At the moment of the incarnation, the divine light was concentrated, so to speak, in Christ, the God–man, 'in whom dwelleth the whole fullness of the Godhead bodily'. That is to say that the humanity of Christ was deified by hypostatic union with the divine nature; that Christ during His earthly life always shed forth the divine light—which, however, remained invisible to most men. The Transfiguration was not a phenomenon circumscribed in time and space; Christ underwent no change at that moment, even in His human nature, but a change occurred in the awareness of the apostles, who for a time received the power to see their Master as He was, resplendent in the eternal light of His Godhead.[3] The apostles were taken out of history and given a glimpse of eternal realities. St. Gregory Palamas says, in his homily on the Transfiguration: 'The light of our Lord's Transfiguration had neither beginning nor end; it remained unbounded in time and space and imperceptible to the senses, although seen by

---

[1] St. Symeon, *Hom. LVII*, i. Athonite ed. II, p. 36. Palamas, 'Cap. physica, etc., c. 67', *P.G.*, CL, 1169 A.

[2] *P.G.*, CLI, 268 AB.

[3] 'Hagioritic Tome', *P.G.*, CL, 1232 C.

bodily eyes . . . but by a change in their senses the Lord's disciples passed from the flesh to the Spirit.'[1]

To see the divine light with bodily sight, as the disciples saw it on Mount Tabor, we must participate in and be transformed by it, according to our capacity. Mystical experience implies this change in our nature, its transformation by grace. St. Gregory Palamas says explicitly: 'He who participates in the divine energy, himself becomes, to some extent, light; he is united to the light, and by that light he sees in full awareness all that remains hidden to those who have not this grace; thus, he transcends not only the bodily senses, but also all that can be known by the intellect . . . for the pure in heart see God . . . who, being Light, dwells in them and reveals Himself to those who love Him, to His beloved.'[2]

The body should not be an obstacle in mystical experience. The manichean contempt for our bodily nature is alien to orthodox asceticism: 'We do not apply the word *man* to body and soul separately, but to both together, for the whole man was created in the image of God,' says St. Gregory Palamas.[3] The body must be spiritualized and become (in the words of St. Paul) 'a spiritual body'. Our ultimate destiny is not merely an intellectual contemplation of God; if it were, the resurrection of the dead would be unnecessary. The blessed will see God face to face, in the fullness of their created being. That is why the Hagioritic Tome already grants certain 'spiritual dispositions' to our purified bodily nature here below: 'If the body is to partake with the soul in the ineffable benefits of the world to come, it is certain that it must participate in them, as far as is possible, now. . . . For the body

[1] *P.G.*, CLI, 433 B.

[2] *Homily on the Presentation of the Holy Virgin in the Temple.* Ed. Sophocles, 22 *Homilies of St. Gr. Palamas*, Athens, 1861, pp. 175–7.

[3] *P.G.*, CL, 1361 C. The authenticity of this *Dialogue* has been questioned: it belongs in any case to the same spiritual family.

also has an experience of divine things, when the passionate forces of the soul are—not put to death, but transformed and sanctified.'[1]

Just because it is light grace, the source of revelation, cannot remain within us unperceived. We are incapable of not being aware of God, if our nature is in proper spiritual health. Insensibility in the inner life is an abnormal condition. One must know how to recognize the stages, and assess the phenomena of the mystical life. That is why St. Seraphim of Sarov begins his spiritual teachings with these words: 'God is a fire which warms and kindles our hearts. If we feel in our hearts the cold which comes from the devil—for the devil is cold—let us pray to the Lord, and he will come and warm our hearts with love for him and love for our neighbour. And before the warmth of his face, the cold of the enemy will be put to flight.'[2] Grace will make itself known as joy, peace, inner warmth and light. States of dryness, of the dark night of the soul, do not have the same meaning in the spirituality of the Eastern Church, as they have in the West. A person who enters into a closer and closer union with God, cannot remain outside the light. If he finds himself plunged in darkness, it is either because his nature is darkened by sin, or else because God is testing him to increase his ardour. We must rise above these states, by our obedience and humility to which God will respond, showing himself anew to the soul, and communicating His light to the person who was for a time forsaken. Dryness is a state of illness which must not last; it is never thought of by the mystical and ascetical writers of the Eastern tradition as a necessary and normal stage in the way of union. It is but an accident on this way, frequent

---

[1] *P.G.*, CL, 1233 BD.

[2] *Account of the Life and Works of Fr. Seraphim, of blessed memory, hieromonk and hermit of Sarov*, 3rd. ed., Moscow, 1851, p. 63 (in Russian).

indeed, but always a peril. It has too great a likeness to ἀκηδία—*accidia* or tedium, the coldness of heart which leads to insensibility. It is a trial which drives the human being to the verge of spiritual death. For the ascent towards holiness, the struggle for the divine light is not without danger. Those who seek the light, conscious life in God, run a great spiritual risk, but God will not let them wander in darkness.

'I often saw the Light'—says St. Symeon the New Theologian—'sometimes it appeared to me within me, when my soul possessed peace and silence; sometimes it only appeared afar off, and even hid itself altogether. Then I suffered an immense sorrow, thinking that I should never see it again. But when I began to weep, and witnessed to my complete detachment from everything, and to an absolute humility and obedience, the Light reappeared like the sun which chases away the thick clouds, and which gradually discloses itself, and brings joyfulness. Thus didst Thou, O Thou, Ineffable, Invisible, Intangible Mover of all things, present in all things, at all times, filling all things, showing Thyself and hiding Thyself at every hour, thus didst Thou appear to me, and disappear, by night and by day. Slowly didst Thou disperse the mists around me, and dispatch the clouds which covered me. Thou didst open my spiritual ear, and didst purify the sight of my soul. At last, having done as Thou didst will, Thou didst reveal Thyself to my cleansed soul, coming to me, but still invisible. And suddenly Thou didst appear as another Sun, O ineffable and divine condescension!' This passage shows us that aridity is a transitory condition, which cannot become a constant attitude. In fact, both the heroic attitude of the great saints of Western Christendom, a prey to the sorrow of a tragic separation from God, and the dark night of the soul considered as a way, as a spiritual necessity, are unknown in the spirituality of the Eastern Church. The two traditions have separated on a mysterious doctrinal point, relating to the Holy Spirit, who is the source of holiness. Two different dogmatic conceptions correspond to two different experiences, to two ways of sanctification which scarcely resemble one another. Since the separation, the ways which lead to sanctity are not the same in the West as in the East. The one proves its fidelity to Christ in the solitude and abandonment of the night of Gethsemane, the other gains certainty of union with God in the light of the Transfiguration.[1]

A passage taken from 'The Revelations' of St. Seraphim of Sarov, written at the beginning of the nineteenth century, will make us understand, better than any number of theological expositions, wherein this certainty consists, this 'gnosis' or consciousness of union with God. In the course of a conversation which took place in a clearing in the forest, one winter morning, a disciple of St. Seraphim, the author of the passage quoted, said to his master:

'All the same, I don't understand how one can be certain of being in the Spirit of God. How should I be able to recognize for certain this manifestation in myself?'

'I've already told you', said Father Seraphim, 'that it's very simple. I've talked at length about the state of those who are in the Spirit of God; I've also explained to you how we can recognize this presence in ourselves. . . . What more is necessary, my friend?'

'I must understand better everything that you have said to me.'

[1] In thus opposing the ways of sanctification proper to East and West, we would not wish to make any absolute distinction. This is much too delicate and subtle a matter to lend itself to any kind of schematization; thus in the West, the experience of the dark night is in no way characteristic of St. Bernard, for instance; on the other hand, Eastern spirituality provides us with at least one clear enough example of the dark night, in St. Tikhon Zadonsky (eighteenth century). 'Cf. N. Gorodetsky, *St. Tikhon Zadonsky*', (S.P.C.K., 1950.)

'My friend, we are both at this moment in the Spirit of God. . . . Why won't you look at me?'

'I can't look at you, Father—I replied—your eyes shine like lightning; your face has become more dazzling than the sun, and it hurts my eyes to look at you.'

'Don't be afraid,' said he, 'at this very moment you've become as bright as I have. You are also at present in the fullness of the Spirit of God; otherwise, you wouldn't be able to see me as you do see me.'

And leaning towards me, he whispered in my ear, 'Thank the Lord God for His infinite goodness towards us. As you've noticed, I haven't even made the sign of the cross; it was quite enough that I had prayed to God in my thoughts, in my heart, saying within myself: "Lord make him worthy to see clearly with his bodily eyes, the descent of your Spirit, with which you favour your servants, when you condescend to appear to them in the wonderful radiance of your glory." And, as you see my friend, the Lord at once granted this prayer of the humble Seraphim. . . . How thankful we ought to be to God for this unspeakable gift which He has granted to us both. Even the Fathers of the Desert did not always have such manifestations of His goodness. The grace of God—like a mother full of loving kindness towards her children—has deigned to comfort your afflicted heart, at the intercession of the Mother of God herself. . . . Why then, my friend, do you not look me straight in the face? Look freely and without fear; the Lord is with us.

'Encouraged by these words, I looked and was seized by holy fear. Imagine in the middle of the sun, dazzling in the brilliance of its noontide rays, the face of the man who is speaking to you. You can see the movements of his lips, the changing expression of his eyes, you can hear his voice, you can feel his hands holding you by the shoulders, but you can see neither his hands nor his body—nothing except the blaze of light which shines around, lighting up with its brilliance the snow-covered meadow, and the snowflakes which continue to fall unceasingly.

'What do you feel?' asked Father Seraphim.

'An immeasurable well-being,' I replied.

'But what sort of well-being? What exactly?'

'I feel', I replied, 'such calm, such peace in my soul, that I can find no words to express it.'

'My friend, it is the peace our Lord spoke of when he said to his disciples: "My peace I give unto you," the peace which the world cannot give; "the peace which passeth all understanding." What else do you feel?'

'Infinite joy in my heart.'

Father Seraphim continued: 'When the Spirit of God descends on a man, and envelops Him in the fullness of His presence, the soul overflows with unspeakable joy, for the Holy Spirit fills everything He touches with joy. . . . If the first-fruits of future joy have already filled your soul with such sweetness, with such happiness, what shall we say of the joy in the Kingdom of Heaven, which awaits all those who weep here on earth. You also, my friend, have wept during your earthly life, but see the joy which our Lord sends to console you here below. For the present we must work, and make continual efforts to gain more and more strength to attain "the perfect measure of the stature of Christ. . . ." But then this transitory and partial joy which we now feel will be revealed in all its fullness, overwhelming our being with ineffable delights which no one will be able to take from us.'[1]

In this simple account of an experience are contained all the doctrines of the Eastern Fathers on 'gnosis', that knowledge of grace which reaches its highest degree in the visions of the divine light. This light fills the human person, who has attained to union with God. No longer is it an ecstasy, a passing condition which snatches a human being away from his habitual experience, but a conscious

[1] 'Conversation of St. Seraphim on the End of the Christian Life.'

life in light, in endless communion with God. We have indeed already quoted a passage from St. Symeon the New Theologian which asserts that ecstatic states belong primarily to those whose nature has not yet become changed and adapted to the divine life. The transfiguration of created nature begun here is an earnest of the new heaven and the new earth, the entry of the creature into eternal life before death and resurrection. Few, even of the great saints, reach this state in their earthly life. The example of St. Seraphim is all the more striking in that it revives in quite recent times the sanctity of the Desert Fathers, which appears almost fabulous to our reasonable and lukewarm faith, to our mind which, owing to the fall, has become 'Kantian', and is always ready to push back everything which transcends the laws, or rather the habits of fallen nature, into the noumenal realm, that of 'objects of faith'. The philosophical defence of the autonomy of our limited nature, closed to the experience of grace, is a conscious affirmation of our unconsciousness, it is the 'antignosis', the 'anti-light', the opposition to the Holy Spirit which opens up in human persons a perfect awareness of communion with God. In the spiritual conversation which we have just quoted, St. Seraphim said: 'In the times in which we live, we have reached such a degree of lukewarmness, almost everywhere, in the holy faith in our Lord Jesus Christ, such an insensibility towards communion with God, that really one can say, we have departed almost entirely from the true Christian life. Passages of the Bible seem strange to us today. . . . Some people say: "These passages are incomprehensible; can one admit that men can see God in so concrete a way?" But there is nothing about them at all incomprehensible. Our lack of understanding results from the fact that we have departed so far from the primitive simplicity of Christian knowledge. Under the pretext of education, of enlightenment, we are involved in such an obscurity of ignorance that today we find inconceivable those things of which the ancients had so clear an understanding, that they were able to speak to each other of God's appearances to men, as of things well known, and not at all strange.'[1]

It is where knowledge and love are one, in the secret experience, hidden from the eyes of the world, in the life of those who are united to the eternal light of the Holy Trinity, that we rediscover the simplicity of Christian understanding; but this experience is unutterable. 'The realities of the world to come', says St. Isaac the Syrian, 'have no proper and direct nomenclature. One can only have a certain simple knowledge, above all words, elements, images, colours, pictures, or names of whatever sort.'[2] 'This is the ignorance which passes all knowledge.'[3] Once again we find ourselves in the apophatic realm, where we commenced our study of Eastern tradition. But instead of the divine darkness there is now light, instead of forgetfulness of self, the full flowering of personal consciousness in grace. What is here at issue is a perfection which has been acquired, a nature which has been transformed by union with grace, a nature which has itself become light. How can we make this experience comprehensible to those who have not had it? What St. Symeon is attempting to express, leaves us to discern in the contradictory terms which he uses those things which remain hidden from our unillumined minds. 'When we arrive at perfection, he says, God no longer comes to us, as before, without image or appearance. . . . He comes with a certain image, but it is an image of God; for God could not appear under any image or figure; but he makes himself seen in his simplicity, formed in light without form, incomprehensible, ineffable. I can say no more. As he makes himself to be clearly seen, he is perfectly recognizable, he

[1] *Idem.*
[2] Ed. Wensinck, *Hom. II*, pp. 8–9; cf. *Hom. XXII*, p. 114.
[3] Ibid., *Hom. XXII*, p. 118 (ed. Theotoki, *Hom. XXXII*).

speaks, and listens in a manner which cannot be expressed. He who is God by nature holds converse with those he has made gods by grace, as a man talks with his friends, face to face. He loves his sons like a father; he is loved by them without measure; he becomes a strange spectacle in them, a yet more awful hearing (ξένον θέαμα ναί φριντότερον ἄνουσμα). They cannot speak of him as they should, but neither can they keep silence. . . . The Holy Spirit becomes in them all that the Bible says about the Kingdom of God—the pearl, the grain of mustard seed, the leaven, the water, the fire, the bread, the life-giving draught, the couch, the marriage chamber, the bridegroom, the friend, the brother, the father. But what shall I say of that which cannot be spoken of? What eye has not seen, nor ear heard, neither has it entered into the heart of man—how can it be expressed in words? Although we have received all this within ourselves, by a gift of God, we are completely unable to measure by our intellect, or express it in words.'[1]

According to the defenders of the uncreated light, this experience of the realities of the world to come cannot be dogmatically defined. Thus, the Old Testament had prophetic insights of the realities which were revealed and became dogmas in the Church, as well as dogmas and commandments of the law. In the same way, in the age of the Gospel in which we live, besides the dogmas, or rather in the dogmas themselves, a hidden depth appears to us as a mystery of the age to come, of the Kingdom of God.[2] One can say equally well, that the Old Testament lived by faith, and moved towards hope; that the age of the Gospel lives in hope and moves towards love; that love is a mystery which will only be fully revealed and realized in the age to come. For him who acquires love 'the darkness is past and the true light now shineth' (I John ii, 8).

[1] *Homily XC*, Russian ed. from Mt. Athos, pt. II, pp. 488–9.
[2] 'Hagioritic Tome', *P.G.*, CL, 1225–7.

The Divine Light

The divine light manifests itself in this life in space and in time. It is revealed in history, but it is not of this world; it is eternal, it involves going out from historical existence; 'the mystery of the eighth day', the mystery of true knowledge and the perfection of gnosis, whose fullness the world cannot contain before the last day. It is the beginning of the parousia in holy souls; the first-fruits of the final revelation, when God will appear to all in His inaccessible light. That is why, according to St. Symeon the New Theologian, 'for those who have become the children of light, and sons of the day which is to come, for those who walk at all times in the light, the day of the Lord will never come, for they are always with God and in God. Thus, the day of the Lord will not appear to those who are already enlightened by the divine light, but it will be suddenly revealed to those who dwell in the darkness of passions, to those who live conformed to this world, attached to the things that are perishing. For these, that day will come suddenly, unexpectedly, and it will be terrible to them, terrible as fire, which cannot be borne.'[1]

The divine light becomes the principle of our understanding; in it we come to know God, and we come to know ourselves. It searches out the depths of the person who attains to union with God, it is for that person the judgement of God, before the Last Judgement. For, according to St. Symeon, there are two judgements: one, in this life, the judgement to salvation; the other, after the end of the world, the judgement to condemnation. 'In this present life, when by repentance, we enter freely and of our own will into the divine light, we find ourselves accused and under judgement; but, owing to the divine love and compassion the accusation and judgement is made in secret, in the depths of our soul, to purify us, that we may receive the pardon of our sins. It is only God and ourselves who at that time will see the hidden depths

[1] *Homily LVII*, 2 (Russian ed. of Mt. Athos, pt. II, p. 37).

233

of our hearts. Those who in this life undergo such a judge-ment will have nothing to fear from another tribunal. But for those who will not, in this life, enter into the light, that they may be accused and judged, for those who hate the light, the second coming of Christ will disclose the light which at present remains hidden, and will make manifest everything which has been concèaled. Every-thing which today we hide, not wishing to reveal the depths of our hearts in repentance, will then be made open in the light, before the face of God; and the whole world, and what we really are will be made plain.'[1]

At the second coming of Christ, all will be made fully conscious, in the power of the divine light. But this con-sciousness will not be one which opens up freely in grace, according to the divine will; it will be a consciousness coming, so to speak, from outside, and developing in per-sons against their will, a light being united to beings ex-traneously, that is to say, 'outside grace', as St. Maximus has it.[2] The love of God will be an intolerable torment for those who have not acquired it within themselves. Accord-ing to St. Isaac the Syrian, 'those who find themselves in gehenna will be chastized with the scourge of love. How cruel and bitter this torment of love will be! For those who understand that they have sinned against love, under-go greater sufferings than those produced by the most fearful tortures. The sorrow which takes hold of the heart which has sinned against love, is more piercing than any other pain. It is not right to say that the sinners in hell are deprived of the love of God. . . . But love acts in two different ways, as suffering in the reproved, and as joy in the blessed.'[3]

The resurrection itself will reveal the inner condition of beings, as bodies will allow the secrets of the soul to shine through. In his vision of the last things, St. Macarius

[1] Ibid.   [2] See above, p. 178.
[3] Ed. Theotoki, LXXXIV, pp. 480–1; Wensinck, XXVII, p. 136.

of Egypt expresses this thought: 'The heavenly fire of the divine nature', he says, 'which Christians receive in this world, where it works within their hearts, this fire will work from outside, when the body is destroyed; it will restore again the disjointed limbs, and will bring to life the bodies which have decayed. . . .'[1] At that time, everything which the soul has stored up in its inner treasure, will appear outwardly, in the body. All will become light, all will be penetrated by uncreated light. The bodies of the saints will become like the glorious body of the Lord, as it appeared to the apostles on the day of the Transfiguration. God will be all in all, and divine grace, the light of the Holy Trinity, will shine forth in the multitude of human hypostases, in all those who have acquired it; they will become like new suns in the Kingdom of the Father, resembling the Son, transfigured by the Holy Spirit, the Giver of Light. 'The grace of his most Holy Spirit', says St. Symeon, 'will shine like a star on the just, and in the midst of them thou wilt shine forth, O Thou, Inaccessible Sun! Then all will be enlightened according to the measure of their faith and their works, of their hope and their charity, in the measure of their purification and illumination by the Spirit, O, Thou only God, infinite in lovingkindness.'[2]

In the parousia, and the eschatological fulfilment of history, the whole created universe will enter into perfect union with God. This union will be realized, or rather will be made manifest, differently in each of the human persons who have acquired the grace of the Holy Spirit in the Church. But the limits of the Church beyond death and the possibilities of salvation for those who have not known the light in this life, remain a mystery of the divine mercy for us, on which we dare not count, but to which we cannot place any human bounds.

[1] 'Spiritual Homilies, XI, I', *P.G.*, XXXIV, 544.
[2] *Discourse*, XXVII.

CHAPTER TWELVE

Conclusion: The Feast of the Kingdom

In our introduction we insisted that there is a deep and indissoluble bond between theology and mysticism, between doctrinal tradition and spirituality. It is impossible to expound spirituality otherwise than in a dogmatic form, dogma being its outward expression, the only objective evidence of an experience which the Church affirms. Personal experience and the common experience of the Church are identical by virtue of the catholicity of Christian tradition. Now tradition is not merely the aggregate of dogmas, of sacred institutions, and of rites which the Church preserves. It is, above all, that which expresses in its outward determinations a living tradition, the unceasing revelation of the Holy Spirit in the Church; a life in which each one of her members can share according to his capacity. To be in the tradition is to share the experience of the mysteries revealed to the Church. Doctrinal tradition—beacons set up by the Church along the channel of the knowledge of God—cannot be separated from or opposed to mystical tradition: acquired experience of the mysteries of the faith. Dogma cannot be understood apart from experience; the fullness of experience cannot be had apart from true doctrine. It is for this reason that in the present work we have sought to present the tradition of the Eastern Church as a mystical theology—doctrine and experience mutually conditioning each other.

Conclusion: The Feast of the Kingdom

We have examined in succession the basic elements of orthodox theology while never losing sight of its final goal: that of union with God. Directed as it is towards this goal, always soteriological in its intent, this doctrinal tradition has emerged as remarkably homogeneous despite the richness of its accumulated experience and of the diversity of cultures and periods which it embraces. It forms a single spiritual family whose members are easily recognizable even though they are separated from one another by time and space. As witnesses to the same spirituality we have been able to refer, in the course of our study, to Dionysius the Areopagite and to Gregory Palamas, to Macarius the Egyptian and to Seraphim of Sarov, to Gregory of Nyssa and to Philaret of Moscow, to Maximus the Confessor, as well as to modern Russian theologians, without receiving the impression of a change of spiritual climate in passing from one epoch to another. The Church within which human persons fulfil their vocation, within which their union with God is accomplished, is always the same; though her *economy* in regard to the outside world must needs change according to the differences of historical period and environment in which the Church fulfils her mission. The Fathers and Doctors who, in the course of her history, have had to defend and formulate different dogmas belong none the less to a single tradition; they are witnesses to the same experience. This tradition remains common to the East and to the West as far as the Church witnesses with power to those truths which are connected with the Incarnation. But those dogmas which are, so to speak, more inward, more mysterious, those which relate to Pentecost, the doctrines about the Holy Spirit, about grace, about the Church, are no longer common to the Church of Rome and to the Eastern Churches. Two separate traditions are opposed one to another. Even those things which down to a particular moment were held in common receive in retrospect a different stress, appear in a different light as spiritual realities belonging to two distinct experiences.

Henceforth a St. Basil or a St. Augustine will be differently interpreted according as they are considered within the Roman Catholic tradition or in that of the Orthodox Church. This is inevitable, for one cannot recognize the authority of an ecclesiastical writer except in the spirit of the tradition to which one owns allegiance. We have tried in this essay to bring out those characteristics which are proper to the tradition of the Orthodox Church; and in order to avoid all possible confusion and misunderstanding we have based ourselves exclusively upon the testimony of the Eastern Fathers.

We have had again and again, in the course of our study of the mystical theology of the Eastern Church, to refer to the apophatic attitude which is characteristic of its religious thought. As we have seen, the negations which draw attention to the divine incomprehensibility are not prohibitions upon knowledge: apophaticism, so far from being a limitation, enables us to transcend all concepts, every sphere of philosophical speculation. It is a tendency towards an ever-greater plenitude, in which knowledge is transformed into ignorance, the theology of concepts into contemplation, dogmas into experience of ineffable mysteries. It is, moreover, an existential theology involving man's entire being, which sets him upon the way of union, which obliges him to be changed, to transform his nature that he may attain to the true *gnosis* which is the contemplation of the Holy Trinity. Now, this 'change of heart', this μετάνοιά, means repentance. The apophatic way of Eastern theology is the repentance of the human person before the face of the living God. It is the constant transformation of the creature tending towards its completeness: towards that union with God which is brought about through divine grace and human freedom. But the fullness of Godhead, the ultimate fulfilment toward which all created persons tend, is revealed in the Holy Spirit. It is He, the Mystagogue of the apophatic way whose negations attest the presence of the Unnameable, the Uncircumscribed, the absolute Plenitude. *This* is the secret tradition within the tradition which is manifested to all and preached from the house-tops. This is the mystery which lies hid within the precepts of the Church, even while it confers upon them their character of certitude. This is the inner evidence, the life, the warmth, the light which properly belong to Christian truth. Without Him, dogmas would be but abstract truths, external authorities imposed from without upon a blind faith, reasons contrary to reason, received by obedience and afterwards adapted to our mode of understanding, instead of being revealed mysteries, the principles of a new knowledge unfolding within us and moulding our nature to the contemplation of those realities which surpass all human understanding. The apophatic attitude in which one can see the fundamental character of all theological thought within the Eastern tradition, is an unceasing witness rendered to the Holy Spirit who makes up all deficiencies, causes all limitations to be overcome, confers upon the knowledge of the Unknowable the fullness of experience, and transforms the divine darkness into light wherein we have communion with God.

If the incomprehensible God reveals Himself as the Holy Trinity, if His incomprehensibility appears as the mystery of the Three Persons and the One Nature, it is the Holy Spirit laying open to our contemplation the fullness of the divine being. This is why, in the Eastern rite, the day of Pentecost is called the festival of the Trinity. This is the absolute stability, the end of all contemplation and of all ascents, and, at the same time, the principle of all theology, primal verity, initial datum from which all thought and all being take their origin. St. Gregory Nazianzen, Evagrius Ponticus, St. Maximus, and other

Fathers identified the perfect knowledge of the Trinity with the Kingdom of God; the ultimate perfection to which all created beings are called. The mystical theology of the Eastern Church is always trinitarian. The knowledge of God is always for the Eastern Church a knowledge of the Trinity, the mystic union—a unity of life with the three divine Persons. Eastern apophaticism jealously safeguards the antinomy of the trinitarian dogma, the mysterious identity of the Three-and-One; resists the Western formula of the procession *ab utroque* that it may not stress the unity of nature to the detriment of the personal plenitude of the 'thrice repeated Holy, meeting in one ascription of the title Lord and God'.[1] The monarchy of the Father—the unique source of the Persons in whom exist the infinite riches of the one nature—is always asserted.

Eastern theology—straining always to conceive a greater fullness and to pass beyond the conceptual limitations which determine the divine being in terms proper to human reason—refuses to ascribe to the divine nature the character of an essence locked within itself. God—one essence in three persons—is more than an essence: He overflows His essence, manifests Himself beyond it, and, being incommunicable by nature, communicates Himself. These processions of deity outside the essence are the energies: the mode of existence proper to God in so far as He pours the fullness of His deity upon all those who are capable of receiving it by means of the Holy Spirit. This is why a hymn for Pentecost calls the Holy Spirit *stream of divinity flowing from the Father through the Son.*

The same aspiration towards plenitude is shown in those doctrines which relate to the creation. If the existence of the created world has no character of necessity, if all creation is contingent, it is precisely in this absolute freedom of the divine will that the created universe finds its

---

[1] St. Gregory Nazianzen, 'In Theophaniam, Or. XXXVIII, 8', *P.G.*, XXXVI, 320 BC.

perfection. For God created out of nothingness something that was absolutely new, a world which is not an imperfect copy of God but a deliberate work 'excogitated' by the 'divine counsel'. Indeed, in Eastern theology, as we have seen, the divine ideas present themselves under the dynamic aspect of forces, wills and creative words. They determine created beings as their outward causes, but, at the same time, they call them to perfection—to perfect being (εὖ εἶναι)—in union with God. Thus, the created universe appears as a dynamic reality tending towards a future plenitude which for God is always present. The unshakable foundation of a world created out of nothingness consists in the fulfilment which is the end of its becoming. Now, He who fulfils and who bestows plenitude upon all created being is the Holy Spirit. Created being, considered in itself, will always be an implenitude: considered in the Holy Spirit it will appear as the fullness of the deified creature. Throughout the course of its history the created world will be set between these two limits without our being able ever to apprehend 'pure nature' and grace as two juxtaposed realities which are added the one to the other. The tradition of the Eastern Church knows the creature tending towards deification, transcending itself continually in grace. It knows also the fallen creature, separating itself from God to enter upon a new existential plane—that of sin and death. It avoids, however, the attribution of a static perfection to created nature considered in itself. For this would be to ascribe a limited fullness, a natural sufficiency, to beings which were created that they might find their fullness in union with God.

In anthropology and the ascetic theology which derives from it, the limitation which has to be overcome is that of the individual, a particular being resulting from a confusion between person and nature. The fullness of nature demands the perfect unity of humanity, one body which is realized in the Church; the virtual fullness of persons expresses itself in their freedom in regard to all natural qualifications and all individual character: a freedom which makes each one of them a unique and unparalleled being—a multiplicity of human hypostases having a single nature. Within the unity of the common nature the persons are not parts, but each a whole, finding the accomplishment of its fullness in union with God. The person, the indestructible image of God, tends always towards this fullness, even though it sometimes seeks it apart from God, for it knows, desires and acts through that nature which is darkened by sin and no longer has the divine likeness. Thus, the mystery of the divine Being, which is the distinction between the one nature and the persons, is graven upon humanity, called to participate in the life of the Holy Trinity. The two poles of human being—nature and persons—find their fullness the one in unity the other in absolute diversity; for each person is united to God according to the mode which is proper to him alone. The unity of the purified nature is recreated and 'recapitulated' by Christ; the multiplicity of the persons is confirmed by the Holy Spirit who gives Himself to each member of the body of Christ. The new fullness, the new existential plane that entered the universe after Golgotha, the Resurrection and Pentecost is known as the Church.

It is uniquely in the Church and through the eyes of the Church that Eastern spirituality sees Christ. In other words, He is known in the Holy Spirit. Christ always appears in the fullness of His Godhead, glorified and triumphant: even in His Passion; even in the Tomb. The κένωσις is always balanced by the splendour of the deity. Dead and laid in the tomb, He descends as a conqueror into Hades and destroys for ever the power of the enemy. Risen and ascended to Heaven, He can be known by the Church under no other aspect than that of a Person of the Holy Trinity, seated at the right hand of the Father, having overthrown death. The 'historical Christ', 'Jesus of Nazareth', as He appears to the eyes of alien witnesses; this image of Christ, external to the Church, is always surpassed in the fullness of the revelation given to the true witnesses, to the sons of the Church, enlightened by the Holy Spirit. The cult of the humanity of Christ, is foreign to Eastern tradition; or, rather, this deified humanity always assumes for the Orthodox Christian that same glorious form under which it appeared to the disciples on Mount Tabor: the humanity of the Son, manifesting forth that deity which is common to the Father and the Spirit. The way of the imitation of Christ is never practised in the spiritual life of the Eastern Church. Indeed, for the Orthodox Christian this way seems to have a certain lack of fullness: it would seem to imply an attitude somewhat external in regard to Christ. For Eastern spirituality the only way which makes us conformable to Christ is that of the acquisition of the grace which the Holy Spirit confers. No saint of the Eastern Church has ever borne the stigmata, those outward marks which have made certain great Western saints and mystics as it were living patterns of the suffering Christ. But, by contrast, Eastern saints have very frequently been transfigured by the inward light of uncreated grace, and have appeared resplendent, like Christ on the mount of Transfiguration.

The source of this fullness which makes it possible to surpass all rigid limitations—whether it be in doctrine, experience, or the life of the Church—the fount of this richness and this freedom is the Holy Spirit. Fully *Person*, He is never in His hypostatic being, considered as a 'bond of love' between the Father and the Son, or as a function of unity within the Trinity—where there is no place for functional determinations. The tradition of the Eastern Church, in confessing the procession of the Holy Spirit from the Father alone, the hypostatic independence of the Spirit in relation to the Son, asserts the personal fullness of the work of the Paraclete who comes into the world. The Holy Spirit is no mere unitive force whereby the Son imposes Himself upon the members of His mystical body. If He bears witness to the Son, it is as a divine Person, independent of the Son; a divine Person who communicates to each human hypostasis, to every member of the Church, a new fullness, wherein created persons unfold and confess freely and spontaneously the divinity of Christ made plain in the Spirit: 'where the Spirit of God is, there is liberty'—the true liberty of the persons who are not blind members within the unity of the body of Christ, who are not annihilated in this union, but who acquire their personal fullness; each one of them becomes a whole in the Church, for the Holy Spirit descends separately upon each human hypostasis. If the Son brings His hypostasis to the renewed human nature, if He becomes the Head of a new body, it is the Holy Spirit, coming in the name of the Son, who confers deity upon every member of this body, upon every human person. In the κένωσις of the incarnate Son the person is plainly manifested, but the nature remains hid beneath the form of the slave. In the coming of the Holy Spirit, the deity is revealed as a Gift, while the person of the Giver remains undisclosed. In thus annihilating Himself, so to speak, in hiding Himself as Person, the Holy Spirit appropriates uncreated grace to human persons. Man is united to God as he adapts himself to the fullness of being which opens up in the depths of his very person. In the ceaseless struggle of the way of ascent, the way of co-operation with the divine will, created nature is more and more transformed by grace until the final deification which will be fully revealed in the Kingdom of God.

This same fullness of the Holy Spirit, this same reaching out towards the final consummation, leaving behind all that is fixed and stagnant, is to be found in Eastern ecclesiology. The historic Church, concrete, well-defined in time and space, encompasses within herself earth and heaven, men and angels, the living and the dead, sinners and saints, the created and the uncreate. How can we recognize beneath the outward failings and weaknesses of her historic existence the glorious Bride of Christ: 'Having neither spot nor stain nor any such thing' (Eph. v, 27)? How could one escape from the temptation to doubt? Did not the Holy Spirit constantly remedy our human failings, were not the limitations of history continually transcended, our emptiness always transformed into fullness, as the water was changed into wine at Cana of Galilee? How many people pass by the Church without recognizing the splendour of the eternal glory beneath the outward aspect of humiliation and weakness? Yet, how many recognized in 'the man of sorrows' the eternal Son of God? One must have eyes to see and an understanding opened in the Holy Spirit to recognize the fullness there where the outward sense perceives only limitations and want. It is not only in the 'great ages' of the Church's life that one can detect this fullness of divine life always present within her. In the age of the apostles, during the times of persecution, and during the period of the great councils, there were always certain *esprits laïcs* who remained blind in the face of the evidence of the manifestations of the Spirit of God in the Church. We may mention à more recent example of the same insensibility. Within the last generation the Church of Russia has brought forth thousands of martyrs and confessors who will bear comparison with those of the first centuries. In every place where the faith has been put to the test there have been abundant outpourings of grace, the most astonishing miracles—icons renewing themselves beneath the eyes of the astonished spectators; the cupolas of churches shining with a light not of this world. And—greatest miracle of all—the Church has been enabled to triumph over all difficulties, and to emerge renewed and strengthened from her fiery trial. Nevertheless, all this was scarcely noticed. The glorious aspect of what had taken place in Russia remained almost without interest for the generality of mankind. There were protests at the persecution; there were regrets that the Russian Church did not act like a temporal or a political power; excuses were put forward on behalf of this 'human frailty'. The crucified and buried Christ will always be judged in similar fashion by those who are blind to the light of His resurrection. We must, in the words of St. Paul, receive, 'not the spirit of the world, but the Spirit which is of God; that we may know the things that are freely given to us of God,'[1] that we may be enabled to recognize victory beneath the outward appearance of failure, to discern the power of God fulfilling itself in weakness, the true Church within the historic reality.

So, finally, the apophaticism which characterizes the mystical theology of the Eastern Church appears as a witness to the fullness of the Holy Spirit—to this Person who, though He fills all things and brings all things to their ultimate fulfilment, yet remains Himself unknown. In the Holy Spirit all becomes fullness: the world which was created that it might be deified, human persons called to union with God, the Church wherein this union is accomplished; finally, God makes Himself known in the fullness of His Being—the Holy Trinity. The faith which is an apophatic sense of this fullness cannot remain blind in the persons who come to union with God. The Holy Spirit becomes in them the very principle of a consciousness which opens up ever more and more in the discernment of the divine realities. As we have seen in the last two chapters, the spiritual life is always, according to the Eastern ascetic writers, a life of awareness. This awareness of grace and of God's presence in us, is generally called *gnosis* or spiritual understanding (γνῶσις πνευματική), defined by St. Isaac the Syrian as 'the knowledge of

---

[1] I Cor. ii, 12.

Conclusion: The Feast of the Kingdom

eternal life' and 'the knowledge of secret realities'.[1] This *gnosis* dispels all limitations of consciousness; banishes that ἄγνοια which has the twilight of hell at its farthest margin. The perfecting of gnosis is the contemplation of the divine light of the Holy Trinity; that full consciousness which is the parousia, the judgement, and the entering into eternal life, being fulfilled here and now (according to St. Symeon the New Theologian), before death and the resurrection, in the saints who live in uninterrupted communion with God.

The consciousness of the fullness of the Holy Spirit, given to each member of the Church in that measure to which he has attained, banishes the shades of death, the terrors of the Judgement and the abyss of Hell, in turning our attention solely to the Lord coming in His glory. This joy in the resurrection and the life everlasting makes of the paschal night 'a banquet of faith', wherein all may participate—though but feebly and for a few moments—in the fullness of that 'eighth day' which shall have no end. A homily attributed to St. John Chrysostom, and read every year during the matins of Easter Day, perfectly expresses the sense of this eschatological fullness to which Eastern Christendom aspires.[2] No words could more eloquently bring to a close our study of the mystical theology of the Eastern Church:

'If any be pious and a lover of God, let him partake of this fair and radiant festival.

'If any be a faithful servant, let him come in rejoicing in the joy of his Lord.

'If any have wearied himself with fasting, let him now enjoy his reward.

'If any have laboured from the first hour, let him today

---

[1] Ed. Theotoki, XLIII and LXIX. Wensinck, *Hom. LXII*, p. 289, and *Hom. LXVII*, p. 316.

[2] 'Paschal Homily of St. John Chrysostom', *P.G.*, LIX, 721–4 (spuria).

receive his rightful due. If any have come at the third, let him feast with thankfulness. If any have arrived at the sixth, let him in no wise be in doubt, for in nothing shall he suffer loss. If any be as late as the ninth, let him draw near, let him in no wise hesitate. If any arrive only at the eleventh, let him not be fearful on account of his slowness. For the Master is bountiful and receives the last even as the first. He gives rest to him of the eleventh hour even as to him who has laboured from the first. He is merciful to the last, and provides for the first. To one He gives, and to another He shows kindness. He receives the works, and welcomes the intention. He honours the act, and commends the purpose.

'Enter ye all, therefore, into the joy of our Lord, and let both the first and those who come after partake of the reward. Rich and poor, dance one with another. Ye who fast and ye who fast not, rejoice today. The table is full-laden: do ye all fare sumptuously. The calf is ample: let none go forth hungry.

'Let all partake of the banquet of faith. Let all partake of the riches of goodness.

'Let none lament his poverty; for the Kingdom is manifested for all.

'Let none bewail his transgressions; for pardon has dawned from the tomb.

'Let none fear death; for the death of the Saviour has set us free.

'He has quenched death, who was subdued by it.

'He has despoiled Hades, who descended into Hades.

'Hades was embittered when it tasted of His flesh, and Isaiah, anticipating this, cried out saying: Hades was embittered when it met Thee face to face below. It was embittered, for it was rendered void. It was embittered, for it was mocked. It was embittered, for it was slain. It was embittered, for it was despoiled. It was embittered, for it was fettered.

Conclusion: The Feast of the Kingdom

'It received a body, and it encountered God. It received earth, and came face to face with Heaven. It received that which it saw, and fell whence it saw not.

'O Death, where is thy sting? O Hades, where is thy victory?

'Christ is risen and thou art cast down.

'Christ is risen and the demons have fallen.

'Christ is risen and the angels rejoice.

'Christ is risen and life is made free.

'Christ is risen and there is none dead in the tomb. For Christ is raised from the dead, and become the first-fruits of them that slept. To Him be glory and dominion from all ages to all ages. Amen.'

Index

Index

Index